Reclaiming Difference

Reclaiming Difference

CARIBBEAN WOMEN REWRITE
POSTCOLONIALISM

Carine M. Mardorossian

New World Studies

A. James Arnold, editor

University of Virginia Press

Charlottesville and London

University of Virginia Press
© 2005 by the Rector and Visitors of the University of Virginia
All rights reserved
Printed in the United States of America on acid-free paper
First published 2005

9 8 7 6 5 4 3 2 1

Library of Congress Cataloging-in-Publication Data
Mardorossian, Carine M., 1966-
  Reclaiming difference : Caribbean women rewrite postcolonialism / Carine M.
Mardorossian.
      p. cm. — (New World studies)
  Includes bibliographical references and index.
    ISBN 0-8139-2346-8 (cloth : alk. paper) — ISBN 0-8139-2347-6
(pbk. : alk. paper)
    1. Caribbean fiction—Women authors—20th century—History and criticism.
I. Title. II. Series.
PN849.C3M34 2005
810.9'9287'09729—dc22
                                                              2004028932

To Lonny,
Cédric, and Delphine

Contents

Acknowledgments

FOR READING and rereading drafts of my work and for their insightful comments, I thank Amanda Anderson, Chris Bongie, Greg Dimitriadis, Peter Garrett, Danny Hack, Jim Holstun, Bénédicte Ledent, Deidre Lynch, Janet Lyon, Jane Morse, Lonny Morse, Adlai Murdoch, Mireille Rosello, Margarita Vargas, and my two readers at the University of Virginia Press. I am extremely fortunate to be surrounded by the most intellectually stimulating colleagues one could wish for at the University at Buffalo. I am grateful to them for creating the kind of environment where scholarship and friendship, lively conversation, and rigorous learning go hand in hand and fuel my thinking daily.

At the University of Virginia Press, Cathie Brettschneider provided the most generous attention to the manuscript (and its author). I am also grateful to Susan Brady for making this manuscript much more readable than it would otherwise have been. For their early mentorship, continuing support and friendship, I am indebted to Robert Leroy, Ena Maes-Jelinek, Lyn Petrie, and Amanda Anderson.

I thank my parents and sister for opening up the unconventional path that took me where I am, and my best friend, Pascale, for making the journey with me. Finally, I dedicate this work to Lonny, Cédric, and Delphine, who teach me daily and concretely about the value of rethinking difference.

PORTIONS OF this volume previously appeared as "Opacity as Obeah in Jean Rhys's Work" (*Journal of Caribbean Literatures* 3, no. 3 (summer 2003): 133–43) and "From Literature of Exile to Migrant Literature" (*Modern Language Studies* 32, no. 2 (fall 2002): 15–34). An earlier version of chapter 2 was published as "Shutting Up the Subaltern: Silences, Stereotypes, and *Double-Entendre* in Jean Rhys's *Wide Sargasso Sea*" in

Callaloo: A Journal of African-American and African Arts and Letters 22, no. 4 (fall 1999): 1071–90 (John Hopkins University Press). I am grateful for permission to reprint.

Unless otherwise noted, all translations are my own.

Reclaiming Difference

Introduction

From Postcolonial Rewriting to Rewriting the Postcolonial

LIKE MANY of the authors that constitute the postcolonial canon today, contemporary Caribbean women writers are producing their best sellers from the heart of colonial and neocolonial centers, whether it is England or the United States. Indeed, none of the writers discussed in *Reclaiming Difference* relates to her island of origin as her "home" or makes it the exclusive focus or setting of her fiction. Instead, Jean Rhys (Dominica/UK), Maryse Condé (Guadeloupe/USA), Julia Alvarez (Dominican Republic/USA), and Edwidge Danticat (Haiti/USA) stage and identify with transcultural experiences that undermine the usual classification of literary texts in terms of national and regional literatures. Having left their Caribbean birthplaces to live and write elsewhere, these women embody and write about the emergent political, economic, and cultural configurations of the late twentieth and twenty-first centuries. They exemplify a new aesthetics that urges us to rethink postcolonial approaches to literature in light of the global changes that have transformed our world. They revise in so doing the key categories that have defined postcolonial studies and that have been used to analyze postcolonial culture. Understanding these authors has therefore broad implications for our perception of postcoloniality and postcolonialism writ large.

Reclaiming Difference: Caribbean Women Rewrite Postcolonialism highlights the ways in which these Caribbean women writers radically reformulate the meanings of the national, geographical, sexual, and racial concepts through which postcolonial studies has been configuring difference. Their aesthetics as well as their experiences fall outside the designated rubrics of the field and call for a fundamental recasting of its foundational terms: nation and nationalism, race and hybridity, home and exile, agency, voice, and resistance. Their novels stage fictional worlds where the transgression of national, racial, gender, and class boundaries radically challenges the categorical affirmations of identity that defined earlier anticolonialism. In other words, rather than add a putatively missing (female or Caribbean) dimension to postcolonialism, these women writers modify, unsettle, and call into question the very terms of postcolonial discourse. Their reconfiguration of postcolonialism's key concepts exemplifies a new paradigm for the study of literature and culture that works across conventional representations of identity by challenging the view that racial and cultural identities are stable points of reference. As such, these writers transform postcolonial reading strategies as well as our understanding of colonialism and its aftermath and represent a brand-new phase in the field of postcolonial studies.

The standard narrative of postcolonialism, as offered by K. Anthony Appiah, proposes a two-stage sequence in the development of postcolonial literature: anticolonial national narratives followed by narratives of delegitimation. The corpus examined in *Reclaiming Difference* belongs to a new phase of rewriting—or, more precisely, a strategy of rereading—that contests Appiah's tidy paradigm. Appiah identifies the first phase as the literature produced during the decolonizing era of the 1950s and 1960s, when postcolonial prescriptions for change were based on unitary notions of cultural and national identity. The colonized nation was perceived as a community of people of the same race whose common linguistic, class, and cultural interests constituted the basis of their opposition to the colonizing nation.[1] Appiah singles out African novels like Chinua Achebe's *Things Fall Apart* and Camara Laye's *L'Enfant Noir* as exemplary of this stage insofar as they are "imaginative re-creation[s] of a common cultural past that is crafted into a shared tradition" (433). From the late 1960s on, however, this celebratory fiction was supplanted by "novels of delegitimation." As a result of the utter disappointment with the dictatorships and neocolonial regimes that took over ex-colonized countries after independence, the literature produced during the second stage no longer considers nationalism as a serious alternative to imperialism. It questions the assumption of a shared ethnic and cultural identity as representative of the nation-state and exposes the concept of the nation itself as a European invention.[2] Most important, in rejecting the nationalist project, it helps make visible the internal gender, racial, religious, and cultural differences that the myth of the nation had previously obscured through its production of a unified imaginary community.

While the works examined in this project certainly also qualify as "novels of delegitimation," their revisionist practices are not just a version of the delegitimation story told by Appiah. They represent a third phase in postcolonialism insofar as they revise the second stage's reconceptualization of culture and identity and take us beyond settled spatial, linguistic, discursive, and literary configurations. Indeed, even though the literature of the second phase does identify racial, gender, religious, and ethnic differences as constructions that set the norms of the nation, it tends to treat these identities as discrete and preexisting categories that define and divide groups of people in predictable and stable ways. Gender or race function as a common bond or identity between individuals who are excluded from the imagined community of the nation by virtue of their constructed but no less determining and invariable difference.

By contrast, I argue that the writers of the third phase of rewriting transform such approaches to identity (and correlatively our reading strategies) by making them more attuned to the contingent workings of difference. Instead of "freezing" identity into racial, cultural, or gender difference, they open it up to re-imagination by representing it as in constant flux rather than fixed, as multiple rather than dualistic. They challenge the idea that racial and cultural identities function as stable points of reference in our unstable world and represent subjects as constituted by a network of interdependent identities that cannot be adequately accounted for by identity-bound differences. In contrast to the novelists of the previous stage, they show that identities do not preexist the particular symbolic economy that deploys them but are very much constituted by its operations. In this context, race, gender, and class are no longer viewed as discrete categories of identity (whether deemed natural or constructed) that can be discussed in isolation from each other but are seen instead as relational entities that come into being *through* rather than *prior to* their interrelationships. What matters, in other words, is no longer whether *Wuthering Heights*'s Heathcliff and his Caribbean counterpart, *Windward Heights*'s Razyé, are respectively "dark-skinned" and "black" but how each of these racial identifications shifts during the narrative according to its changing articulation with other categories of difference. This relational model offers a useful model for thinking about the world today insofar as it challenges the separatism of identity politics, cultural purism, and ethnic absolutism in favor of mappings of identity that emphasize the deep interconnectedness of our lives across the globe.

Reading through such a model means foregrounding "relation identity" as an alternative to the static "root identities" that perpetuate fixed and exclusionist notions of nation, race, or culture. It subverts the binaries and inflexible categorizations (same/other, colonial/postcolonial, black/white, male/female) through which official cultures and languages operate, proposing instead a rhizomatic network that emphasizes the new, global interrelationships that are increasingly defining the world in multilayered ways. In contrast to modern liberal narratives, however, this approach does not challenge categories of difference in the name of an abstract form of personhood that treats individuals in abstraction from their social attributes. Rather, it highlights the ideological and material effects of race, gender, sexuality, etc., even as it exposes the limits and contingency of these identities.

This groundbreaking approach exemplifies the alternative aesthetics showcased in *Reclaiming Difference,* but it also extends the usual meaning of the "New World" vision we have come to associate with Caribbean authors from a trans-American to a global one. A New World perspective is traditionally perceived as one that highlights the interconnectedness of the dynamics of creolization in the Americas, that is, of the transnational and cross-cultural processes of intermixing and transformation that produce a Creole society. In so doing, it brings together literatures from the anglophone, hispanophone, and francophone Caribbean and locates Caribbean literature in the regional context of the Americas rather than in individual Caribbean nations; it thus challenges the linguistic blocks and colonialist divisions that were imposed by colonial powers.

The Caribbean region provides a unique perspective into these interconnected cultural dynamics of creolization because it reflects a history of social struggles—divided among native-born whites, foreign whites, free and enslaved blacks, free and enslaved mulattos—that has always resisted binaries. As a result of the history of slavery as well as of the major ethno-cultural and migratory displacements (particularly from South Asia) that followed emancipation, creolization in the Caribbean occurred and continues to occur in a compacted and accelerated way. According to the influential Martinican writer Édouard Glissant, the Caribbean "may be held up as one of the places in the world where Relation presents itself most visibly, one of the explosive regions where it seems to be gathering strength" (*Poetics* 33). At the same time, this hybrid condition or "Relation" is also increasingly "making itself visible everywhere . . . notably in the West's megalopoli" (Confiant 266), so that the rest of the world has much to learn from the condensed "workshop" of the Caribbean archipelago, where the processes of cross-cultural interaction and exchange are eminently visible and researchable. That the region functions as the exemplar of the new global order explains why its literature is seen as especially representative in postcolonial studies today.[3]

The Caribbean women's writings I analyze embody the radical revisionary venture of this New World culture insofar as, in linking the dynamics of Caribbean creolization to the complexities of diversity in our postmodern world, they recast our understanding of culture and identity as a global and relational process. In addition, this renewed focus has regenerative implications for our readings of postcolonial and colonial artifacts alike. Indeed, in going beyond the settled spatial, temporal, and literary boundaries that typically define New World culture, these works represent a new strategy of rereading that illuminates canonical works such as Brontë's *Wuthering Heights* or Rhys's *Wide Sargasso Sea*. Once our conceptualization of identity changes to account for practices of relationality, new cultural and literary dimensions emerge in earlier works like Brontë's and Rhys's that have traditionally been analyzed in terms of the dichotomous hierarchies of colonialist thinking. In rereading these two canonical texts anew, *Reclaiming Difference* thus marks out a new transgenerational, transracial, translinguistic, and translocal analytical territory that treats the earlier writers as precursors of the present. And through this genealogical operation, it traces the beginnings of our own moment and of contemporary constructions of migrant identity back to the twentieth and nineteenth centuries. It transcends national, linguistic, historical, and geographical boundaries, and in thematizing the crisscrossings that have defined the Atlantic world since the Middle Passage, it reflects its exemplary Caribbean authors' own transnational meanderings.

Maryse Condé moved to the United States after having spent a number of years in Africa and France, and her novels often explicitly link the Caribbean to the United States. Her rewriting of Brontë's *Wuthering Heights* in particular opens with the United States' 1898 intervention in the Spanish-Cuban conflict, a momentous event that marked the onset of twentieth-century neocolonialism. Julia Alvarez and Edwidge Danticat settled in North America in their early teens, and their autobiographical novels fictionalize their stories of transplantation to this country. Last but not least, Jean Rhys moved to England when she was sixteen, and her novels relate her heroines' struggle to survive the emotional and financial hardships of exile as they drift from one European metropolis to another. In fact, like many imaginative postcolonial writers today, these Caribbean women qualify so well for the category of "migrant authors" that, as Kutzinski remarks, the U.S.-centric discipline of American Studies does not know what to do with them: "Do Caribbean writers belong to the province of American Studies only if they reside in the United States, as opposed to the United Kingdom, Canada, or heaven forbid, the Antilles themselves? . . . Can [they], then, be brought into the fold without adulterating the predominantly nationalistic body of knowledge that fold seeks to represent and protect, at times rather imperiously?" ("Borders" 57).

This unsettling New World perspective is one where the connections within and between the Americas and the rest of the world challenge the nationalist and identitarian rubrics through which disciplines such as American or postcolonial studies have traditionally framed their subject; where an attention to transcultural exchange inside and outside national and international boundaries is central, not incidental, to questions of culture and identity; and where a novelist's transnational status does not question her Caribbeanness so much as constitute it. This is a vision where works of art speak to each other through boundaries of time, space, language, and race in a cross-cultural and intertextual dialogue to which New World writers have always been particularly attuned by virtue of their histories of cultural contact. Unlike appeals to universal modes of aesthetic inquiry, however, this alternative approach remains rooted in the specificities of a politics of location and positionality. Rather than transcend identities without due regard for their effects on cultural production, it works through them to arrive at a representational politics that recognizes the cross-cultural interdependence, relationality, and plurality that is obscured by identity-bound thought. The answer to the boundaries arbitrarily erected between peoples, cultures, and countries is consequently not, as the Caribbean women writers of my corpus show, to turn a blind eye to difference but to recast it as a fluid concept that binds rather than blinds, connects rather than isolates, and enriches rather threatens. In such an alternative paradigm, identification replaces identity; "Relation" defines community; and multiplicity supplants singularity. Only when such an overhaul of our relationship to otherness as constitutive rather than incidental (or derivative) takes place will we be in a position to visualize an ethical world whose interdependent features form the basis of transformative hope rather than paralyzing fear.

We live at a historical juncture where such a reconceptualization of identity and difference is more urgent than ever. Differences today have become eminently representable, consumable, and marketable, while the other is endlessly made visible and promoted. Yet this proliferation of alterity is no cause for celebration. It is not a function of the realization of new ethical forms of human relatedness but evidence of successful capitalist appropriation and commodification. As critics such as Prakash and Braidotti have powerfully shown, far from homogenizing difference, capitalism is perfectly capable of generating heterogeneity in the service of the consolidation of the dominant subject. In fact, this identity-bound version of difference is instrumental in producing the "Majority-Subject" through its very alterity. An acceptance of difference then often amounts to nothing more than to its "tolerance," leaving the same/other opposition intact, since without a devalued (or, for that matter, revalorized) difference, there would be no center. In other words, it is simply no longer sufficient to accept or celebrate difference by valuing conventional manifestations of racial, gendered, or religious otherness. Instead, it is imperative that we reconfigure difference as a relational concept that, insofar as it reveals the irreducible interdependence of self and other, is better equipped to resist hegemonic cooptation. The purging of otherness is only conceivable when difference is visualized as a site of categorical alterity. In a relational mode, the other becomes that to which one is related rather than opposed.

This revision of "difference" from concept into process constitutes the trademark of the new group of postcolonial writers I examine in this book. Yet it also evokes a long-standing tradition in postcolonialism, namely that of "rewriting" Western texts and representations. The practice of rewriting has been seen as exemplary of the field since its inception, since postcolonialism in all its guises has similarly been concerned with replacing colonialist images of difference with more empowering representations from the margins. It is therefore not surprising that the first sustained theoretical investigation of postcolonial literatures should have been entitled *The Empire Writes Back* (1989), and that with—and since—its publication, literary rewritings of English and European canonical texts have been treated as paradigmatic instances of the postcolonial project as a whole.

This representative status was enhanced by the fact that literary rewritings have served as a metaphor for the two (diametrically opposed) theories of cultural resistance that have dominated postcolonial studies since its turn to theory in the 1980s.[4] On the one hand, anticolonial theories that emphasize the oppositionality between the colonial and the postcolonial cultures (Achebe; Parry) have used postcolonial rereadings of the canon as metaphors for the opposition between the empire and its margins. On the other hand, more recent theories that stress the hybrid nature of postcolonial culture and therefore question the possibility of retrieving a precolonial and oppositional cultural tradition (Spivak; Harris) have paradoxically turned to the same writings in order to substantiate their own claims. For the first group, the focus is on how postcolonial rewritings write *against* colonial culture, while for the second, it is on how they write *from within* or *in symbiosis with* the dominant discourse whose claims they undermine internally rather than oppositionally.[5]

Nevertheless, despite the important place literary rewritings have occupied in postcolonial studies, there has been a dwindling number of postcolonial revisions of European classics over the last decades. Whereas the earlier generation of Caribbean writers produced a fair number of revisions of the Western canon (Aimé Césaire's *The Tempest;* Wilson Harris's *Palace of the Peacock;* George Lamming's *Water with Berries;* V. S. Naipaul's *A Bend in the River* and *Guerrillas;* Jean Rhys's *Wide Sargasso Sea*), the writers of the new Caribbean diaspora (with the exception of Maryse Condé) have tended to limit their engagement with the classics to a few intertextual references. This subdued relationship to colonialist texts signifies, I argue, a loosening of the past's hold on the future, since it downplays postcoloniality's relation to colonialism, while implying that postcolonial writers have not transcended colonial history and discourse once and for all. In fact, the writers of the new Caribbean diaspora continue to engage the categories of racial, gender, and class identities that are the legacy of colonialism.

What distinguishes them from previous generations is, I argue, the way in which they appropriate and constantly rework these categories of identity. They challenge the separatism of identitarian thought by highlighting not only the interconnectedness of the cultures and races that came into contact through colonialism but also the representational interdependence of race, gender, sexuality, and nationality (whereby the figuration of one stands as a double for the other). They envision the future by questioning the terms in which the colonial past has been cast rather than by reacting against it. In this way they create a new paradigm that questions the assumption that canonical counterdiscourse is a vital and inescapable task for the postcolonial field. This renegotiation challenges the conceptualization of a Caribbean experience and aesthetics in terms of reductive oppositions such as colonial past/postcolonial future, or similar binaries that posit the possibility of a future entirely freed from colonialism. It exposes as fallacy the Hegelian concept of History as linear progression that underwrites such accounts and that has been the dominant paradigm in much of (post)colonial history.[6] It resists defining the postcolonial as a reversal of colonialist discourse because such oppositional framework ultimately reproduces the very binary system that grounds colonial thinking. Instead, it offers a genuine alternative to colonialist configurations by rewriting not colonial texts and discourses but the colonial/postcolonial relationship itself.[7]

Although the practice of "rewriting" no longer refers to the same corrective process of revision it used to evoke after decolonization, it remains a guiding paradigm in postcolonial studies. In *Reclaiming Difference,* I use the term "rewriting" to conjure up these different manifestations and implications of the process for postcolonialism—whether it be the process of revisiting the past from a postcolonial perspective—the kind of revision to which the field of postcolonial studies itself has recently been subjected—or the literal or literary rewriting of European discourses and texts as in Jean Rhys's *Wide Sargasso Sea* and Maryse Condé's *Windward Heights.* I also use the term "migrant" to distinguish, as Belinda Edmondson suggests in *Making Men,* the writings of the first (mostly male) generation of exiled Caribbean writers from the work of the (mostly female) members of the second generation. As Edmondson explains, "migration out of the Caribbean, particularly in the last twenty-five years, has been of a heavily female nature, owing particularly to the burgeoning market in domestic work," which, as a result, "figures prominently in [contemporary Caribbean women writers'] personal narratives and in their fictions" (156). By contrast, the first generation of mainly male Caribbean writers went into exile to pursue "a specifically English 'vision' of intellectual [and literary] authority" (5) associated with Oxford and Cambridge even as, ironically, their aesthetics are dominated by a black nationalist and revolutionary rhetoric.

Edmondson's distinction between exile and migrancy draws attention to the shifting conditions of displacement that increasingly characterize our global and interdependent world. In *Reclaiming Difference,* I aim to raise a similar contextual awareness by using the term "migrant" rather than "exile" to describe the process of rewriting that continues to define postcolonialism today. I argue that the different but interconnected historical and geopolitical contexts in which we read postcolonial rewritings necessarily affect both our understanding of the works themselves and their relation to their canonical source-texts. In chapter 1, for instance, I show how Maryse Condé's 1995 rewriting of Emily Brontë's *Wuthering Heights* transforms the kind of "postcolonial revisionism" with which Jean Rhys's 1966 rejoinder to Charlotte Brontë's *Jane Eyre* has been associated. I use "postcolonial revisionism" as shorthand for the practice of reading Victorian texts as paradigms of a colonialist perspective awaiting overhaul by timely postcolonial rewritings. I offer instead a model of reading that takes its cue from Condé's *Windward Heights* and opens our analyses of both colonial and postcolonial texts to the challenges offered by contemporary relational paradigms.[8]

Reclaiming Difference illustrates how contemporary reading strategies that highlight the interdependence of identity structures transform our interpretations of novels that have been read through the lens of earlier forms of anticolonial postcolonialism. Once our conceptualization of identity changes, new cultural and literary dimensions emerge in earlier works like Emily Brontë's *Wuthering Heights* and Jean Rhys's *Wide Sargasso Sea* that have traditionally been analyzed in terms of the dichotomous hierarchies of colonialist thinking. In rereading these two canonical texts anew, *Reclaiming Difference* thus highlights how postcolonialism has evolved from a practice of reading texts belatedly for "the traces of colonial memory" (Behdad 77) to a "provoking rediscovery of [colonialism's] new traces today" (79). It makes visible an analytical space that crosses racial, linguistic, local, national, and historical boundaries by presenting the earlier writers as precursors of the later ones. This genealogical operation resets the genesis of our present ethos and of contemporary constructions of migrant identities back to the twentieth and nineteenth centuries.

In devoting a chapter to the rereading of a Victorian classic, this book also participates in an emerging field of criticism that takes the Caribbean as a point of departure to creolize readings of literary and philosophical canonical texts. Books such as Bongie's *Islands and Exiles* and Nesbitt's *Voicing Memory* are cases in point. Bongie juxtaposes contemporary francophone Caribbean writings and nineteenth-century French literary classics in order to bring to light the Creole identities of "post/colonial" fiction. Nesbitt examines the ways in which Aimé Césaire's writings engage and cannibalize Hegelian philosophy. Both resist casting the postcolonial in opposition to the colonial discourse with which it is always necessarily imbricated and detect in the canonical texts the very structures of creolized and relational identity that the Caribbean texts help make visible. This approach avoids reifying the binaries that ground colonialist discourse and that readings of postcolonial texts as "corrective" necessarily evoke. It reinterprets the practice of rewriting not in opposition to a dominant culture but in light of a new Caribbean sensibility that replaces divisiveness with multiplicity and redefines fragmentation not as the opposite of wholeness and harmony but as their only possible incarnation.

Emily Brontë's only novel is particularly well-suited for such a renewed emphasis since, maybe more than any other novel of the Victorian canon, it makes explicit the workings of a relational model of identity that is covertly embedded in the period's literature. In fact, the creolized dynamics that infuse the Victorian masterpiece explain why the novel has been so significant to New World writers in general. The Mexican Carlos Fuentes's first encounter with *Wuthering Heights,* he vividly recalls, marked *the* turning point in his intellectual development:

For it was on rereading *Wuthering Heights* in the mid-1950s that I came to understand the *other* possibility of that Western culture I had come to see as both mine and alien, nurturing and poisonous, magnificent and decadent. But above all, this other possibility enabled me to make use of my Western inheritance without giving up my own Latin America, mestizo, Indian-colored realities. For what was Emily Brontë but the outcast within the center, the visionary writer who dissolved the hypnosis of the future by the consecration of the instant of passion, preferred love to property, clung to the reality of myth as a constant present, and shunned the illusion of progress. (212)

Wuthering Heights's "eccentric" approach to narration, time, love, and morality epitomized for Fuentes "the *other* possibility of . . . Western culture" (212). He recognizes in Emily Brontë's writing an alternative epistemology that helped him reconcile his Western with his Latin American inheritance and that, as Dash reminds us, ultimately defines New World culture. This is an epistemological shift that allows us to "conceptualize the diversity of peoples and the unity of the human race at one and the same time" so that "identity is no longer imagined as a single tree rooted in the landscape" (Dash, *The Other America* 151). Significantly, Jean Rhys's correspondence shows that she shared Fuentes's admiration for the novel. Ironically, it was *Wuthering Heights* she wanted to emulate when she was rewriting the other Brontë masterpiece, Charlotte Brontë's *Jane Eyre*. Similarly, the revolutionary rhetoric of V. S. Naipaul's *Guerrillas* is infused with references to Emily Brontë's text. *Wuthering Heights* thus occupies a paradigmatic status for New World writers that is comparable to the tremendous impact Faulkner's "eccentric writing" has had on Caribbean and Latin American writers alike.[9]

In highlighting how new models of identity and relationality affect our interpretations of colonial and postcolonial texts alike, *Reclaiming Difference* defines postcolonialism as a reading practice rather than as a body of texts produced after decolonization. Rather than review the various literary responses to colonial discourse or the different types of literature or theories that have been grouped under the aegis of postcolonialism,[10] it surveys the reading strategies that have dominated the field and highlights their transformation under the pressure of the relational approaches and historical problematics that earlier paradigms obscured. In thus making visible the developments that have defined postcolonialism since the 1980s, it also challenges the field's much bemoaned splitting into literature and theory by setting in motion a critical and transformative dialogue between the two. Specifically, *Reclaiming Difference* reenacts the three forms of textual analyses that became popular in the 1980s and that continue to characterize postcolonial approaches today. The nonchronological order in which I discuss the novels aims to reflect the contemporary lens and cultural perspectives through which we necessarily read and reread the past as well as past readings. To this end, the 1990s fiction analyzed in the first (Condé) and last chapters (Alvarez and Danticat) frames the discussion of the earlier novels by Rhys and Brontë (in chapters 2 and 3, respectively).

The first of the three forms of textual analyses I undertake involves the rereading of canonical texts.[11] It assesses the extent to which literary classics reproduce or contest the ideological categories of representation that justified colonialism. It is exemplified, in *Reclaiming Difference,* by my rereading of Emily Brontë's novel in chapter 3, where I draw out the implications of Rhys's and Condé's configurations of racial crossing for our interpretations of the Victorian novel. The second form of analysis consists of reading colonial texts (including nonliterary ones) against the grain in order to discover moments when these representations failed to suppress the resistance of the colonized subject. This approach characterizes Gayatri Spivak's and Homi Bhabha's 1980s writings and is exemplified in chapter 2 by my analysis of obeah in Jean Rhys's *Wide Sargasso Sea,* a novel that, despite its anticolonial aspirations, has been read as harboring a colonialist perspective.[12] The third form of analysis focuses on how the new literatures that have emerged from the once colonized countries "are writing back to the center." This particular reading practice represents all four Caribbean women writers I discuss, even as they are shown to revise what the practice of writing back entails. Indeed, they are all engaged in a process of "writing back" whether or not they do so explicitly by rewriting a canonical text, or whether the center from which their rewriting originates and which it addresses is colonial Europe or the neocolonial United States. Restaging these three standard approaches to postcolonial literature provides a unique lens into how the new mappings of identity that are a trademark of these Caribbean women's diasporic writings can and do transform our previous readings of both colonial and postcolonial literature, anticolonial and more recent postnational theories.

Although it singles out Caribbean women writers, this book is not a project of recovery. It seeks to make no claims about a missing female perspective in postcolonial studies. It is certainly true that throughout postcolonialism's history, the reworkings of the colonial canon have predominantly been by male writers, so that the rewritings examined here are all the more interesting for the dialogue they establish with their male predecessors and contemporaries. Similarly, the theories of hybridity, mestizaje, creolization, and Créolité, judging by the leading thinkers who have coined these terms and made them fashionable (Benítez-Rojo, Bernabé, Confiant, Chamoiseau, Glissant, Martí, Retamar), have largely been a male affair. In her *Black Women, Writing and Identity,* Carole Boyce Davies remarks: "it seems so far that the discourses of postcoloniality are not, at this point in history, overly populated by 'postcolonial women'" (80). Nevertheless, my project suggests that while Caribbean women writers seem to occupy a marginalized position in relation to theory, it is indirectly but no less forcefully in and through their fiction that their contributions to theoretical debates surrounding hybridity and creolization occurs. In this respect, I echo Deborah McDowell's important essay "Transferences." McDowell argues that theory has been defined narrowly and constructed institutionally to exclude women of color even though their imaginative as well as nonfictional works constitute a form of "theory in the flesh."[13] Similarly, I argue that the Caribbean writers in my corpus are making radical theoretical interventions through their fiction and transform our reading practices in ways that cannot be adequately addressed when we emphasize their marginality in relation to theory.[14] Their fictional writings respond to and engage an already existing Caribbean poetics whose principles and assumptions they affirm, refine, and extend as they go along. They complicate postcolonial categories and discursive moves whose all-too-solid history has unduly circumscribed our approaches to the Caribbean literary archive. In the rest of the introduction, I expand on the transformation of these particular tropes and concepts in three sections; each focuses on a cluster of related terms: (1) race and hybridity, (2) agency, voice, and resistance, and (3) nation, home, and exile.

Race and Hybridity

Academic discussions of race today seem to entail an inevitable double gesture. On the one hand, critics preface their analysis of the category by underlining its arbitrariness and constructedness. In "Writing 'Race' and the Difference It Makes," for instance, Henry Louis Gates Jr. explains that: "Race, as a meaningful criterion within the biological sciences, has long been recognized to be a fiction. When we speak of 'the white race' or 'the black race,' 'the Jewish race' or 'the Aryan race,' we speak in biological misnomers and, more generally, in metaphors" (4). Similarly, in *Beginning Postcolonialism,* John McLeod begins his analysis of nationalism's collusion with racism by reminding us that "it is important to realise [*sic*] that all constructions of racial difference are based upon human invention and not biological fact" (110). On the other hand, this insistence on the constructedness of the category is also almost always accompanied by a caveat—namely, that while race is certainly a fiction, it is no less a determining and constraining force at that. Indeed, social hierarchies are still generated along racial lines that are therefore invoked to justify the production of sites of political solidarity based on race. For such identity politics, the term "blackness" continues to function as a unifying discourse that aims to challenge and reverse racist stereotypes and hierarchies.

In his controversial *Against Race,* Gilroy distances himself from this model of politicized identity by calling it "the pious ritual in which we always agree that 'race' is invented but are then required to defer to its embeddedness in the world and to accept that the demand for justice requires us nevertheless to enter the political arenas it helps to mark out" (52).[15] He further qualifies this automatic deferring gesture as a "capitulation to the lazy essentialisms that postmodern sages inform us we cannot escape" (53). According to Gilroy, a politics of identity and solidarity based on race is reactionary because race has in fact long ceased to be the stable and fixed entity it used to be. Global biotechnological developments such as the transracial trade in internal organs or the engineering of transgenic animals and plants as well as the recent changes in consumer culture where the black body has gained a new hypervisibility have ensured that "the history of racism is a narrative in which the congruency of micro- and macrocosm has been disrupted at the point of their analogical intersection: the human body" (53). In light of race's increasing instability in the twenty-first century, Gilroy sees race-based politics as a reactive attachment to an elusive category of identity whose origins can be traced to the dubious racist pseudosciences of the eighteenth and nineteenth centuries (craniometry, phrenology, etc.). For Gilroy, a race-based politicized identity is bound to reproduce the assumptions that derive from the term's questionable history and to consolidate the naturalization of social hierarchies. As such, the reliance on race as fuel for politics implicates the progressive movements that deploy the concept within the very power relations they aim to undo. Gilroy therefore urges us, as his book's subtitle makes explicit, to imagine a "political culture beyond the color line."

I argue that the Caribbean women writers I focus on in *Reclaiming Difference* help us to envision precisely such a renewed political culture. The progressive deployments of race Gilroy criticizes belong to a tradition of social constructionism that seeks to counter the essentialism of biological determinism. This constructionist position is not biologically deterministic because it sees society, not biology, as determining character formation, and it recognizes that different societies can impose different norms of personality and behavior on racially marked bodies. It does usually assume, however, that the cultural construction of the body functions as a predictable variable that provides the ground for certain commonalities in personality formation or reaction across certain historical and cultural contexts. It therefore still reproduces a form of biological "foundationalism" since such generalizations based on race necessarily resort to the body to justify them, even if it is not in a biologically essentialist way. Whether the body is perceived as a "coat rack" upon which various psychological and moral attributes have been superimposed over time (social constructionism) or as a naturalized site that is determinative of certain commonalities or differences (biological determinism), it is nonetheless invoked as an unchanging foundation to which meanings are attached. The biological is invoked even when it is being undermined.[16]

This socially constructed model gets transposed in literary criticism into readings that see race as preceding and transcending the patterns of meaning created through narrative and literary form. A character is "black" or not, and it is only after his/her racial identity has been ascertained that his/her role in the narrative is examined, a role that is seen as circumscribed by the stereotypical racial meanings that preexist individuals and their development. A character's "blackness" is then seen as a fixed and indelible marker of his or her identity that controls his or her function in the text. In this sense, race serves as the basis of group distinction; it is interpreted as invariable in its narrative function and effects, whether it attributes somatic visibility to social and behavioral characteristics or vice versa. And because racially marked characters are seen as different once and for all, the shifting and multilayered ideological work performed by the racializing logic of the narrative itself goes unnoticed. That "blackness" is not a pre-given identity but a crucial aspect of the workings of narrative does not occur to us because we have been conditioned to think of race as a preexisting, stable, coherent—if not visible—identity.

By contrast, Caribbean writers' revision of the category shakes our investment in "regimes of corporeal visibility" (Wiegman 4), that is, regimes that anchor race in signs of corporeal difference (size, skin or hair color, nose, etc.). As Wiegman points out, race is "rendered 'real' (and therefore justifiable) through the naturalizing discourses of the body, those discourses that locate difference in a pre-cultural realm where corporeal significations supposedly speak a truth which the body inherently means" (4). Caribbean writings have always challenged this tendency to "visualize" race as a fixed, because "natural," site of difference anchored in the body. Similarly, the Caribbean women writers examined here expose race as a constructed and unstable category of social belonging, but in contrast to many of their contemporaries, they present this instability not only as a function of the intermingling of various races or cultures but also of the crossing of race with other categories such as gender and class. In fact, racial crossing in their novels serves as a figuration for the transgressions of class and gender boundaries so much so that the notion of race itself has to be reinscribed as a complex set of crossing categories (gender, class, ethnicity, nationality, etc.) rather than in terms of the simplified binaries of black/white and self/ other (that ultimately derive from post-nineteenth-century views of race and nation). This logic affects individual characters whose own relation to a particular "race" changes as they are "blackened" or "whitened" according to their shifting relation to categories of class, gender, nationality, and so on. It reveals that interpretations of characters as either black or not fail to do justice to the fluctuating meanings of race in narrative. It challenges our deep-seated investments in normative figurations of identity and forces us to develop new reading strategies that emphasize not *whether* but *when* characters are "black" or "white." Simply put, this recasting of race reveals that diverse configurations of difference cannot be read in isolation since they acquire meaning through one another. It also shows that while identificatory structures such as race are indeed fluid and variable, they are not arbitrarily so. Rather, they fall into patterns that can be traced through a sustained attention to race's inseparability from other categories of social analysis.

In chapter 1, I expand on the way in which the description of Cathy's race in Maryse Condé's *Windward Heights* illustrates this racial problematic. On her deathbed, Cathy's corpse undergoes a dramatic fluctuation in skin color that can only be understood, I argue, in relation to her crossing and recrossing of class and gender boundaries. In thus redefining the very notion of race as racial crossing rather than racial difference, Condé's description exposes it as a fluid variable that changes in different contexts and at different times rather than as a persistent variety of difference determined by lines of blood or descent. Unlike conventional social constructionist approaches, this alternative view treats the body as a variable rather than as a constant that grounds claims about the black/white distinction across history and culture. It also throws new light on the workings of race in both Rhys's *Wide Sargasso Sea* and Emily Brontë's *Wuthering Heights,* two novels that tend to be read as invested in a normative reinscription of race as a black/white binary. In fact, Condé's text can arguably be said to be as much a rereading of Rhys's rewriting as of its canonical Victorian counterpart. It is indeed highly unlikely that the Guadeloupean author undertook her rewriting of the *other* Brontë masterpiece without having Rhys's paradigmatic and now canonized revision in mind.[17]

In chapter 2, I examine *Wide Sargasso Sea*'s racial/textual politics and argue that Rhys's white Creole protagonist, Antoinette, like Condé's "black" Cathy, undergoes a process of racialization that, although not as condensed and dramatic as Condé's heroine, is a manifestation of the same racial logic. I show that the shifting racial meanings that affect Antoinette are rooted less in her family's mixed racial origins than in her own transgression of gender expectations. Antoinette is "blackened" the moment she takes charge of her sexual relationship with her new husband, thus confounding the crossing of gender boundaries with racial crossing. Such reinscription of race also characterizes Rhys's other novels. In *Voyage in the Dark,* for instance, the white Creole heroine, Anna Morgan, undergoes a similar process of darkening as she drifts in and out of sexual relationships. It is, I argue, in the context of her violation of gender norms rather than merely of her Antillean origins that she is called "the Hottentot" and that her lilting voice is compared to that of a black woman's.

In the same way as Rhys's representation of race reads differently when examined through this alternative racial logic, so does the Victorian novel's relation to the discourses of race prevalent in nineteenth-century England. In chapter 3, I trace the implications of the recasting of race as crossing for postcolonial analyses of Emily Brontë's *Wuthering Heights*. Whereas postcolonial criticism tends to foreground the English literary canon's investment in maintaining separate racial and cultural boundaries, reading the racial dynamics of the mid-Victorian novel through Condé's Caribbean rewriting reveals not a racial but an interracial problematic that affects characters whose relation to a particular race is shifting and contingent. This re-articulation of race brings into relief a logic to which both "white" and "nonwhite" characters are subjected as they cross boundaries of class, gender, or national belonging. It thus emphasizes something the dominant culture is often too wont to forget, namely, that whiteness too is a racial category in need of ideological analysis. Previous characterizations of *Wuthering Heights*'s protagonists as either "nonwhite" or "white" are exposed as a continuation of the kind of racialist thinking that Gilroy's *Against Race* urges us to move beyond because they ultimately fail to do justice to the complex workings of narrative form. Race is no longer approached as descriptive sociological data whose meanings can only be extrapolated metaphorically but rather as a narrative whose structures of meaning perform ideological work even as they fluctuate according to context.

Significantly, this postcolonial reconfiguration of race as crossing also extends and revises recent models of hybridity and creolization offered by contemporary theorists of relationality. Indeed, whereas creolization—the racial and cultural process that defines Caribbean reality and that is at the forefront of postcolonial studies today—signifies the intermixing of several races, cultures, or languages, the Caribbean writings I examine dramatize a blurring of boundaries both *within* a single race and its representative(s) *as well as* in relation to other categories of identity. They represent race not as a composite of "European, African, or Asiatic" solidarities (as the authors of the influential *In Praise of Creoleness* do) but as a figuration of crossing whose patterns of meaning emerge only in light of the crossing of other categories such as class, gender, nationality, and sexuality. As it is typically conceived, the concept of hybridity cannot help but evoke the product of sexual intercourse between members of different "races," and as such, it is ultimately based on a biological phenomenon. It is seen as a form of transgression through sexual reproduction. By contrast, my project foregrounds a model of hybridity that resists anchoring the concept in the biological as it reveals the inseparability of the economies of visibility that generate the racial meanings attached to bodies from the symbolic operations of other identity categories. On the one hand, then, this book brings the issue of the interrelations of identities to the forefront of discussions of racial and cultural hybridity. On the other hand, it extends in so doing the notion of hybridity itself from a mixture of races or cultures to a structural interdefinition of racial, national, class, and gender identities. In the tales of interracial encounters it singles out, race, always already internally hybridized, crosses with identities whose meanings change as they interact with each other. This logic reveals categories that have no meaning outside of their interrelationships but are very much constituted by these. As Judith Butler explains in *Bodies That Matter,* "Though there are good historical reasons for keeping 'race' and 'sexuality' and 'sexual difference' as separate analytic spheres, there are also quite pressing and significant historical reasons for asking how and where we might not only read their convergence, but the sites at which the one cannot be constituted without the other" (168).

In *Against Race,* Paul Gilroy points out that the question of how "race" interrelates with sex, gender, and sexuality is "something that is further than ever from being settled and that defines a new and urgent need for future work" (45). That Gilroy himself should not have undertaken such work while calling for a postracial order is understandable since examining the interaction of racial and gender differences usually posits and hence runs the risk of reifying the very categories of identity that ought to cease serving as the basis of belonging. It is one thing to expose how discrete categories dissolve and lose their constricted meanings in light of contemporary global developments; it is another to conceptualize a transformed symbolic order in which destabilized categories interact with each other in a meaningful pattern. The vision of inexhaustible hybridity and blurring of post-identitarian postcolonialism is more easily assumed and abstracted than theorized and illustrated.[18] Yet it is precisely such a fundamental contribution to the study of the interrelatedness of identity categories that, I argue, this new generation of Caribbean writers is making.

Voice, Resistance, Agency

Other standard maneuvers of postcolonial revisionism interrogated and reconfigured by the Caribbean women writers of this study revolve around the interlinked issues of voice, resistance, and agency. Postcolonial practices have always been concerned with recovering the silenced voices of the underprivileged, about "looking at history through the prism of people who have nominally been written out of it" (Phillips, "Crossing the River" 26) and "disrupting that structure of colonial amnesia that denied the colonized his or her history" (Behdad 75). As phrases such as "coming to voice" and "finding one's voice" indicate, the metaphor of voice (in life as in fiction) evokes acts of resistance to the forces of domination that seek to suppress it. Voice is celebrated as the means through which an alternative truth can emerge through spontaneous expression and replace the lies of dominant representations. By extension, the character in possession of a narrative voice in fiction is traditionally the one with whom the reader identifies and the one who consistently moves closer to an "authentic" self as the story progresses. We expect the narrator to work toward achieving full autonomous subjectivity as she successfully bridges the gap between speech and thought, representation and emotion.[19] Earlier forms of feminist and postcolonial literary criticism tended to privilege this personal mode of narration precisely because it draws its authority from the speaker's right to tell her story by giving the evidence of her experience, whereas the generalizing and judgmental stance of the authorial mode emulates male imperialist authority.[20]

As the editors of *Out of the Kumbla* (1990) point out, a consideration of voice and voicelessness is crucial to understanding Caribbean women's writings since women were subjected to both colonial and patriarchal power structures that deprived them of voice. Nevertheless, the privileged position of contemporary female Caribbean authors complicates even if it does not invalidate their attempts at giving a voice to history's unheard. Authors such as Maryse Condé, Julia Alvarez, and Edwidge Danticat have all generated best sellers and have been affiliated with North American institutions of higher learning, while Rhys and Condé are today two of the most revered and canonized figures in postcolonial studies.[21] In light of their newly anointed status in the field on the one hand and the institutionalization of postcolonial studies on the other, these writers' engagements with voicelessness might thus appear problematic, especially in relation to the Caribbean people represented in their fiction. I argue that while this new generation's involvement in Western literary and academic institutions is certainly significant, it does not just turn them into the "color-baiters" and "culture vultures" (83) that Lamming so stridently criticizes in *The Pleasures of Exile*.[22] As Mignolo argues, it is important to distinguish "*postcolonial theories* as an academic commodity . . . from *postcolonial theorizing* as particular colonial critics subsumed under subaltern reason and border gnosis. The latter is a process of thought that people living under colonial domination enact in order to negotiate their life and subaltern condition" (93). What Caribbean writers' status in the West has effected then is not the invalidation of the process involved in resurrecting suppressed modes of expression but an anxious recognition of the mediated nature of such a process. Rather than unproblematically link voice and power, or literary and social authority, contemporary Caribbean women authors attend to the complexities of "finding a voice" and "breaking the silence" in the context of the conflicting legacies of colonialism. Issues of voice and representation remain an imperative in their postcolonial narratives, but they are no longer seen as necessarily tantamount to possessing historical or narrative authority.

Partly because of their "relational positionality,"[23] these authors are now generating narratives where the metaphor of voice is raised as a site of contradiction rather than as a unidirectional trope of power and authority. Instead of narratives whose central preoccupation is the coming to voice of the other, they generate questions surrounding the process of voicing: Is narrative voice tantamount to narrative authority? Can the dispossessed's voice be in fact heard? To what extent does speaking in one's voice in a postcolonial context amount to being possessed by Western ideals of embodied subjectivity? Is telling one's story a "ventriloquist's tale" (to borrow Pauline Melville's title) that ultimately reproduces colonialist terms often unbeknownst to the speaker herself? Do alternative Afro-Caribbean cultural practices (obeah, Santeria) constitute an authentic mode of expression and a site of oppositional resistance? Or do appeals to such practices merely serve to appease the conscience of critics anxious to skirt the charge of imperialism?

Critics today are eager to identify sites of subaltern agency in cultural and textual artifacts because the recognition of victimization is increasingly conflated with the denial of subaltern agency. Colonial discourse has always represented the other as a passive and malleable being who cannot be the maker of his or her own history. By extension, Western discussions of the subaltern as victims of a dominant structure have become suspect as well. Anxious not to be accused of reproducing imperialism's systematic erasure of the evidence of subaltern agency, postcolonial critics have consequently been busy celebrating representations of subaltern insurgency and its unsettling effects. As a result, their determination to detect these sites of resistance often obscures the power relations in which the subaltern voices are imbricated and celebrate agency independently of the context in which it operates. Whether or not slave or ex-slave revolts are successful does not seem to affect the strength such militant opposition embodies in the postcolonial imaginary. What matters is the recognition that the racial other is no victim. Never mind that such recognition obscures the oppressive effects of colonialism and its aftermaths, and that it ultimately reproduces the very binaries it should be undoing, namely those that oppose victimization and agency, agency and passivity, or voice and silence. What was once tacitly understood, namely, that someone can be an agent and a victim at the same time, now requires sustained theoretical elaboration to be recognized as a reasonable and cogent argument.[24]

By contrast, the contemporary Caribbean fiction discussed in *Reclaiming Difference* deconstructs these complacent views of agency and resistance, which too often only serve to give scholars a good conscience. It challenges, for instance, the Western notions of embodied subjectivity and speech that often unproblematically motivate readings of subaltern agency and resistance. It questions the "simple binary stereotype of resistance" (Ashcroft 25) such views propound, along with the notions of unified racial and national identity on which they are based. These narratives are peopled with oppressed individuals who oppress, oppressors who are disenfranchised, silences that speak louder than words, whites who are described as black, and shifting racial identities that turn the usual narrative of blacks passing for whites into a story of whiteness *as* passing. Last but not least, they shift the focus away from the recording of alternative voices, which, they reveal, do not necessarily provide evidence of decentered histories and subjectivities. They show instead that how history and instances of resistance are recorded and read, how they are disseminated and received, is as determining as the process of recovering suppressed knowledges and experiences.[25]

Home, Nation, Exile: Rewriting the Postnational

In chapter 4, I juxtapose two contemporary Caribbean migrant authors, Edwidge Danticat (Haiti/USA) and Julia Alvarez (Dominican Republic/ USA), whose stories of transplantation to the United States provide a unique perspective into the reconfiguration of the tropes of home and exile in Caribbean and postcolonial studies. Indeed, the meaning and scope of these categories have radically changed in light of the supplanting of nationalist modes of representation by a trans- and postnationalist focus in postcolonial studies. As *Reclaiming Difference* testifies, over the last two decades, postcolonialism has become primarily identified with terms like diaspora, migration, hybridity, and creolization, and has moved from an oppositional stance to an emphasis on the changing identities of both colonized and colonizers. This shift is all the more noticeable in contemporary migrant fiction where the nation as a unified imaginary community in all its manifestations seems to have been exploded once and for all, its constructions dissected, and its presuppositions laid bare. Scholars such as Kutzinski (*Sugar's Secrets*), Handley, and Dash (*The Other America*) have provided illuminating analyses of this development. In this chapter, I examine Danticat's and Alvarez's autobiographical novels, *Breath, Eyes, Memory* and *Yo!*, to highlight how, in light of this focus on transnational forms of cultural and racial exchange, these writers revise the core concepts of home and exile (with home functioning as a metaphor for the nation).

Exile and nostalgia have been dominant tropes in Caribbean texts ever since Kenneth Ramchand's pioneering *The West Indian Novel and Its Background* (1970) demarcated the paradigms for a critical approach to the Caribbean literary canon. As Ramchand points out, the birth and development of a West Indian consciousness and aesthetics in the 1950s and 1960s is bound to the experience of exile experienced by the first generation of Caribbean writers such as Lamming, Harris, James, Naipaul, and Selvon. These authors produced oppositional narratives of exile that assumed the shape of cultural nationalist romances and that, whether they advocated a return to the homeland or not, "remain[ed] preoccupied with the *meaning* of the native land in one way (Naipaul) or another (Lamming)" (Edmondson 141). Exile for these writers was a necessary aspect of nationalism, a paradox Edward Said highlighted in his "Reflections on

Exile": "All nationalisms in their early stages develop from a condition of estrangement" (quoted in Gikandi 71). As critics such as Edmondson, Kaplan, and Sugg have noted, this notion of exile is also rooted in colonialist discourses of Euro-American modernity that conceptualize it in terms of modernist fantasies of the mobile (white, privileged, and male) self at liberty. This tradition represents exile as a condition that allows the author to "objectively" assess his society and his relation to it and is hence deeply gendered since travel has always been "the privileged terrain of the errant male" (Nair 185).

In their tales of transplantation, Caribbean migrant women writers such as Danticat and Alvarez challenge the opposition between home and exile that motivates such discourses, offering powerful alternatives to the problematic masculinist identifications of the female self to the home/land. They complicate the binary geographical categories of U.S. and Caribbean identity prescribed by nationalist nostalgias by introducing an alternative third space that transforms Caribbeanness into a hybrid identity. Significantly, they both do so by writing in the language of their host country, which is at once a profound statement of cultural displacement and a paradoxical expression of rootedness in the creative syncretism that has been a hallmark of Caribbean and New World cultures for centuries. These writers relinquish "all idea, desire or nostalgia for fixity" (Braidotti, *Nomadic Subjects* 22) and reconfigure the relationship between American and Caribbean spaces in the face of global trends. They refuse to be either assimilated or marginalized, and insist on redefining Americanness itself rather than on integrating discrete versions of otherness into its misconceived dominant incarnations. In this sense, they echo Bharati Mukherjee's important critique of the idea of "America" as a multicultural space or a melting pot. Multiculturalism, Mukherjee explains, implies "the existence of a central culture, ringed by peripheral cultures . . . , of one culture as the norm and the rest as aberrations . . . [which] reinforce[s] an 'us' versus 'them' mentality" (135).

At the same time as both Danticat and Alvarez encourage us to rethink American culture and nationhood "as a constantly re-forming and transmogrifying 'we'" (Mukherjee 136), they also, I argue, allow us to differentiate between its various formulations. Indeed, postcolonialism's recent preoccupation with the supplanting of nationalist by postnationalist representations has also contributed to obscuring important differences within the new transnational ethos of New World fiction. To evoke Barbara Johnson's deconstructive language, it could be argued that the difference between the national and postnational produces and is produced by the repression of differences within the postnational. Indeed, the processes of intermixing and cross-fertilization that postcolonialism is so keen on today often generate "a bland interactive model" (Dash, "Madman" 1) or "a facile postmodern hybridity" (8) that tends to homogenize the differences among various postcolonial interventions.[26]

In chapter 4, I show how the expression of a creolized postnationalism takes quite different shapes in Alvarez's and Danticat's respective narratives. While both North American and Dominican societies are shown to partake of a hybridizing impulse in Alvarez's novel, the creolizing ethos among the cultures that come into contact in Danticat is unevenly spread; it is the black Atlantic cultures with a common history of slavery that are shown as open to an unceasing transformation, whereas "white" North America remains, by contrast, mired in a sterile focus on purity and homogeneity. Creolization in Danticat's work defines the regenerative black Atlantic, not the dominant "white" culture. Her representation of hybridity thus enacts a partial derailment of the white/other binary as she explodes "black culture" into its dynamic and heterogeneous parts and emphasizes the role of gender as a central mediating factor in her national and cultural histories of displacement. While Danticat thus apparently reifies a notion of black solidarity, she also complicates any facile conflation of a "black" consciousness with essentialism or nationalism. Her view challenges any attempt to dilute creolization into a metaphor for all humanity and emphasizes instead the history of slavery and oppression that underlies its processes.

Together, these writers remind us that like any other disciplinary formation, postcolonial studies runs the risk of creating orthodoxies that homogenize different writers' representational politics by virtue of a common experience of transplantation and a common history of colonialism. As Boehmer points out, "writers and texts from different continents, nations, and cultures are often indiscriminately blended together as being migrant or polyphonic" (246), a tendency that is even more pronounced when these writers are from the Caribbean, that is, the site where "a regional identity . . . assumes a greater importance than that of any single territory within the archipelago" (Dash, *The Other America* xi). The four migrant tales I examine in *Reclaiming Difference* all contribute to recasting postcoloniality in terms of relation rather than opposition and are as such exemplary of the creolized aesthetics that constitutes an "ideological breakthrough" in relation to previous identitarian thought (Dash, *Édouard Glissant* 148). Their departure from a preexisting anticolonial paradigm does not, however, merely make them exemplary of a circumscribable "migrant aesthetics." The different modalities of their creolizing imperative are as important as the way in which this new aesthetics distinguishes itself from Euro-American etiologies of exile.

Ten years ago, Ahmad's influential critique of Jameson reminded us that not "*all* third-world texts" are "national allegories" (Ahmad 107). Today, we need to remind ourselves that not all postcolonial authors writing from a privileged position in the West are producing the same kind of transnational narrative, let alone the kind of postmodern hybrid and muddled view of the world that Ahmad identified as a trademark of Rushdie's fiction. In fact, despite Rushdie's own frequent endorsements of migrancy and hybridity as universal and regenerative conditions, not even he can be accused of indiscriminately endorsing an amorphous hybridity that blindly valorizes the experience of "unbelonging" (Ahmad 152). In *The Satanic Verses,* the protagonist's forceful Indian mistress and art critic Zeeny Vakil is both a staunch defender of the hybrid nature of India's national culture (borrower of "whatever clothes seemed to fit, Aryan, Mughal, British, take-the-best-and-leave-the-rest") and the harshest critic of Saladin's own hybridic layering of identities (she calls him "Salad"). This recognition that not all cultural cross-fertilizations are equivalent also defines Rushdie's *The Moor's Last Sigh,* where the hybrid cultures resulting from the encounter between invading Muslim forces and the local populace in Moorish Spain as well as Mughal India are contrasted with the imperialist nature of the British-Indian colonial encounter.

Similarly, *Reclaiming Difference* highlights the different forms of narrativity that creolization and hybrid identities take in contemporary Caribbean women's fiction. My juxtaposition of Condé and Rhys in the first and second chapters emphasizes the ways in which Condé rewrites the kind of revisionism with which Rhys's novel is associated even as it reveals striking parallels between these two novels' rewriting of racial identity as a relational concept. In chapter 3, I use this reconceptualization of race— a notion that is at the core of postcolonial studies—to reread Emily Brontë's *Wuthering Heights.* Last but not least, my juxtaposition of Danticat's and Alvarez's autobiographical narratives in chapter 4 emphasizes the dramatically different ways in which two migrant writers with a similar experience of transplantation challenge the nationalist ethos of earlier postcolonial representations. Specifically, I discuss this discrepancy in their narratives of legacy in light of their respective ethnic backgrounds and experience of exile.

Provided it remains attentive to the differences resulting from divergent colonial histories, the New World perspective I have outlined in this book allows us to look anew at a reality whose contours are too often ossified and to redraw its configurations in a way that frees us from the tyrannies of race and nation. In *Losing Isaiah,* a film about an African American boy adopted by a white family, when Isaiah is asked to name the difference between his and his white sister's hand, he responds: "Yours is bigger." His inability to recognize the contrast in skin colors as a primary mode of identification is surprising if not inconceivable to an audience well trained in viewing race as a somatic site of difference. The child's blindness to his own racial difference is symptomatic of the kind of symbolic economy in which he was brought up (where difference based on race was suppressed) and which will no doubt be replaced by a system based on color as he gets socialized and racialized. *Reclaiming Difference* foregrounds moments such as these, when concepts such as nation and race that are at the core of postcolonialism have to be rethought and re-conceptualized. These are moments when silences reconfigure passivity as agency, when home is neither here nor there but in both places, when the racial difference of a "black" character is visibly "invisible" or alternatively, when the invisible (because naturalized) "white" norm is rendered visible in such a way as to radically redefine the concept of "blackness." These are also moments when the vision of a culturally and ethnically homogeneous nation is exploded in favor of a nonexclusionary and relational mode of thinking that best represents the dynamics of our interdependent post/colonial world.

1 Maryse Condé's *Windward Heights*

A Rewriting of Postcolonial Revisionism

> Mine will be the story of very ordinary people who in their very ordinary ways had nevertheless shed the blood of others. . . . A book with neither great torturers nor lavish martyrdoms. But one that would still be heavy with its weight of flesh and blood. The story of my people.
>
> Maryse Condé, *Tree of Life*

IN "Order, Disorder, Freedom, and the West Indian Writer," the Guadeloupean Maryse Condé emphasizes the importance of challenging the ideological dogmas established by male authors and of replacing their masculinist tenets and "constraining order" with "disorder" and "freedom." Caribbean women writers, she argues, "displease, shock, or disturb. Their writings imply that before thinking of a political revolution, West Indian literature needs a psychological one. What they hope for and desire conflicts with men's ambitions and dreams. Why, they ask, fight against racism in the world when it exists at home among ourselves?" (131–32). In this chapter, I argue that Condé's *Windward Heights,* her imaginative rewriting of the Victorian classic *Wuthering Heights,* does precisely what the Guadeloupean author advocates in her essay, namely "disorder" some of the most foundational concepts in Caribbean and postcolonial studies: race and hybridity, resistance and agency. To do so, Condé engages the various models of cultural and racial identity—from Négritude to Antillanité and Créolité—through which Caribbeanness has been articulated over the last few decades and uses fiction to forcefully intervene in contemporary theoretical debates on postcoloniality.[1] She sets in motion a critical and productive dialogue between postcolonial theory and criticism by making us question the reading strategies through which we read postcolonial fiction. By generating and revising current theoretical configurations, she also transforms the act of "rewriting" itself.

Indeed, *Windward Heights* distinguishes itself from previous postcolonial rewritings (and more specifically from Jean Rhys's *Wide Sargasso Sea*) insofar as it is dedicated to the author of its source-text: "To Emily Brontë, who, I hope, will approve of this reading of her chef-d'oeuvre. With honor and respect!"[2] As Françoise Lionnet has remarked, instead of writing "back to the expected *destinataire,* Condé crosses borders and boundaries to find inspiration and to articulate unexpected affiliations" ("Narrating" 71). The Victorian classic is a source not of indignation but of inspiration for the Guadeloupean author, and as a result, the expectations of contemporary readers well trained in postcolonial revisionism or "anticolonial literary militantism" (Bernabé, Chamoiseau, and Confiant 106) are derailed. Rather than rewrite the colonial text as if it were a static object waiting to be decoded by its enlightening postcolonial sequel, Condé's novel stages a salutary double-take that rewrites not colonialism so much as postcolonialism's most time-honored maneuvers. Indeed, as a "postcolonial" novel, *Windward Heights* raises expectations it flagrantly refuses to fulfill.[3] It is a revision of a European classic from a "black" perspective that seeks neither to correct its source-text nor to valorize blackness. Rather than challenge racism's conflation of cultural and physical elements by separating them, it rewrites race by paradoxically reinforcing the inseparability of these two dimensions. In fact, it defies the tenets of postcolonial revisionism so unashamedly that it makes readers question their own assumptions rather than the colonialist representations it is rewriting. It highlights *how* rather than *what* we read when we read postcolonial fiction. It makes us self-conscious about our reading practices, so much so that it replicates in fiction the self-reflexive turn that has defined postcolonialism since its turn from literature to theory in the 1980s. Indeed, as Moore-Gilbert points out, postcolonial theory has not only become a field in its own right but seems to thrive at the expense of the criticism of postcolonial literature. In light of this splitting, Condé's reconciliation of criticism and theory through her fiction is all the more unique and momentous.

In *Windward Heights,* Condé transposes the plot of the Brontë text from the harsh windblown Yorkshire moors of eighteenth-century England to the tropical setting of the nineteenth-century Caribbean to illuminate not the past text and context but contemporary racial and neocolonial relations. Wuthering Heights is now located in La Guadeloupe in the late 1890s and is renamed "L'Engoulvent." The novel begins with Razyé's return from Cuba after a three-year exile and relates the story of his revenge on his rival and the latter's descendants. Whereas in Brontë's text this rivalry is represented predominantly in terms of class conflict, it is now overlaid with a racial dimension that forcefully illustrates the intertwined racial and class hierarchies of Caribbean societies.[4] As a black Creole of unmixed African ancestry, Razyé (Heathcliff's counterpart) is a member of the lowest class, while at the other end of the social spectrum, his rival, the white planter (or *béké*) Aymeric de Linsseuil (alias Edgar Linton), owns 20 percent of Grande-Terre's lands.[5] The object of both men's obsession, Cathy Gagneur (Brontë's Cathy Earnshaw), belongs to the mulatto, or "colored," class who gained their freedom during slavery and often aspire to the same status as the *békés*. Throughout the novel, what remains remarkably consistent with the original is Razyé's unrelenting passion for his childhood love, Cathy, and his unrepentant cruelty toward everyone else. What is radically different is the second generation's fate, since *Windward Heights*'s young lovers do not get to experience the domestic bliss that concludes *Wuthering Heights:* the second Catherine, Cathy II, dies in childbirth like her mother after realizing that Razyé II, the man whose child she is having, is her own half-brother. Furthermore, Condé explodes the double narration of *Wuthering Heights* into a multitude of narrators whose first-person "récits" alternate with the third-person narration. Most of her narrators are black Creoles who are at the bottom of the social hierarchy, that is, servants, ex-slaves, nannies (called *mabos*), housekeepers, fishermen, obeah men (*babalawos*), or helpers. Significantly, they give their own version of events as they meet Brontë's revamped characters without, however, subordinating their own experiences to that of the protagonists. Condé thus ensures that her most disenfranchised characters have a narrative voice, thus evoking but also, I will show, reformulating postcolonialism's investment in "giving a voice" to the silenced oppressed.

If she paradoxically turned to a Victorian classic to represent contemporary concerns, it is because Condé recognized in *Wuthering Heights* elements that strongly resonate with the Antillean cultural context. In her own words, she took what was "a sketch in the original and went further in relation to the culture to which I belong" (Haubruge 18). While Condé does not specify the nature of this "sketch" in her interview, her rewriting makes it amply clear that she is referring to the racial and class hybridity embedded in Emily Brontë's narrative. In Lionnet's words, Condé "foregrounds the racial scripts that are barely hinted at in Brontë's tale of guilty passion" ("Narrating" 71). She displaces the geographical and historical frames of Brontë's canonical narrative to a late-nineteenth-century Caribbean context in order to reconceptualize the complex issues of racial and cultural identity endemic to the "contact zone" produced by colonization.[6] Specifically, her interracial narrative transforms our conventional understanding of racial identity by challenging earlier anticolonial but also more recent postcolonial deployments of race and hybridity. On the one hand, in line with more recent theories of postcoloniality, *Windward Heights*'s representational politics challenges anticolonialism's use of race as the basis for unified notions of identity and resistance. Instead, Condé demonstrates that ethnicity and race are not fixed constructs or measurable entities and that, as she provocatively put it in a much quoted but insufficiently understood statement that anticipates Gilroy, "there are no races, only cultures" ("Notes" 14). On the other hand, she also challenges more recent postcolonial paradigms of relational identity, such as creolization, since she represents the cross-fertilization of races or cultures as a process that does not occur outside of its relationship with other categories of identity.

Condé's rewriting of race is important because it emphasizes both the contingent configurations of race, class, gender, and nationality and the determining logic through which these identities are deployed to keep social hierarchies in place. What is remarkable is that her dramatization of the potency with which racial ideology conditions history and daily life does not reinscribe the tyranny of race. Instead, she demonstrates how the interdependence of identities allows each category to accrue meaning through contingent but not arbitrary patterns. In *Windward Heights*, Condé urges us to detect and trace these patterns, and in replacing normative configurations of difference with a complex model of relational identity, she instigates a new reading strategy that alters our traditional approaches to both colonial and postcolonial texts. I will now account for this intervention by emphasizing Condé's engagement with the leading theories of identity in Caribbean studies.

From Négritude to Antillanité to Disorder

Condé's revised models of identity and resistance cannot be properly understood unless they are examined in the context of two intellectual movements, Antillanité and Créolité, which emerged respectively in 1981 and 1989. The proponents of Antillanité and Créolité formulated their theories of difference in reaction to Négritude's model of racial identity, which they claimed failed to do justice to the cultural and geopolitical complexity of the West Indian space. The Martinican Édouard Glissant was among the first to proclaim the specificity of West Indian culture and to reject black universalism in favor of a concept of "créolisation" and "Le Divers," reflecting the concrete realities of cross-cultural fertilization. In *Le Discours Antillais* (1981) and *Poétique de la Relation* (1990) specifically, Glissant proposes a model of West Indian identity that breaks away from notions of (black or African) origins and rootedness to foreground the complexity, heterogeneity, and polysemy of the Caribbean context. Caribbeanness, he insists, is a mosaic of infinitely multiplying "relations" that cannot be accounted for in terms of essences. For Glissant, the constitutive principle of Caribbean identity is thus the intermingling of languages, races, religions, and customs that cannot be subsumed under a totality. He further explains:

> Today, the Antillean no longer denies the African part of her being; neither does she need to proclaim it as an exclusive identity. She must recognize it. She understands that our history (even if we have lived it as non-history) has resulted in *another reality*. She is no longer constrained strategically to reject its Western components, even if they are still alienating, because she knows that she can choose from them. She sees that alienation lies first and foremost in the impossibility of making a choice, in the arbitrary imposition of values, and perhaps in the very notion of "Values." She realizes that synthesis is not the process of bastardization that she was led to believe but a fertile practice through which the constituent elements get enriched. She has become Antillean. (*Le Discours Antillais* 25–26)

Similarly, in a literary manifesto entitled *Éloge de la Créolité* (1989), Bernabé, Chamoiseau, and Confiant promote a cross-cultural poetics of liberation that celebrates hybridity and "the conscious harmonization of preserved diversities" as the basis of Caribbean identity (Bernabé, Chamoiseau, and Confiant 114). Inspired by Glissant's Antillanité, Créolité rejects a racial definition of identity and underlines African, European, Chinese, Indian, and Lebanese contributions to West Indian cultures: "In multiracial societies, such as ours, it seems urgent to quit using the traditional raciological distinctions and to start again designating the people of our countries, regardless of their complexion, by the only suitable word: *Creole*. Socioethnic relations in our society ought to take place from now on under the seal of a common creoleness, without, not in the least, obliterating class relations or conflicts" (90).

Windward Heights's defining cross-cultural imagination echoes Créolité's representation of the Caribbean as multiethnic and syncretic. Condé, like Glissant and the Créolistes, posits a cross-cultural sensibility and hybrid culture that conveys the immigrant experience as key to Caribbeanness. Because of her fictional explorations of pan-Caribbean and transcultural spaces as well as of her own personal peregrinations from Guadeloupe to Africa, Europe, and the United States, her work is often discussed as an embodiment of celebratory notions of creolization, all the more so since she has explicitly and repeatedly distanced herself from black consciousness movements such as Négritude.

Throughout her fictional and critical writings, Condé has consistently interrogated the premises of the Négritude movement, and *Windward Heights* is no exception to this rule. While she gives the movement credit for fundamentally changing the way Caribbeans perceived themselves, her work never fails to foreground the dangers inherent in its myth of rootedness in a racial past. Aimé Césaire and Léopold Senghor, the founders of Négritude, introduced the notion of racial pride at a time when the majority of Caribbeans sought to emulate European ways of being and thinking. Both men called for the solidarity of the peoples of the African diaspora based on a common ground of blackness and advocated the renewal of the black world through the revalorization of Mother Africa.[7] As Condé herself acknowledges, Négritude's anti-assimilationism and emphasis on the resurrection of black values and culture was an important and necessary step in the decolonizing process: "Without Césaire, we might not be who we are. He was the first to give us racial pride, a racial conscience, and the realization that the Caribbean islands are not just 'specks of dust' in the Caribbean Sea. . . . I think that we are all children of Césaire. I consider him the Founding-Ancestor" (Pfaff 61). In her study of Césaire's germinal 1939 *Cahier d'un Retour au Pays Natal* (*Notebook of a Return to the Native Land,* 1983), she nonetheless also explains why the utopian project of Négritude, whether biologically based or not, needs to be thoroughly revised if it is to dismantle colonialist discourse and practice: "Negro/African values are only countervalues. They are the opposite of what Europe possesses and when it is time to make a positive inventory, our writers are stuck. Refusals and oppositions are not constructive" (48).[8]

While recognizing the liberating contribution of Négritude to later postcolonial analyses, Condé exposes the impossible choice it establishes between two basic ideological premises, namely the white and the black myths, or Europe and Africa. The very opposition itself is revealed as problematic through the representation, for instance, of the first Cathy, who is asked to choose between the "black" and "white" sides of her identity, two terms whose opposition her very existence has already scrambled. She lives in a world that demands that she either repress or reclaim her African ancestry despite the process of transculturation that defines her experience. As Condé explains elsewhere: "Caribbeans tell themselves they have to choose. And choose what? Because the basic premise has taken on a political implication. That which gives prevalence to African elements is immediately defined as progressive. Reclaiming its African heritage, it is opposed to the assimilationist, defender of European values, and hence, contemptible. Let us explain that things are not that simple. This basic premise, Africa against Europe, is in fact a racist premise inherited from colonial times and which includes the opposition Savagery/ Civilization" (*La Civilisation du Bossale* 6).[9] Trapped in Négritude's model of cultural duality, Catherine has to choose between an identification with the African worldview or with the colonizers' historical and cultural hierarchies. It is this artificial forced choice that ultimately signifies and generates her dementia and death. As her dramatic and posthumous change in skin color reveals, a model of identification and rootedness that foregrounds race as an immutable category of social existence is bound to fail.

Like her previous novels, *Windward Heights* includes direct textual citations from Césaire's work. The chapter entitled "Return to My Native Land" echoes his important poem by the same name (as well as, inevitably, Condé's now famous essay about it)[10] and emphasizes the difficulty of recovering one's past and of determining one's future alliances based on them. Razyé II, Isabella and Razyé's first son, returns to La Pointe to discover that his "indestructible" father is dead and that the newly rich Irmine is "lactifying" her children (to borrow Fanon's phrase) even as she is idealizing the memory of her late husband and pitiless tormentor. The novel shows that in fact, one's "return to the native land" can only result in yet another form of exile: "Every displacement, every attempt to return, every new departure renders the 'I' more and more aware of the gap, of his or her difference" (Rosello, "One More Sea" 181). Return for Razyé II, as for his father before him, brings on consciousness and alienation, not reconciliation with and recovery of the past. Origins and roots are themselves exposed as constructed narratives that are told retrospectively.[11] The chapter "Return to My Native Land" gives way to the last section entitled "Return to L'Engoulvent," and in thus repeating and deferring the completion of an actual "return" represents the act of returning as a process, a series of "detours" (to borrow Glissant's term) rather than as a self-contained event or outcome.[12] As Rosello explains in her analysis of the theme of exile for Antillean writers, what we have is "a 'land' that is not one, . . . a 'native land' that is not an origin, . . . a 'return' that would only be another departure and a new detour . . . and become little by little the acceptance of 'wandering,' . . . an infinite and irremediable exile" (177–78). Razyé II's "return" takes him to L'Engoulvent, where he had in fact never set a foot before and does in no way provide either him or us with a satisfying sense of closure. Instead he has entered "l'univers taraudant, non de la conscience malheureuse mais, bel et bien, de la conscience torturée" (the piercing universe, not of the unhappy but of the tortured conscience) (Glissant, *Le Discours Antillais* 53). He stops changing, shaving, or washing himself, and, as far as we know, will be forever tormented both by the suspicion that his union with Cathy was incestuous and by the devouring concern for his daughter, Anthuria: "Une si belle enfant ne pouvait pas être maudite" (Such a lovely child could not be cursed) (348).

Windward Heights's radical reworking of Césairian themes thus exemplifies the kind of demystification of "essentialist glorifications of unitary origins, be they racial, sexual, geographic, or cultural" (Lionnet, *Autobiographical Voices* 8–9) that the proponents of creolization and Créolité also advocate in their writings. But the commonalities between *Windward Heights*'s representation of Caribbean complexities and the model of identity set forth by "Le Groupe de la Créolité" only go so far.[13] In fact, Condé deliberately transgresses the edified strictures suggested by this group as a model for West Indian fiction. For instance, while Glissant focuses on rehabilitating the (male) Marron as the true hero of West Indian history, and the writers of *Éloge* on celebrating the male storyteller, Condé takes issue with the very assumption that literature should provide Caribbeans with an idealized image of themselves and their islands.[14] The manifesto *Éloge de la Créolité* decrees that literature should recover the dignity of Caribbean realities from their debased rendition in white texts:

> The Creole literature that we are elaborating takes it as a principle that there is nothing petty, poor, useless, vulgar, or unworthy of a literary project in our world. . . . We want, thanks to Creoleness, to name each thing in it, and to declare it beautiful. To perceive the human grandeur of the djobeurs. To grasp the depth of life in Morne Pichevin. To understand the vegetable markets. To elucidate the functioning of the tale tellers. To accept, again without any judgment our "dorlis," our "zombis," our "chouval-twa-pat," "soukliyan." (100–101)

By contrast, Condé objects to any process of recovery that glosses over the vulgar and immoral aspects of Antillean societies. Whereas Bernabé, Chamoiseau, and Confiant ask for a representation of the Caribbean space and its people that accepts without judging, she offers an "aesthetics of the reprehensible" that advocates both judgment and acceptance and refuses idealized heroes.

In *Éloge de la Créolité,* the authors further call for a Caribbean poetics that "look[s] for our truths" (101) in order to enhance the collective ability to fight neocolonialism. To this end, they encourage the celebration of the "bursts of our rebellions" and of the "opaque resistance of Maroons allied in their disobedience" (98). They urge writers and readers to resurrect these "insignificant heroes, anonymous heroes . . . who are forgotten by the colonial chronicle" and "have nothing in common with the Western or French heroes" (101). Condé's novel conforms to the tenet that Antillean literature should foreground the daily life of ordinary people and draw on the Creole people's memory. Like her male contemporaries, she is invested in recovering *"these impenetrable areas of silence where screams were lost"* to replace the official history that has feigned to be Caribbean history (Bernabé, Chamoiseau, and Confiant 99). And like them, she aims at resurrecting "the insignificant . . . [and] anonymous heroes" whose model of heroism diverges from Western notions of agency (101). In Condé, however, the masculinist notions of heroism and agency, marronnage, and storytelling with which the Créolistes offer to replace Western myths are themselves exposed as the same thing, myths. What the critic Ian Strachan points out about novelists such as Michelle Cliff and Paule Marshall is also true of the Créolistes: "These writers have written eloquently about the need for buried truths to be unearthed and for certain myths to be destroyed. It seems counterproductive to offer new myths in their place" (255). Similarly, in both criticism and fiction, Condé takes issue with any new orthodoxy offered to replace the old ones. Specifically, she criticizes the injunctions that Creole literature should celebrate folk heroes or underclass characters, necessarily represent a "collective voice" by using the Creole vocabulary, and be anchored in a mono-insular West Indian setting. She asks: "Are we condemned *ad vitam aeternam* to speak of vegetable markets, story tellers, 'dorlis,' 'koutem' . . . ? Are we condemned to explore to saturation the resources of our narrow islands? We live in a world where, already, frontiers have ceased to exist" (Condé, "Order" 130).[15]

In transgressing the principles suggested by her predecessors as a model for West Indian fiction, Condé's work offers a trenchant critique of the masculinism and heterosexism inherent in such models. As James Arnold points out

> On reading Bernabé, Chamoiseau, and Confiant, not to mention Glissant, we would be hard pressed to account for all those grandmothers or elderly aunts, those repositories of oral history, folk medicine, and stories of all sorts who have been credited by nearly all women writers in the Caribbean with stimulating their writing careers. None of these female figures of cultural transmission

find their way into the history of oraliture that Chamoiseau and Confiant have constructed. ("Gendering" 30)

In *Windward Heights,* Condé's gendering of Créolité goes further, however, than simply introjecting female protagonists or storytellers into her fiction. She also rewrites core concepts of postcolonialism such as race, resistance, and history by accounting for their gendered and contingent structures. Most important, she disengages race from the inescapable regime of visibility that underlies many contemporary discussions of race. In extending the notion of hybridity from a mixture of races or cultures to a structural interdefinition of racial, national, class, and gender identities, she frees us from the tyranny of race, which is ultimately one of the most sessile legacies of colonialism.

Cathy's Race

While it is a matter of debate whether Emily Brontë's darkening of Heathcliff in *Wuthering Heights* is a metaphorical or literal reference to race, Condé does away with the uncertainty by physically marking both Heathcliff and Cathy as "black" and "mulatta," respectively. Unlike his gypsylike Victorian counterpart, Razyé's physical attributes unequivocally evoke features associated with the Negro race in the nineteenth century; his skin is described as "black, that shiny black they call ashanti" (7). Similarly, Cathy's darker skin is explicitly and repeatedly ascribed to her African ancestry, while the representation of the second Cathy puts an end to speculations concerning her origins by confirming the assumption that Brontë critics could not substantiate in the source-text. Condé's Cathy II is unequivocally identified as Cathy and Razyé's child, and she herself enters an incestuous union with her half-brother Razyé II, alias Premier-Né. If there are identity crises in the novel, they do not derive from any ambiguity of origins since even the most "minor" characters begin their respective narrative sections with a detailed account of their own personal history. Lineages are minutely traced in the narrative, and racial difference is visibly and unambiguously established.

   In other words, Condé does not challenge racist and colonial ideologies by evoking the biological "errances of hybridity" to expose the falsity of a pure and static identity. She represents a world where the dominant ideology does not repress the truth of miscegenation but reappropriates it in service of its own imperialist agenda. In turn-of-the century Guadeloupe, blood-mixing is not, as in Victorian England, the vestige of a repressed past whose unearthing threatens naturalized rigid binary identities but a staple of the present and of its reconfigured hierarchical structure. The tripartite social system of the Caribbean keeps track of genealogies and holds people accountable for the slightest suspicion of racial transgression. This is a world where the crossing of racial barriers does not necessarily constitute a threat to the color hierarchy. The process of racial and cultural creolization that defines Caribbean reality is mobilized by hegemonic discourse as individualized perversion rather than as a function of a repressed history and cultural contact.

In this context, celebrating hybrid forms of race for their ability to destabilize binary oppositions and hegemonic categories of race becomes a futile gesture. And indeed, Condé's recasting of race does not tread such a beaten path since she resists representing race as a category whose meanings and boundaries can simply be transgressed or reversed through interracial or intercultural paradigms. In her narratives, race does not come under fire because her hybrid characters "pass" or undermine the use of physical phenotypes as the basis of group distinctions. Neither do the meanings of race get disrupted because "black" characters challenge racist culture's attribution of social and behavioral importance to physical markers. In fact, Condé's interracial narratives are so unorthodox that they often appear to be reclaiming rather than—to borrow the title of Mireille Rosello's book—"declining the stereotype."

Far from deviating from hegemonic representations of race, *Windward Heights* paradoxically seems to amplify some of the most egregious stereotypes of blackness that postcolonialism has so painstakingly worked to undo. The oversexualization of her nonwhite male characters and their massive promiscuity (in stark contrast to the monogamous white Aymeric) is a case in point. The novel abounds with graphic phallic imagery detailing the vitality and health of a particular character's sexual organs, so much so that the relative firmness of a particular man's member appears to be directly commensurate with his prospects and dealings. Everyone's member is always about to take over, and all the women watch, fascinated. To Aymeric's question, "Is [sic] a man's qualities measured by the lustiness of his member?" (86), the novel appears to answer with a resounding "yes."

Condé's focus on the body as a determinative site of visible (sexual or racial) differences is deeply unsettling to a postcolonial audience trained to balk at the oversexualization of blackness in stereotypical discourses of race. Her descriptions of the meanings attached to the body—the attention to skin, penis size, and breast size, for instance—are not parodic enough to be read as denunciations of "doudouiste" stereotypes. The insistence on male virility and black female sexuality seems to reify stereotypes of "real" blackness all the more since the significations linked to corporeality are not exposed as misrepresentations.[16] How then does Condé show us that there are indeed "no races, only cultures"?

Instead of overturning racial stereotypes, Condé exposes race as culture by recasting the concept of race itself. The hegemonic reading of these corporeal meanings is questioned not by attacking the meanings attached to the body (which would leave the body intact in its prediscursive essentiality) but by reconceptualizing corporeality itself. *Windward Heights* questions the notion that race is a stable identity whose crossing destabilizes its meaning *after* race has first been visualized in its hegemonic wholeness. When it is viewed as a coming together of discrete categories, the logic of crossing actually reinforces the very norms it is supposed to undo and loses its subversive force. It merely reproduces exclusionary configurations of difference. By contrast, crossing in the novel is depicted not as what follows from but as what constitutes the very category of race itself. Whereas other writers define the concept by presupposing that a set of phenotypical characteristics identifies groups of people who are oppressed on that basis, Condé explores the concept as a social construction that shifts as her characters interact. In other words, it is not because of a character's preexisting racial identity that certain gendered traits/stereotypes come to be ascribed to him/her, but because of the crossing of gender categories (or class, or nationality) that race comes to matter (and be) at all. Race crossing thus becomes a figuration for class and/or gender crossing in an economy that redefines what were once perceived as discrete categories as sets of crisscrossing ones (gender, class, nationality, etc.).

This reconfiguration challenges the view of race as a stable identity circumscribed by a visible taxonomy of skin to which various traits and behaviors are attached a posteriori. Instead, *Windward Heights* exposes the supposed incontrovertibility of the regime of visibility through which race is produced and which is constantly reinforced culturally. It reveals that when postcolonialism destabilizes the stereotypical traits associated with race rather than the concept itself, it implicitly acquiesces with the notion of race as an unassailable identity and colludes with its hegemonic deployments. To demonstrate the shifting nature of the term and its necessary interdependence with other identities, Condé focuses then on the visible and changing taxonomy of skin in a way that radically challenges our conventional understanding of race. In her novel, race is no longer a backdrop of visible and invariable difference on which social meanings are imposed but itself a site of visible transformation. The description of

Cathy I in *Windward Heights* powerfully illustrates this reconceptualization of race as crossing.

Windward Heights's Cathy is the daughter of a "tallow-colored"
mulatto in late-nineteenth-century Guadeloupe whose changing status in
Caribbean society translates into remarkably physicalist transformations.
When we are first introduced to her character, she is "the colour of hot
syrup left to cool in the open air, with black hair like threads of night"
(19). She is so dark-skinned that, unlike her light-skinned brother, Justin,
she cannot pass as a white Creole. Yet pass is exactly what she does when
she marries into the upper echelons of the white Creole class. What is remarkable about this social elevation is that Cathy manages to pass not
despite her skin color but because of it. She undergoes in life as well as in
death such dramatic epidermic changes that they rival Michael Jackson's
phenotype-modifying antics, only maybe in a more accelerated fashion.
Her phenotype reflects her social status rather than determines it. On the
day of her wedding, she is so "pale" as to draw an expression of surprise
from her own brother. Years later, her corpse undergoes yet another striking somatic transformation—her black features literally take over her
white blood: "First of all the colour of her skin was not white. It was as if
her black blood could no longer be contained and was taking its revenge.
Victorious, it was flooding through her. It thickened her facial features,
distended her mouth, giving a mauve touch to her lips, and with the stroke
of a pencil redefined the arch of her eyebrows" (84). This description of
retransformation is the way Condé chooses to highlight the cultural nature
of race as a category. It is not merely, I argue, an outcome of the artistic
license writers use to describe the social world in a hyperbolic or parodic
way. Classified as an exaggeration, it fails to affect let alone threaten our
commonsense understanding of race, and the implications of Cathy's final
transformation are neutralized. They are safely interpreted, for instance,
as the inescapability of racial meanings one can only vainly attempt to
evade and as the reinstatement of the heroine's racial identity by a "black"
writer. Cathy's victorious "blackness" then would merely recast her earlier
passing as wishful thinking in a society where racial hierarchy overlaps
with class inequality. Such a predictable interpretation does not do justice
to Condé's pyrotechnics, which, I argue, goes further through its revision
of race as culture.

Far from duplicating racialist thinking, the description of Cathy's race
epitomizes Condé's explosion of our most deep-seated assumptions about
race and urges us to explore the far-reaching implications of such "disorder."
Cathy's epidermal mutation points to a racial logic in which the issue is

not *whether* but *when* one is "black." What matters to the author of the statement "there are no races, only cultures" is not the recognition of Cathy's "rightful" racial identity but the capacity of her identity to shift in the first place. Her recasting of the notion of race distinguishes itself from other forms of postessentialist analyses in that it takes place, as it were, on top of a familiar essentialist scenario that anchors race in bodily characteristics. This emphasis on the physicalist aspects of race shows that Condé is not merely pointing to the ways in which transgressive light-skinned "blacks" are metaphorically and metonymically associated with "whiteness" (or vice versa), but that she also is questioning the very "economies of visibility" (Wiegman 4) in which our understanding of race is anchored. Readers are urged to question a facile critical reliance on referential and metaphorical meanings of "race" and to see both of these as part of the same racial logic.[17]

In describing Cathy's "darkening" as a literal transformation, the narrative highlights the imbrication of two fields, vision and the visible—that is, what is part of one's field of vision (but not necessarily seen) and what one actually sees. It dramatizes the importance of recognizing how contingent the shift is from one to the other of these modalities. According to Robyn Wiegman, while it is true that "the economies of visibility that produce the network of meanings attached to bodies" have always worked to "anchor whiteness in the visible epistemology of black skin" (21), it is only in the sixteenth century that race was defined as a visible economy. Before the Renaissance, it did not function as the main organizing criterion to divide human beings. Condé reveals race as a contingent production whose visibility itself needs to be scrutinized as the basis of difference among human beings. Like other corporeal signs with which it is used interchangeably (hair, palms, nose, etc.), race is revealed as an arbitrary means of maintaining social hierarchies and as the site of a slippage between the visual and the visible. What determines race's shift from one economy into the other, *Windward Heights* reveals, is its relation to other categories of identity. The visibility to which Cathy's race becomes subjected is a function of her crossing of class and gender boundaries.

Condé confirms this reconceptualization of race when the narrator informs her readers of something they thought they already knew, namely that "First of all the color of her skin was not white." This statement immediately precedes the description of Cathy's metamorphosis back into blackness and emphasizes as a result not her racial identity but its instability. The narrator is imparting a piece of information that she assumes will or should surprise her readers when the very fact of having to make it at all highlights a fluidity that is usually considered antithetical to racial difference. It highlights the corpse's physical permutation rather than its putatively predetermined racial difference: "What was this girl of African descent doing here, you might well have asked, and how did she get laid out on a sheet surrounded by all these white Creoles trying to put on an appropriate face for the occasion?" (84). Cathy's shifting race is inseparable from her crossing of class boundaries and from the *békés'* anxious production of categorical difference in the face of destabilized social hierarchies. Her "black" body is not the origin of racism and requires us to question the "recurrent and . . . violent equation between the idea of 'race' and the 'black body'" (Wiegman 21). The visual and the visible are different economies whose conflation is part and parcel of the workings of these "regimes of visibility." Just as the visual does not necessarily lead to visibility, neither does the visible necessarily require the visual to establish difference. As Frantz Fanon's insights make clear, "below the corporeal schema" is a "historical-racial schema," a racial narrative through which we come to understand and interact with our world. "The fact of blackness" (Fanon 109), in other words, lies not in the body but in the cultural disciplining that teaches us what to see. This model of reading powerfully exposes the very processes through which racially marked subjects get fixed within visibility or excluded from it.[18]

This is why the extreme pallor of Justin-Marie, the child of the light-skinned Justin and the white and blonde Marie-France La Rinardière, does not prevent him from being racialized in the narrative. The presence of black blood in his veins—the Indian character Sanjita insists—is immediately detectable in his physiognomy: "He may be as white as a sheet, but he's no white Creole. You can see that straightaway: his mouth is too big and there is something about the shape of his cheekbones" (167). Condé reveals the unstable nature of these corporeal significations through the crossing of gender and class boundaries that this effeminate and socially transgressive character represents. Juxtaposed with the depiction of Cathy's race, Justin-Marie's "black" status powerfully illustrates the contingency of the visible economies that accompany the production of race in Caribbean society. In *Les Derniers Rois Mages,* the protagonist Spéro muses about the significance of being black and asks: "Pourtant, cela a-t-il encore une signification?" (But does this really still mean anything?) (176). Condé's *Windward Heights* reveals that while race still means a lot, the way in which it accrues meaning needs to be revisited in light of the crossings that constitute it. Race is profoundly influenced by the fluid nature of its false dichotomy.

The novel demonstrates that defining difference on the basis of race does not do justice to the social complexities of New World societies. Race is not the only indicator in the Caribbean. Racial categories are not challenged, however, in light of incontrovertibly mixed racial origins that undermine dominant conceptions of national identity; their arbitrariness as an explanation of difference is also exposed through the characters' own alternative relation to the concept. Married to a de Linsseuil, the white *béké* Jean nonetheless boasts: "The only white you see in me is the colour of my skin. I eat like a nigger; I swig my rum like a nigger; I swear and I fight like a nigger; as for fucking, I fuck like a nigger" (182). Justin's white-skinned mulatto son, Justin-Marie, adopts the rhetoric of black revolutionaries and socialists, yet treats black Creoles like slaves. The reworking of the crossed familial and racial genealogies of *Wuthering Heights*'s Hareton, Linton, and the second Catherine through those of Justin-Marie, Razyé II, and Cathy in *Windward Heights* is another way in which the novel powerfully dramatizes the cultural constitution of subjectivity. Whereas Brontë's final pair of lovers at least partly carry traits "inherited" from the previous generation, Cathy's and Justin-Marie's identifications with their putative "fathers" play on culturally influential notions of paternity and disengage subjectivity from inherited identity. As a mulatto who calls Irmine "mother" and looks forward to the day his "father" Razyé will kill all the whites (170), Justin-Marie functions as a foil to the "black" Cathy who has completely assimilated the values and norms of her "father" Aymeric. Indeed, despite Razyé II's attempts at making her aware of an alternative black history and culture, she never reclaims her African heritage and remains a de Linsseuil until the end.

As Henry Louis Gates Jr. points out in *"Race," Writing, and Difference,* "Race, as a meaningful criterion within the biological sciences, has long been recognized as a fiction" (4). At the same time, despite the fictional nature of its "essence" and pseudobiological configuration, attempts at dissolving the category have been received with much apprehension and resentment in various critical circles. For instance, Alexander and Mohanty argue that "if we dissolve the category of race, for instance, it becomes difficult to claim the experience of racism" (xvii). Like many critics of postmodernist discourse, these feminists are concerned that in its "haste to dissociate itself from all forms of essentialism," postmodernist theory obscures the way skin color frequently determines one's social, political, and economic status. This is why most commentators who emphasize the metaphorical nature of race and promote its "denaturing" nonetheless defer to its importance as the foundation from which antiracist political solidarities are forged. This is why Paul Gilroy's call to end such deferring gestures in *Against Race* has been so controversial.

Condé's reinscription of race as indeterminate and fluid exemplifies what Paul Gilroy has identified as "the crisis of raciology" in *Against Race*. This crisis "has ensured that racialized bodies . . . are never going to be enough to guarantee that racial differences remain what they were when everyone on both sides of the line between white and colored knew what 'race' was supposed to be." As far as race goes, Gilroy insists, "what you see is not necessarily what you get" (23). Gilroy locates the source of the crisis in global biotechnological developments as well as in recent changes in consumer culture. Through the representation of Cathy's race, Condé reveals that while such contemporary developments might indeed have contributed to crystallizing race's indeterminacy, its fluid variability can in fact be traced in narrative as far back as the nineteenth century when race mythologies were arguably at their most tenacious. Her rewriting not only reconceptualizes race as a variable that shifts according to con-text but also identifies a similar racial logic embedded in her Victorian source-text, Emily Brontë's *Wuthering Heights*. She challenges readings that interpret the presence of "race" in "black" fiction as a contribution to a classic sociology of race relations and emphasizes instead how the patterns of meaning that emerge through literature shed light on nonliter-ary racial and social discourses and practices. Race, Condé reveals, is a discourse whose workings might be best elucidated through a study of narrative form. Her approach thus resists separating postcolonial specu-lations from the consideration of the literariness of the literary text and analyzes fiction not as an investigation of real historical circumstances but as a practice that, in the process of evolving its own myths and para-digms, demythologizes history and its naturalized categories. It is then, as Eagleton has argued, "no longer a question of debating whether 'litera-ture' should be related to 'history' or not: it is a question of different read-ings of history itself" (*Literary Theory* 209).

Fire and Resistance

Windward Heights's challenge to accepted meanings of race leads to the unsettling of other widely used concepts of postcolonialism such as history and correlatively, resistance, and agency. These notions have traditionally been based on unified notions of race and ethnicity and are too often, as Ashcroft argues in *Post-colonial Transformation*, "conceived in terms of a simplistic view of colonization, of postcolonial response, and of postcolo-nial identities" (22). Resistance denotes opposition (armed or ideological) to oppressive structures and is often associated with Marxist models of "liberation" in postcolonial states. The post-independence era in Africa showed, however, that as a "simple binary stereotype" (Ashcroft 25), resistance led not to social change but to new tyrannies in the hands of equally oppressive indigenous elites. As a result, this core trope of postcolonialism has been challenged in recent years.

Windward Heights problematizes militant opposition through its representation of one of the most powerful symbols of postcolonial resistance, namely the burning of cane fields and plantation houses, which was historically carried out by slaves and exploited workers. In postcolonial studies, these fires have come to symbolize the agency of the oppressed insofar as they challenge the stereotyped view of colonized people's "victimage" (to borrow Ashcroft's term). In *Windward Heights,* however, the ruining of targeted planters through fires is part of a much more complex ideological picture than the idea of straightforward resistance typically offers. Indeed, the novel is set in 1898, a year that, with the U.S. intervention in the Spanish-Cuban conflict, marks the onset of neocolonialism in the region. This is a time when both the old planter class and the exploited laborers became the pawns of the neocolonial and metropolitan-based companies that were acquiring Guadeloupe's sugar plantations at the end of the nineteenth century. In this context, the "black" protagonist's final and victorious torching campaign does not cause but accelerates the ruin of an already hopeless Caribbean cane sugar industry. This is also a time that has caused much controversy in Caribbean historiography. Scholars cannot seem to agree whether the burning of crops in Guadeloupe at the end of the nineteenth century was in fact politically motivated. On the one hand, some argue that the fires were indeed the workers' response to labor exploitation and poverty and symbolized effective lower-class resistance. On the other hand, Foucauldian critics like Claude Thiébaut argue that most of these fires were motivated only by personal vendettas, so that what had political and historical import was not the burning of crops but its ideological appropriation by the Guadeloupean and French press.[19] Indeed, the white planters were overwhelmingly invested in publicizing the fires that were ravaging Guadeloupe as acts of savagery that justified withdrawing the right to vote from the black population. Throughout 1899, they campaigned to modify the Constitution on the grounds that universal suffrage gave too much power to the section of the population that was ruining the island. These descendants of the first colonizers longed for the days before the French Revolution when political power was based on economic power. Some were even plotting for the annexation of

Guadeloupe by the United States because the new neocolonial power adhered to a more racist structure in its governance. U.S. intervention would have helped reestablish the racial boundaries that French egalitarian ideals had eroded.

In *Windward Heights,* Justin-Marie's claim that "Razyé's name is in every paper, without exception. He is terrorizing the whole of Guadeloupe. He works for the Socialists. . . . He is going to kill the white folks down to the very last man" (168) seems to confirm Thiébaut's theory of a white colonial conspiracy. The press is shown to be advertising the fires as part of a socialist ploy to ruin the planter class. At the same time, the character of Razyé fuses the two seemingly incompatible historiographic theories, since he instigates the cane-field fires both as a socialist and as a vengeful neighbor. His personal vendetta against Aymeric implies that the fires are personal, his association with the deputy-mayor that they are political. While Thiébaut emphasizes the *békés'* ideological appropriation of localized acts as a means of furthering their racist agenda, *Windward Heights* represents both the individual appropriation of political activity for personal reasons and the socialist exploitation of personal animosity for political purposes. This reveals the extent to which the torching of cane fields is a discursive ploy that various actors can and do appropriate for their own ends rather than an unproblematical symbol of resistance. Even at their most destructive, the fires do not threaten the power structure so much as expedite the arrival of neocolonialism. Clearly, the binary notion of resistance bears reexamination. *Windward Heights*'s interweaving of historical material with Razyé's private predicament challenges traditional historiography's focus on landmark events and glorified heroes as catalysts of change. Instead, the novel emphasizes the fraught but intricate relations between the individual and the collective, the personal and the political, the private and the public, and exposes the ideological processes through which historical "convulsions" like wars and revolutions get disentangled from the webs of individual life and sanitized to write History.

This kind of sterilized approach to history challenged in the novel is epitomized, for instance, by Paul Hamilton's preface to *Historicism,* where he cites the following passage from Ernst Robert Curtius's *European Literature and the Latin Middle Ages* (1979):

> The protagonists of progress in historical understanding are always isolated individuals who are led by such historical convulsions as wars and revolutions to put new questions. Thucydides was induced to undertake his history because he regarded the Peloponnesian War as the greatest war of all times. Augustine

wrote his *City of God* under the impact of Alaric's conquest of Rome. Machiavelli's political and historical writings are his reaction to the French expeditions into Italy. The revolution of 1789 and the Napoleonic wars provoked Hegel's *Philosophy of History*. . . . The end of the First World War was responsible for the resonance Spengler's *Decline of the West* found in Germany. Deeper in intent and saturated with the entire yield of German philosophy, theology, and history was Ernst Troeltsch's unfinished work, *Der Historismus and seine Probleme.* (Curtius, quoted in Hamilton 1)

While Hamilton's main point here is to promote a historicist perspective whereby historical context is important to the interpretation of texts of any kind, he does not, however, challenge Curtius's assumptions that historical "convulsions" such as wars and revolutions are indeed the catalysts of change in historical consciousness, that the "protagonists of progress" are "isolated" individuals reacting to the context, or that they all happen to be ungendered male subjects. The "protagonists of progress in historical understanding" are thus strikingly reminiscent of the protagonists of masculinist history whose preeminence feminists and postcolonial critics have exposed as patriarchal bias.

Razyé's involvement with a radical organization for social justice forces us to reconsider the motivations of the black heroes and glorified leaders that have historically been hailed as liberators of the people or, inversely, as martyrs for the cause. He is utterly dominated by selfish interests and concerns, yet he is perceived by other characters as a powerful agent in a significant social movement.[20] After all, as the paternalist priest at Petit-Canal puts it, he is "guilty of having stirred up social unrest and sown thoughts of revenge in the childlike souls of the former slaves" (280). Similarly, the leader of the "Parti Nègre" Endomius, whose speech and presence ignite *mabo* Sandrine's political consciousness and cause her to go into a trance from excitement, is revealed as an ambitious man who does not hesitate to compromise his principles in order to reach his goal.[21] He too wants to ruin the planters, and despite his claim that education and politics are the only way the black majority will redress power imbalances, it is Razyé's physical strength and violent tactics that the socialist counts on to achieve his ends. Furthermore, he recruits Razyé even though he knows of the atrocities his new acolyte committed during the 1895–98 Civil War in Cuba. In fact, he does not even flinch at hearing Razyé matter-of-factly recall fighting for the Spanish and the loyalists and killing not only peasants who were struggling for their country's freedom but runaway slaves in hiding who did not know that slavery was over:

I climbed up to the forest, the *manigua,* to hunt down the rebels and their sup-
porters. In other words, all the peasant folk. For the people had had more than
enough of the Spanish. I didn't have a minute's rest. Every day, even the day of
the Lord, I set fire to villages, I tortured women and children, I slaughtered
cattle. Sometimes, under the acanas and mahoganys I came face to face with
men, hiding naked in the forest, not knowing that slavery was over. They could
no longer speak Spanish and had returned to the languages of Africa. I killed
them even so, but felt bad about it. (116)

Throughout the novel, Razyé's deeds follow a logic that resonates with
one of Heathcliff's most provocative statements in *Wuthering Heights*—
"The tyrant grinds down his slaves and they don't turn against him, they
crush those beneath them" (111)—and leaves the reader wondering "how
many really ordinary [and reprehensible] human beings . . . are the actual
bases of great national and religious movements, [and] just how substan-
tial a part mere chance and erratic behavior have in such movements"
(Bruner and Bruner 12–13).

    While Razyé's interests and experiences link him to the laborers whose
political alliance he has joined, his acts do not stand for an "authentic"
expression of his social position. His vendetta against Aymeric is only
incidentally mapped onto the struggle of the black labor force against the
white *békés'* control of the economy. He does not recognize his connectedness with the workers who have been exploited. In other words, although the novel brings to light the differential structures of power that
are inscribed on the population, it also challenges a politics that anchors
political opposition in one's racial difference and assumes that one's identity and social position will determine how one acts.[22] The irony is that it
is Razyé's active participation in a *political* struggle that undermines this
model of identity politics and its attendant notion of black solidarity.
In this respect, *Windward Heights*'s representation of blackness echoes
Paul Gilroy's notion of the black Atlantic insofar as it repudiates "the
racialised [*sic*] figurations of kinship and connectedness that have appeared in the political discourses through which blacks in the Western
world have worked to answer the brutal potency of white supremacy"
(Gilroy, "Route Work" 25). As in the rest of Condé's oeuvre, the category
of race is scrutinized but not fetishized.[23] Its validity as an explanation of
difference is exposed at the same time as its effects are highlighted. Instead
of a politics of solidarity based on essential or unified identities, Condé
offers a world where personal affinities constantly violate and expose
ideological boundaries set between races and classes. Not surprisingly,

this representational politics has important implications for postcolonial discussions of agency.

Subaltern Agency

Because colonial discourse represents colonized subjects as passive and malleable beings who cannot be the makers of their own history, discussions of the subaltern as victims of a dominant structure have become suspect in literary criticism.[24] As a result, celebrations of acts of subaltern insurgency and their unsettling effects abound in postcolonial criticism, all the more so since contemporary critics are particularly anxious about unwittingly reproducing imperialism's systematic erasure of signs of subaltern agency. Whether slave or ex-slave revolts are quelled or not does not seem to affect how postcolonial scholars perceive such militant opposition. What matters is the recognition that the racial other is no victim. I argue that this emphasis on a reductive understanding of agency can only obscure the oppressive effects of colonialism and its aftermaths; it also reproduces the very binaries we should be challenging, namely, those that oppose victimization and agency on the one hand, and agency and passivity on the other.

Maryse Condé's intervention deconstructs such facile views of agency and resistance whose main function often seems merely to be to give Western scholars a good conscience. She exposes postcolonialism's investment in identifying liberationist cultural codes and emblems of resistance at all costs including those that were ineffectual. It is significant, in this respect, that *Windward Heights* opens with the murder of the *babalawo,* the Santeria priest whose Afro-Caribbean religion has become yet another powerful symbol of resistance in anticolonial criticism. The *babalawo*'s power might impress the protagonist Razyé and the Spanish governors but cannot prevent a lurking ruffian from murdering the clairvoyant priest. Furthermore, whereas the imperative of an "authentic" postcolonial perspective has been the recreation of counterheroes such as Toussaint l'Ouverture who take action on a grand scale and shape others, Condé's lower-class characters subvert the expectations raised not only by colonial stereotypes (through the novel's recasting of race) but also by anticolonial discourse.

As critics have convincingly shown, colonialist discourse tends to confine black agency to the dichotomous historical roles of "good docile" and "bad rebellious" blacks.[25] In response, anticolonial discourse developed its own opposition between the "good rebellious blacks" who resist colonization and the bad self-alienated "mimic men" who have internalized white values but whose mimicry can sometimes destabilize the dominant discourse.[26] What is remarkable about *Windward Heights*'s representation of the black Creoles is the way in which it mimics and explodes both sets of binaries and the roles assigned to racially marked people by both colonialist and anticolonial discourse, that is, the Ariel versus Caliban opposition.[27]

Most of *Windward Heights*'s narrators invoke the representation of blacks as self-alienated laborers (the Ariel paradigm) insofar as they are devoted to the physical care of the white subject. They are servants, black nannies (*mabos*), fishermen, obeah men (*babalawos*) or helpers whose first-person "récits" alternate with the third-person narration and give us access to these witnesses' marginalized and subjective perspectives. This multitude of narrators thus explodes the double narration of *Wuthering Heights* in a way that is quite reminiscent of a Faulknerian narrative structure. Indeed, as in Faulkner, these polyphonic narratives are not integrated through a metadiegetic narrator. Instead, the third-person narrator functions as the tangential link between divergent narratives that are juxtaposed rather than controlled through a focalizing consciousness. The narrator's role, in other words, has evolved from relating as telling to relating as linking. In this universe, the novel's peripheral characters no longer content themselves with recounting the protagonists' tribulations at the expense of their own stories. Unlike typical "witnesses" whose role is usually confined to reporting on the main plot from a particular angle, they all begin with an account of their own personal history and memories. For instance, whereas Nelly Dean's origins in *Wuthering Heights* remain nebulous notwithstanding her narrative dominance, Nelly Raboteur prefaces her account of Razyé's background with the story of her own humble beginnings: "I was born into a poor family in Morne-Caillou, a few miles from Anse-Bertrand, in the most desolate part of Guadeloupe. We were seventeen children around the table, and we seldom ate meat. So when I was sixteen I was only too happy when Monsieur le curé Poissaudeau found a place for me working for Hubert Gagneur" (18). Similarly, Nelly's successor Lucinda Lucius, the housekeeper Sanjita, the second Cathy's *mabo* Sandrine, Madhi the *babalawo,* and Roro the fisherman tell their own and their ancestors' stories of suffering and survival as they encounter the protagonists. Their respective "récits" ensure that we do not reduce their status to mere observers whose function is to channel information about the "main" characters before being forgotten. They are incapable of relating the protagonists' stories without explaining how they were themselves affected by or instrumental to these encounters and relationships.

These "minor" characters' interior lives and mental recollections offer a valuable commentary on the intricate web of environments and relationships that govern their lives. Access to their voices forces us to reevaluate the lens through which we judge their situation. In this respect, Condé's aesthetics parallels that of many contemporary postcolonial writers who, like Caryl Phillips,[28] aim through fiction "to subvert people's view of history by engaging them with character" ("Crossing" 26) and "to look at that history from a different angle—through the prism of people who have nominally been written out of it, or have been viewed as the losers or victims in a particular historical storm. You take something which people presume they know about—like the West from John Wayne or Sergio Leone—and you make them look again from the point of view of people who have been written out" ("Crossing" 26).

Unlike Phillips's "losers and victims," however, the "casualties of our forgetfulness" (to use Michelle Cliff's formulation) whom Condé integrates into the narrative of history are notable precisely because their characterization seems to fit rather than disallow conventional stereotypes.[29] As mentioned earlier, Condé's inscription paradoxically fails to deviate from hegemonic representations of "black people" either as laborers responsible for the physical care of the white subject or, in the case of Razyé and his socialist acolytes, as hostile threats. Her female characters in particular seem hopelessly trapped between the poles of sexless mammy and sexualized woman that have conventionally defined black women. The *mabos* who succeed one another in attending to the de Linsseuil offspring are as devoted to the white children in their care as any stereotypical Aunt Jemima, thus personifying the stereotypical black mammy. And the sexualized and enticing women of the narrative, Cathy, Etiennise, and Asturias, ultimately fit the Jezebel paradigm described by Diane Roberts: "Jezebel does not feed, she entices, she is to be used, penetrated, had, impregnated" (2). These characters are unsettling because they seem to reinforce rather than challenge the Manichean opposition between "good blacks" and "bad blacks."

Yet unlike Caryl Phillips's *Cambridge*, for instance, who has assimilated the colonizer's language and religion to the point of naïvely believing that "through hard work and faith in the Lord God Almighty, my bondage would soon cease" (*Cambridge* 157), the *mabos* of Condé's world are not in the least deluded about the structural inequities that constitute their lives. They are rounded characters whose historical memories and complex ways of conceptualizing themselves are as fascinating as, if not more clear-sighted than, those of the protagonists. By this means, Condé makes it impossible to dismiss their attachments to members of the higher classes as false consciousness or internalized oppression. *Mabo* Sandrine's complete devotion to her master's daughter Cathy, who is like the "dew . . . watering the dryness of [her] heart" (198), does not stop her from feeling a fierce hatred for her master himself, the representative of the old plantocracy. Similarly, even though the seventy-two-year-old *mabo* Julie paradoxically does not hesitate to offer her (free) services to the battered and humiliated Irmine de Linsseuil, she is full of hatred for the white *békés* and the life of subjugation they inflicted on her and her family. The old woman ignores her own daughters' outcry, "Oh no, slavery isn't over for someone [like] you" (111), and follows her old mistress to La Pointe, where she will soon die and be replaced by another *mabo* (Hosannah). When the East Indian housekeeper Sanjita decides to serve and spoil the dying Justin-Marie (Linton) despite his obvious contempt for "her kind," she sees in him not the superior lighter-skinned "master" of colonialist discourse but the son she lost to typhoid fever. Last but not least, the fishmonger Ada in Roseau becomes a surrogate mother to the dejected and pregnant Cathy because she identifies with the isolated and broken girl's fate. At the end of the novel, she maintains that what killed Cathy is her husband's indifference and unfaithfulness, an explanation that links the young girl's story to her own.

Ada and the other *mabos,* the fisherman Roro, the housekeeper Sanjita, and her daughter Etiennise are thus revealed as complex individuals whose capacity for sympathy transcends the colonial and neocolonial lines of forces that traverse their lives. They articulate, within their servitude, the possibility of moving beyond the confines of slavery, "of journeying outside the closed world of racialised being that had been configured in their New World homeland by slavery and maintained there during its white supremacist aftermath" (Gilroy, "Route Work" 18). Their paradoxical ability to feel a commonality with others despite the material conditions that govern their lives highlights the discontinuity between their subjective experience and our expectations. The novel focuses on the lack of conformity between the political and personal dimensions of their lives and explores the unpredictable and often contradictory ways in which the relationship between subjective experience, social practices, and the power relations that organize them manifests itself.

Yet, at the same time as these alliances move beyond constraining and essentializing racial identities and appeal to the reader's communitarian ideals, it is important to recognize that they fail to result in the lower classes' empowerment. Indeed, to the members of the higher classes, the *babalawos, mabos,* and servants that punctuate their lives are very much interchangeable. Hosannah takes over where *mabo* Julie had left off; Razyé II never even thinks back on what might have become of Roro the fisherman or Ada the fishmonger, notwithstanding their devotion to him and his daughter. As one of the chapter titles puts it, "Losers Will Be Losers" in the world of *Windward Heights,* especially when they assume certain moral qualities. By the end of the novel, the reader cannot help but wonder whether, as Condé explains in her study of Antillean folktales, the values of compassion, morality, loyalty, and so on are not indeed those of the "master," and their adoption the downfall of the black population.

In her 1978 book on the oral culture of the Antilles and more specifically on the traditional *contes* (folktales) that the slaves transmitted from generation to generation, Condé explains that what distinguishes the first cycle of "animal tales" from the second and more recent cycle is the assimilation of Christian values of compassion and goodness by the protagonists. According to Condé, the "moral" cycle with its focus on inner improvement entails an internalization of the stereotype of blackness and the beginning of the slave's aspiration to enter the world of the master that was not present in the first cycle. The first cycle centers on the cunning and immoral ways in which the protagonist Compé Lapin repeatedly tricks Compé Zamba and gets his way. The hero is a thief, a liar, sly, cruel, selfish, greedy, vengeful, voracious, cowardly, lazy, arrogant, and lustful. No compassion or punishment checks his behavior, and as Condé points out, the story entreats us to abandon all our usual references and Western values. In the second cycle, on the other hand, the human protagonist Ti-Jean gets himself and others out of trouble not by using cunning and deceit but by displaying qualities like goodness, courage, self-control, and compassion. This transformation, according to Condé, marks the introduction of a Christian code of ethics that, for the slave, meant an adoption of the values of the masters at the expense of his/her own strategies of survival. In a doubly ironic twist, these values, which the masters mouthed but did not practice, kept the slaves enslaved, while making them more humane that their masters.

In light of the focus on the limits of individual agency in *Windward Heights,* it is not surprising that the phrase "la scélératesse de la vie" which invokes Condé's 1987 novel *La Vie Scélérate* (*Tree of Life,* 1992) should be a recurring concept throughout the narrative.[30] Nelly Raboteur starts her tale with a reminder that "Our life is traced out for us long before we are born. Depending on the cradle that rocks us, we are given the gift of wealth or poverty, life's happiness or life's wickedness" (18). When Irmine muses about the blacks' atrocious living conditions during slavery and her own kinfolks' responsibility in causing them, she says: "My father maintained that they should not be trusted; mother recalled the duties of a Christian towards them. In fact, nobody took the trouble to know precisely who they were. . . . Because they have suffered truly, they are susceptible, aggressive and slow to confide and tell the truth. In their minds, nothing will ever free them from life's wickedness" (104). Similarly, when Aymeric's children start laughing at his extreme feebleness, his last thoughts before dying evoke the same fatalism: "Let them laugh, let them go on laughing. They did not know what lay ahead for them. They would see when they were his age and life in its wickedness had dealt them the blows of which she alone had the secret (209). Yet, even when the characters ascribe the wickedness of their existence to the workings of fate, the novel ensures that the reader locates it in the operations of colonial and neocolonial forces that continue to shape their lives.[31]

Windward Heights's portrayal of clear-sighted *mabos* and servants interrogates the Western conceptions of voice and agency that are often called upon in anticolonial criticism. The black Creoles' first-person tales and lucid self-assessments remind us that our celebrations of resistance in the form of voice, autonomy, and self-consciousness often take place at the expense of acknowledging real inequities that can only be redressed at a structural level. The nannies' and servants' voices along with their moral traits mark them in this sense as the least likely agents of social change. The feminist and postcolonial emphasis on narrative voice as a metaphor for the agency and "coming to voice" of the oppressed is radically challenged. Instead, it is Razyé—the least self-conscious and politicized character in the book as well as the character who lacks a "narrative voice"— who comes the closest to successful political resistance. After all, he is, as the paternalist priest at Petit-Canal put it, "guilty of having stirred up social unrest and planted the seeds of revenge in the childlike souls of the former slaves" (273).

Like the disenfranchised characters in the novel, Razyé both invokes and implodes conventional images of blackness. He is both the "bad" black of hegemonic racist discourse and the "good" rebel of oppositional postcolonial criticism. On the one hand, his boundless ignominy reproduces and amplifies the very characteristics that are typically ascribed to stereotypical representations of racial otherness. In many ways, he is even more relentlessly "savage" than the satanic Heathcliff in *Wuthering Heights*. Unlike Heathcliff, who unexpectedly and albeit out of sheer lassitude or an untapped source of compassion gives up his Machiavellian plans at the end of *Wuthering Heights*, Razyé welcomes death only when he has assured himself that his revenge will be carried out through his rival's off-spring.[32] On the other hand, his involvement in the mayor Jean-Hilaire Endomius's socialist party (which refers to the radical "Parti Nègre" historically) also marks him as the resistant rebel of anticolonialism, albeit with a twist (he ironically produces radical effects he neither intended nor foresaw). He is a demonic character who joins a grassroots social movement solely to fulfill his vengeful ends and whose antiheroism generates progressive or political results despite his selfish aspirations. The novel thus disarticulates subjectivity from agency by emphasizing the political impact of this apolitical character who actually never meant to sow "thoughts of revenge" in the souls of the ex-slaves (280).

In light of the procession of "Uncle Toms" and pitiable (ex-)slaves that have peopled hegemonic representations of nonwhite protagonists in classic texts, it is not surprising that a Caribbean writer like Condé should find the infamous "Afreet" of Emily Brontë's novel an empowering source of emulation. Indeed, racially marked characters have historically had to be impossibly good to arouse pity or sustained interest in white audiences, not to mention the string of black or hybrid characters whose fleeting appearance in fiction has been solely instrumental. Brontë's Heathcliff is a remarkable and unprecedented exception to this representational yoke, insofar as he could be both unquestionably bad and the hero of the tale. Furthermore, *Windward Heights*'s similar emphasis on Razyé's unspeakable acts evokes the kind of racialized negativity delineated in Césaire's *Notebook of a Return to the Native Land:*[33] "and the Negro every day more base, more cowardly, more sterile, less profound, more spilled out of himself, more separated from himself, more wily with himself" (Césaire 77). Like Césaire, Condé describes the ugliness and cowardice, the weaknesses and vices of the black world "without reserve" and includes in her representations both "the scum nigger" (81) and "the good nigger" (Césaire 79). Indeed, for Césaire, as for Condé, "the crimes" to be declared and accepted (Césaire 51) are a testimony to the capacity for survival and endurance of the Antillean, for whom just to remain alive was a victory.[34] Their work accepts the experiences and images of the "négraille" at the same time as it denounces the colonial system for generating them.

In contrast to both the "Founding Ancestor" Césaire and the founding ancestress Emily Brontë, however, Condé's acceptance of the vulgar and the immoral in *Windward Heights* does not result in the mystification of her extraordinary protagonist. For instance, Razyé's attempts at resurrecting Cathy through magic or through her look-alike, Justin-Marie. are represented as utterly hopeless and pathetic efforts. The last glimpse we have of Razyé is as a ghost who not only fails to get reunited with his long-sought love but who does not even know why he is still waiting: "Now I'm here and I don't even know why I'm waiting. I can see a path stretching out in front of me. I have to follow it, but I know it leads nowhere and in the end, I will be back where I started. I am tired. I wish it were over. 'What am I going to do with all this time on my hands?'" (287). Like Cathy, Razyé's "ghost" finds eternity and endless time in the afterlife instead of a much-awaited reunion with his beloved. While the dark presence of Heathcliff dominates Emily's novel and his afterlife relationship with Cathy romanticizes if not vindicates his destructive passions, in *Windward Heights,* the cosmic significance of Heathcliff's deeds that has so often electrified readers of the Victorian text is deliberately denied.

In fact, the novel quells any attempt at magnifying and glorifying Razyé's negative qualities "as virtues and titles of glory" (Condé, "*Cahier*" 32) by repeatedly staging the process through which various characters come to be fascinated with such a persona. More than his self-absorption or the failure of his otherworldly romantic reunion, it is the recurring dramatization of this process of mystification by other characters that effectively distances the reader from Razyé. On the boat that brings the "enigmatic" man back to La Guadeloupe, for instance, Nelly's chronicle of his personal background takes place on account of the curious and impatient ladies on board falling "victim to that unaccountable, mysterious attraction white women feel for black males" (23–24). At the workers' socialist meeting, "He didn't speak, he didn't shake hands, he gave no embraces, as if he thought all this a waste of time. . . . As a result, women pressed around him like flies around a honeypot" 198). Later, his widow Irmine's idealized rereading of her lamentable marriage also ensures that we do not romanticize her tormentor along with her: "She had already disguised him as a model father, concerned about his offspring. He who had been nothing but indifferent and savage" (331). Any initial fascination we might have felt for the character soon subsides and gives way to pity for his deluded widow, Irmine, through whose point of view we experience "the death of the wolf." In fact, it is precisely because the scene of his death is mediated through Irmine's idealized perception that we cannot find Razyé even remotely mystical or mesmerizing. Indeed, as *Wuthering Heights* shows, it is easy to sympathize with "the greatest villain in fiction" (Allott 88) when doing so entails distancing ourselves from the conformist and unreliable lens of the meddling narrators, Nelly Dean and Lockwood. Our identification with the fiery romantic plot of the novel is facilitated if not increased by our distrust in their perspectives and motivations. Their urging that we condemn results in our opposite response. By contrast, identifying with Razyé in *Windward Heights* would put us on the same grounding as his self-deceived widow, the swooning ladies aboard his boat, or the political reunion's "flies around a honeypot" (198). Irmine, for instance, sees nobility where he has only displayed self-serving callousness, and the absurdity of her delusion ensures that the reader does not venture to duplicate her misreading. In other words, while in *Wuthering Heights,* readers identify and sympathize with Heathcliff despite his outrageous villainy, in *Windward Heights,* they distance themselves from Razyé despite his intertextual association with the mesmerizing Heathcliff.

In contrast to Césaire's *Notebook,* Condé's acceptance of the moral and historical "ugliness" of the Caribbean does not result in shoring up her protagonist. For Césaire, the "messianic male hero"[35] functions as the guide who self-consciously leads the downtrodden to assume their destiny, reclaim their demeaned black cultural heritage, and leap into "universal brotherhood."[36] Condé offers instead yet another novel about "very ordinary people who in their very ordinary ways . . . nevertheless shed the blood of others . . . , [a] book with neither great torturers nor lavish martyrdoms. But one that would still be heavy with its weight of flesh and blood" (Condé, *Tree of Life* 357). Like its Victorian source-text, *Windward Heights* unsettles and provokes because the most tortured soul in the novel is himself a ruthless torturer. The irredeemable yet demystified Razyé challenges Césaire's vision of a rehabilitated and united black world and aesthetics. Whereas Césaire's vision inscribes the black world as "a *Paradise* perverted by Europe" ("Order" 124; emphasis mine), *Windward Heights*'s indictment of colonialism and its aftermaths does not rely on utopian notions of precolonial bliss or "black solidarity." This refusal to mystify "the exploited Black Man" (to use Condé's formulation) and the idea of a united black world is epitomized by the novel's representation of its revolutionary hero, who turns out to be neither a revolutionary nor a hero. In fact, it is ironically the patronizing *béké* Aymeric de Linsseuil who ultimately does more to empower the black laborers than the "black rebel" Razyé. Aymeric sells his factory to secure his employees' retirement funds rather than bequeath it to his offspring. Although this generosity stems from his paternalism, the irony underlying the outcome of the Razyé-Aymeric conflict can hardly escape the reader.

Conclusion

Through her representation of the black Creole underclass, Condé forces us to rethink anti-imperialist criticism's facile opposition between self-alienated "mimic men" and politicized rebels. Her characters are neither mimics plagued by a mental enslavement to their subservient fate nor rebels whose insights into the workings of power are the basis for political resistance to colonial and neocolonial policies. They are neither indoctrinated passive people nor empowered politicized rebels. Their acute insight into the workings of power does not become the basis of change. Alternatively, their resistance sometimes derives from self-centered and selfish agents who participate in political campaigns for purely personal reasons.

This "aesthetics of the reprehensible" is a timely contribution to postcolonial criticism because it checks the impulse of readers well trained to see justice, freedom, and happiness as an avatar of the strong and the just. Condé's troubling and troubled characters demonstrate instead that liberty and fairness should not be a function of character but inalienable rights to which even the basest and weakest among us are entitled. Inversely, she also reminds us that being a victim is not the result of one's submissive temperament, nor is being a rebel necessarily a sign of heroic agency. This kind of representational "disorder" is precisely what Condé aims to introduce in the postcolonial reading strategies of her predecessors as well as of her more immediate contemporaries. Through rebels who are not quite rebels and mimics who are not quite mimics, she not only rewrites *Wuthering Heights* but also reformulates one of the major preoccupations of postcolonial studies for the last decade or so, namely, the agency of the oppressed. Her novel dramatizes the complexities that arise from our efforts at resuscitating the subaltern's voice/self by invoking historical contexts. On the one hand, it provides the perspectives of oppressed people, while on the other hand, it problematizes Western notions of voice and agency by highlighting their articulation with colonialist strategies. Acts of resistance in the narrative do not occur on behalf of an essential subaltern subject entirely separate from the dominant discourse. Instead, they draw attention to the subject-position of the marginalized in a context where neocolonial forces have replaced old colonial ties and problematize any notion of the subaltern as "historical subject and agent of an oppositional discourse" (Parry, "Problems" 38).

This rewriting of core concepts of postcolonialism such as resistance, agency, and race offers a model of relationality that complicates the influential notions of Créolité and creolization that have dominated Caribbean studies in recent years. As Madeleine Cottenet-Hage points out, it is unclear how the concept of Créolité succeeds in moving beyond the very categories of identity it seeks to undo: "Cependant, à réexaminer une définition qui s'ouvrait, on s'en souvient, sur la declaration liminaire: 'Ni Européens, ni Africains, ni Asiatiques, nous nous proclamons créoles,' il nous semble qu'y fonctionnent encore de 'vieilles catégories de race, nationalité, territoire, auxquelles nous nous accrochons [et qui sont] en train de devenir caduques'" (11). (Nevertheless, when we reexamine the definition which—we remember it well—opened with the proclaiming declaration: "Neither Europeans, nor Africans, or Asians, we proclaim ourselves to be Creoles," it seems to us that it is still motivated by old categories of race, nationality, territory to which we are hanging on [and which are] in the process of becoming obsolete.) By contrast, reading of the intersections of race, sex, class, and nation in *Windward Heights* produces meanings that resist hegemonic inscription and challenge the exclusionary configurations of difference that, as Cottenet-Hage points out, still animate the Créolité model.

The salutary and fertile "disorder" that Condé brings to creolization and Créolité has important implications for our reading of both colonial and postcolonial fiction. As the next chapters will illustrate, such intervention challenges postcolonialism's validation of the categories of race, gender, and class generated by colonialism. It shows that the workings of identity cannot be adequately understood without, as Sedgwick points out, accounting for the ways in which "race, ethnicity, postcolonial nationality criss-cross with [gender and sexuality] *and other* identity-constituting, identity-fracturing discourses" (8–9). It challenges our most deep-seated assumptions about racial and national identity by paying attention to the heterogeneity of culture without glossing over "blemishes such as domestic slavery, tribal warfare, and the subjugation of women" (Condé, "Order" 124). Condé extends this revision of the practices of postcolonial rewriting in her more recent novels: *La Belle Créole* rewrites D. H. Lawrence's *Lady Chatterley's Lover,* while *Célanire Cou-Coupé* is a literary rejoinder to Shelley's *Frankenstein.* Her fiction thus continues to disturb our expectations about postcolonial exemplarity while locating at the heart of both postcolonial and colonial narratives a highly nuanced version of hybridity that challenges the very possibility of establishing racial divisions. Racial hybridity can no longer be thought of as a sum of its various parts; rather, it is better understood as a site of identity crossing whose imbrication with gender and class is constitutive rather than merely incidental.

In 1966, the publication of Jean Rhys's *Wide Sargasso Sea,* the Caribbean rewriting of Charlotte Brontë's *Jane Eyre,* triggered a new era in the evolution of feminist and postcolonial criticism. Indeed, Rhys's novel was instrumental in making Anglo-American feminists sensitive to the issues of race and imperialism that their celebratory readings of *Jane Eyre* had inadvertently precluded. What is remarkable, in light of the watershed quality of *Wide Sargasso Sea,* is that it took almost thirty years for the other Brontë masterpiece, *Wuthering Heights,* to be rewritten from a postcolonial perspective. It is not that Emily Brontë's novel has not been rewritten, since, unlike *Jane Eyre,* it has given rise to not one but many novelistic sequels and revisions.[37] It is thus not *Wuthering Heights* itself but its relation to imperialism and racial difference that has failed to inspire creative writers and postcolonial critics alike.[38] In turning Emily Brontë's only novel into the same kind of (post)colonial artifact as *Jane Eyre,* Condé has once and for all put an end to this indifference to *Wuthering Heights*'s involvement with race and empire. Her intervention generates complex and productive postcolonial reading strategies that challenge the unproblematized colonial/postcolonial opposition through which *Wuthering Heights* and *Wide Sargasso Sea* have both been read. As a result, and insofar as it heralds a new stage in feminist and postcolonial criticism, *Windward Heights* is as much a watershed in postcolonial studies as Rhys's *Wide Sargasso Sea* was more than thirty years ago.

2 Shutting Up the Subaltern

Obeah as Opacity in Jean Rhys's *Wide Sargasso Sea*

THE DOMINICAN-BORN writer Jean Rhys rewrote Charlotte Brontë's *Jane Eyre* because she was "vexed at [Brontë's] portrait of the 'paper tiger,' the all wrong creole scenes" (Wyndham and Melly 262). "I've never believed in Charlotte's lunatic," she explained, "that's why I wrote this book" (1296). "The creole in Charlotte Brontë's novel is a lay figure—repulsive which does not matter, and not once alive which does" (56). In *Wide Sargasso Sea,* Rhys corrects her source-text by giving Brontë's West Indian character a voice and a life story and ensuring that "the woman from the colonies is not sacrificed as an insane animal for her sister's consolation" (Spivak, "Three Women's Texts" 270).[1] Her intervention was a vivid reminder to Anglo-American critics that their exclusive focus on gender in their cult feminist text *Jane Eyre* had assumed an essential female condition at the expense of the non-Western character.[2] *Wide Sargasso Sea* (1966) can thus be said to mark the turning of a new page in the evolution of feminist and postcolonial critical trends, a fact that makes the more recent developments in Rhys criticism all the more ironic. Indeed, the novel has now come under fire for its own construction of racial otherness. Although critics are unanimous in acclaiming Rhys's keen awareness of the ways in which white Creole subjectivity is constructed through the structure of European colonialism, they see her as complicit with the operations of imperial history when it comes to her depiction of the black Creoles. She is guilty of "the usurpation of race/blackness in the service of gender" (46) and of "a Manichean division of 'good blacks'—those who serve—and 'bad blacks'—those who are hostile, threatening, unknown" (Gregg 88).[3] Rhys is believed to identify with her white Creole protagonist's perspective, while her insights into the workings of ideologies are seen as limited to dismantling the nameless man's sexist and colonialist assumptions. (Even though "the man," which is significantly "the black tradition's epithet for the white power structure" [Gates 14], is never named in the novel, I will heretofore refer to him as Rochester).[4] Rhys's otherwise "formidably critical intelligence" (in Gregg's term), in other words, does not extend to her treatment of black subjectivities, and *Wide Sargasso Sea*, critics imply, needs a rewriting for the same reasons as its source-text *Jane Eyre* did.[5]

This chapter reads against the grain of this recent trend in Rhys criticism. I argue that *Wide Sargasso Sea* constantly thwarts an easy identification with the white Creole protagonist Antoinette, showing her as ensnared by colonialist assumptions that she unsuccessfully and often grotesquely attempts to replicate. Although her nameless husband's narrative voice dominates two-thirds of the novel, critics agree that his values do not represent the authoritative ideology of the text. Similarly, I argue that even though the black characters' perspectives are accessible only through the two major narratives, the representation of their practices does not reproduce but challenges the colonialist ways of thinking to which Antoinette and Rochester ascribe. The novel exposes the conventional cultural constructions through which both protagonists represent their racial others. Despite such a focus on colonialist discourse, however, it also resists assigning the subaltern the function of a "mere repository of Eurocentric assumptions" (Parry, "Problems" 38). Rhys represents black Creole agency and locates it, paradoxically, in the inability of whites to understand it. It is ironically the stereotypes and misconceptions through which the white Creole and British classes perceive the black Creoles that become the site of resistance in *Wide Sargasso Sea*. Black cultural traditions and practices such as obeah achieve their potency not through an oppositional strategy so much as through their complex and ambiguous interplay with colonial discourses and strategies. Their subversive power thus lies in their inscrutability and in what the Martinican Édouard Glissant would call their "consensual opacity" (473). Because Rochester cannot understand these alternative epistemologies, his anxious attempts to contain them through Western grids of knowledge keep failing, and he leaves the island, rattled by a space and people he could not control.

In *Le Discours Antillais*, Glissant argues that in light of the "loss of collective memory" and "the careful erasing of the past" resulting from the history "without witnesses" (472) of slavery, it is important for members of ex-slave societies to claim the right to "opacity" (473) and to "a resistance to scrutiny" (227): "More than the declaration of principle, I believe in the production of 'opaque' works. Opaqueness imposes itself and cannot be justified" (455). He further describes how this propensity for obscurity can be understood only in terms of the Western tradition of transparency and facticity: "The only source of light was ultimately that of the transcendental presence of the Other, of his/her Visibility—colonizer or administrator—of his transparency fatally proposed as a model, because of which we have acquired a taste for obscurity, and for me the need to seek out the opaque, that which is not obvious, to assert for each community the right to a consensual opacity" (473).

This principle of opaqueness is what I argue best represents the function of Afro-Caribbean practices in *Wide Sargasso Sea*. If the story of black cultural forms is told at all in the novel, it is indeed "implied, *never* told straight" (Wyndham 233). *Wide Sargasso Sea* reveals that it is when these practices' resistance to opaqueness is articulated with rather than directly opposed to the categories of imperial discourse that colonial authority is destabilized from within. This is why, despite a sustained focus on the preconceived notions of the Euro-Creole and British elites, the novel avoids erasing the political effects of alternative epistemologies such as obeah. Instead, its analysis of Creole colonialism offers a powerful model for rethinking both race and agency in postcolonialism.

Wide Sargasso Sea's alternative racial/textual politics becomes particularly visible when we reread it through the paradigm of relational identity exemplified by Maryse Condé's rewriting of postcolonial revisionism in *Windward Heights*. As I explained in chapter 1, Condé's revisionary novel challenges racist discourse not by questioning the behaviors and traits that supposedly define certain races but by undermining the concept of race itself. What gets exposed is the very assumption that the racial differences to which various moral and psychological traits get assigned are stable and preexisting identities whose visibility precedes the process through which they are given meaning. Instead, Condé reveals race as a shifting category of meaning that is internally hybridized, so that the racial markings of her characters are shown to vary according to their shifting relationship to other categories of identity. This dynamic highlights the inseparability of categories of difference from one another and radically alters our understanding of the racial logic at play in postcolonial rewritings.

In contrast to Rhys critics who see the stereotypical discourse of *Wide Sargasso Sea*'s two "white" narrators as representative of the norm of the text, I see it as dramatizing the process through which shifting racial meanings get attached to bodies as a figuration for other forms of identity crossing. Specifically, I focus on the novel's articulation of race and gender, which I examine in the context of an important theoretical debate around the representation of racial otherness in feminist postcolonial studies. Significantly, this is a debate whose sides have both evoked *Wide Sargasso Sea* and its representation of black Creole culture to illustrate their respective approaches. Placing the novel in such a critical context helps highlight the ways in which Rhys is indeed revising rather than reinscribing racial discourse.

On the one hand, critics like Benita Parry contend that our task as readers of postcolonial literature is to recover historically repressed knowledges and to construct "the speaking position" of the subaltern, that is, a "conception of the native as historical subject and agent of an oppositional discourse."[6] On the other hand, Spivak and her followers argue that our very efforts at recovering such silenced knowledges obscure the impossibility of an unmediated access to alternative histories that are necessarily always constructed according to the critic's Western worldview. According to this side, our intellectual endeavors at resurrecting an authentic past participate in a process of mystification rather than recuperation, and as such, are complicit with imperialist ideology: indeed, they impose on the subaltern Western assumptions of embodied subjectivity and fail to acknowledge that the other has been constructed according to the colonizer's self-image and cannot simply be given his/her voice back.[7] Both Parry and Spivak single out *Wide Sargasso Sea*'s black nurse and obeah woman Christophine to illustrate their respective claims. For Parry, Christophine is the source of a counterdiscourse that is rooted in the historically potent function of black magic in African and West Indian cultures. For Spivak, such an unmediated access to the subaltern history that Christophine represents is impossible because the black Creole woman is ultimately "tangential to a narrative written in the interest of the white Creole protagonist" ("Three Women's Texts" 253).

I argue that each position can only partly account for Rhys's complex delineation of West Indian social and racial relations in *Wide Sargasso Sea*. By analyzing the largely ignored distinction between narration and focalization in the text, I show that the novel does not, as Spivak argues, appropriate blackness in the service of Euro-Creole subject constitution. I agree with Parry's argument that the representation of black Creoles in *Wide Sargasso Sea* does allow for the emergence of countermeanings. I part ways with Parry, however, when she celebrates an unproblematical articulation of the West Indian world from an "authentic" black perspective and puts the defiant Christophine in the role of the self-determining agent that Antoinette failed to become. Indeed, the moment Christophine best represents Western ideals of subjectivity and vehemently speaks up against injustice is also the moment she is made to leave the island and the narrative altogether. The premises of the colonialist discourse do not falter and lose ground when the black subalterns speak but paradoxically when they are silenced and stereotyped. This paradox thwarts our attempts at reading the black subjects as unmediated representations of historical African Creoles by foregrounding the complex and shifting cultural constructions of race, sex, and class through which the black Creoles are perceived in the novel. At the same time, however, it does not preclude the presence of black resistance that is located in the intersection of colonial practices with subaltern strategies. In other words, resistance in *Wide Sargasso Sea* is based on a model of the hybrid nature of postcolonial culture insofar as it is only when it is articulated to the categories of imperial and patriarchal discourse that it has the potential to unsettle colonial authority.

This resurgence of difference through colonial discourse strongly resonates with Homi Bhabha's work on the ambivalence of colonial stereotypes.[8] It shows that while the notion of a homogeneous English identity places white women and minorities on the margins of its norms, it cannot help but provide at the same time the very grounds for the interruption of its ideal of coherence and unity. In *Wide Sargasso Sea,* the colonialist impulse to control discourse and fix meanings is consistently frustrated by subaltern practices like obeah that rely on the ambivalence of colonial authority to "unman" those in power. In addition, questions about "voice," "breaking silence," and first-person narration are made central to a reconceptualization of experience, race, and agency in a way that echoes *Windward Heights*'s textual politics. The models of resistance in both rewritings resonate with one another and show that the meanings of texts are mutually and irremediably transformed when they are set in a dynamic and productive dialogue with new contexts.

CONTEMPORARY CRITICS tend to agree with Spivak's reading that *Wide Sargasso Sea* provides us with a sympathetic representation of white Creole alienation at the expense of the black Creole perspective. By contrast, I argue that the novel's complex delineation of the plural histories and cultures of the Caribbean forecloses a facile celebration of an insulated voice's recovery by hampering the reader's identification with Bertha/Antoinette. By foregrounding the West Indian racial and social divisions, Rhys does to her own protagonist Antoinette what she has been acclaimed for doing to Brontë's Jane Eyre, that is, shows her as constituted within and by the processes of colonization and imperialism. Instead of extolling the unified and autonomous (feminine) subject Jane had—and Antoinette could have—come to embody, *Wide Sargasso Sea* calls forth a model of reading that scrutinizes the negations and devaluations that such a definition of identity may involve. Critics have impressively read against the grain of the husband's narrative in the novel's middle section in order to interpret the white Creole's life and identity; taking into account the representation of the black characters compels us to read against the grain of Antoinette's narrative as well. Rhys distances herself from her protagonist through formal patterns, ellipses, and repetitions that expose Antoinette's colonialist assumptions. Thus, *Wide Sargasso Sea*'s double narrative structure—which gives us access to the black Creole voices and actions only through the consciousnesses of the two major narrators—attests not to Rhys's imperialism but to her insight into the workings of the ideological system and its categories of representation. Binaries are not invoked as central in and for themselves but are flaunted only to be exposed as the historical and discursive constructions through which Antoinette's black others are represented; they ultimately dissolve because we are compelled to take into account the interrelation of axes of power (gender, race, class) that constitute and contextualize cultural identities.

In the first section of the novel, the young Antoinette's perceptual and psychological point of view is considerably confused and confusing. Whereas the initial chapter of *Jane Eyre* raises the question of how an abused and continually humiliated little girl could possibly come up with such psychological vigor and self-esteem, *Wide Sargasso Sea*'s protagonist appears fragmented, insecure, and disoriented so much so that she seems to function merely by internalizing others'—especially her mother's— language and contradictory values. When a black little girl follows her, calling her white cockroach, Antoinette's reaction sounds rather strange ("They hated us. They called us white cockroach. *Let sleeping dogs lie*" [23; emphasis mine]) unless we remember that she is repeating a phrase she heard her mother use in reference to the old gardener Godfrey ("I've learned to let sleeping curs lie" [22]). That Antoinette herself is clueless as to what the "dogs" were doing when they were *not* sleeping becomes clear when we bring the disjointed and fragmentary elements of her narrative together with the other dispersed textual pieces of the patchwork.[9] This reading model provides insight into socially constructed meanings that Antoinette herself lacks and can only grasp intuitively.

The significance of her quarrel with her childhood friend Tia by the pool can only be understood, for instance, once we analyze the white Creoles' interaction with the black Creoles in light of the historical and sociopolitical context of the Caribbean. When Tia takes her money,

Antoinette resorts to cultural stereotypes about black Creoles and Tia retorts accordingly:

> "Keep them then, you cheating nigger," I said, for I was tired, and the water I had swallowed made me feel sick. "I can get more if I want to."
>
> That's not what she hear, she said. She hear all we poor like beggar. We ate salt fish—no money for fresh fish. That old house so leaky, you run with calabash to catch water when it rain. Plenty white people in Jamaica. Real white people, they got gold money. They didn't look at us, nobody see them come near us. Old time white people nothing but white nigger now, and black nigger better than white nigger. (24)

Tia's tirade reveals that race is a historically and discursively constituted identity whose meaning varies according to one's economic status. Antoinette, however, takes her friend's (unwittingly) structural analysis personally, that is, as a comment on her behavior and person rather than as a commentary (albeit a sarcastic one) on the status of the white Creole minority after emancipation. In the middle section of the novel (Rochester's narrative), she refers to this same episode when explaining her background and her past to her estranged husband: "Then there was that day when [my mother] saw I was growing up like a white nigger and she was ashamed of me, it was after that day that everything changed. Yes, it was my fault, it was my fault that she started to plan and work in a frenzy, in a fever to change our lives" (132). This confession underwrites and clarifies her interpretation of Tia's words after their altercation at the pool: "She [my mother] is ashamed of me, what Tia said is true" (26). Antoinette cannot see that "what Tia said" included her mother too, because she has no grasp of the historical and ideological barriers that separate classes in West Indian postslavery society. *Her* personal is not political.

The first section of the novel abounds in scenes that show Antoinette's inability to comprehend the relationships between the broader sociopolitical and discursive fabric of the Caribbean and the few individuals that people her world ("They were all the people in my life—my mother and Pierre [her brother], Christophine, Godfrey [the old gardener], and Sass who had left us" (23–24)).[10] When her mother tells her that had it not been for Christophine, they would all be dead and "that would have been a better fate than being abandoned, lied about, helpless," Antoinette is not aware of the subtext of these comments; she does not pick up on the trope of the gossipy and idle black to which her mother is referring (here and on several other occasions), or else she would not bother to point out that "Godfrey stayed . . . And Sass" in order to console and reassure Annette. Indeed, in the latter's system of belief, the black and colored people are part of the problem, not the solution.

Not surprisingly, Antoinette replicates her mother's racial thinking to the point where it is sometimes hard to determine whether she is transcribing her mother's words (in free indirect discourse) or sharing the beliefs she has internalized and naturalized:

> She still rode about every morning not caring that the black people stood about in groups to jeer at her, especially after her riding clothes grew shabby (*they notice clothes, they know about money*). (18; emphasis mine)

> All Coulibri Estate had gone wild like the garden, gone to bush. No more slavery—why should anybody work? This never saddened me. I did not remember the place when it was prosperous. (19)

> Sass had come back and I was glad. They can smell money, somebody said. (30)

Antoinette's lack of critical and social awareness is partly a result of internal focalization (that is, affected by a child's perception). Indeed, one of the most distinct narrative patterns in *Wide Sargasso Sea* consists of an oscillation between the internal perceptual focalizer (the experiencing child) and the external focalizer (the older, narrating Antoinette).[11] The next excerpt is typical in this respect:

> Quickly, while I can, I must remember the hot classroom. The hot classroom, the pitchpine desks, the heat of the bench striking up through my body, along my arms and hands. But outside I could see cool, blue shadows on a white wall. My needle is sticky, and creaks as it goes in and out of the canvas. "My needle is swearing," I whisper to Louise, who sits next to me. We are cross-stitching silk roses on a pale background. We can colour the roses as we choose and mine are green, blue and purple. Underneath, I will write my name in fire red, Antoinette Mason, née Cosway, Mount Calvary Convent, Spanish Town, Jamaica, 1839. (53)

In the first section of the novel, the adult narrator-focalizer (Antoinette writing in the attic at Thornfield? Or, as I prefer to think, writing before her wedding to Rochester when she is still trying to choose between her cousin Sandi or Rochester) summons images, sounds, and sensations from her past; they first rush back disjointedly, but soon a particular scene is captured, and the internal focalizer takes over ("We can colour, etc.). The change of focalizers is conveyed by the shift in verb tenses within the same sentence or paragraph (I must . . . could . . . is . . . creaks . . . we are cross-stitching . . . I will write) and reveals the psychology of the younger Antoinette from within.

This psychological aspect of focalization might be responsible for the critical assumption that Antoinette is a sympathetic character from the ideological standpoint, all the more so since the adult narrator "fails" to focalize the norms of the text unequivocally. Indeed, in contrast to *Jane Eyre,* whose authoritative ideology is consistently and unambiguously that of the narrator-focalizer (the older Jane), the ideological position of the narrating Antoinette in *Wide Sargasso Sea* is neither transparent nor central. *Wide Sargasso Sea* disrupts the nineteenth-century first-person narrative conventions that tend to subordinate the perspective of the younger focalizer to the ideological point of view of the adult narrator. Instead, the novel offers a narrator-focalizer whose own limited knowledge and problematic values highlight her unreliability as she is shown desperately trying to patch together the fragments of her disintegrating world. Indeed, the older narrating Antoinette in *Wide Sargasso Sea*—in stark contrast to the older Jane—is hardly any less confused and traumatized than the younger one. In fact, she appears to be in a state of "arrested development" in relation to her younger self.

Antoinette's "cluelessness" about the power relations that structure her world is of course also a function of her subject position as a member of the planter class. It cannot be accounted for solely in terms of her sexual and racial domination. Indeed, the relation between metropole and Creole in the novel does not function through a simplified polarity because Antoinette is not simply colonized. While a particular set of oppressions is responsible for her subordination, another is shown to ground her privilege over other groups. Systems of oppression intertwine with each other systematically, so that the oppressions structuring Antoinette and Rochester's relationship necessarily entails examining them in light of the black and mulatto people's "double colonization" (in Spivak's terms). The implications across class, race, and ethnicity of Antoinette's highly selective and emotional perception make it clear that her subjective way of knowing and fragmentary narrative voice partly derive from the planter class's typical amnesia when it comes to their participation in the history of slavery.

Her mother, for instance, does not at any point relate their harassment by the blacks to the historical circumstances of slavery. And when racial history and inequalities are mentioned, she irremediably resorts to stereotypes as "a way out": "We were so poor then, we were something to laugh at. But we are not poor now. You are not a poor man. Do you suppose that they don't know about your estate in Trinidad? And the Antigua property? They talk about us without stopping. They invent stories about you, and lies about me. They try to find out what we eat every day" (32).

It is ironically Mr. Mason, her self-satisfied British husband, who brings up this constantly erased past by mentioning her complicity with the repression of the natives: "Annette, be reasonable. You were the widow of a slave-owner, the daughter of a slave-owner, and you had been living here alone, with two children, for nearly five years when we met. But you were never molested, never harmed" (32).[12] The irony is that he does not in the least mean to justify the blacks' resentment toward her or to ascribe any agency to them: "They are curious. It's natural enough. You have lived alone far too long, Annette. You imagine enmity which doesn't exist" (32). Thus, the text not only invokes the natives' effaced sociohistorical context and agency (independently and even in spite of the speaker's intention), but it also exposes how slavery as a historical event gets constructed and assigned meanings by the colonizer's discourse. Like Rochester, Mason is a haughty and pious abolitionist (he "did not approve of Aunt Cora, an ex-slave-owner who had escaped misery, a flier in the face of Providence" [30]), whose complacent ideals reveal a stereotypical understanding of the blacks that has remained unchanged since before emancipation. Like Rochester, he is incapable of seeing people of color as actors in their own history of liberation.

It is significant in this respect that the novel's evocation of colonial history consists of random and blunt references to place-names, slavery, the Emancipation Act, and historical figures such as Père Labat (Père Lilièvre in the novel). The straightforward historical narrative is replaced by allusions that not only challenge an essential way of ordering reality but also dramatize the process by which "the real" gets obliterated by conflictive representational discourses. And even though the older Antoinette does come to realize the constructedness of notions of the real ("You are trying to make me into someone else, calling me by another name. I know, that's obeah too" [147]), she is mainly shown trying to live up to her husband's preestablished views and submitting to his unshakable belief in the naturalness of his socially sanctioned ways of knowing. After their initial estrangement, for instance, she tries to win him back by telling him the/her truth about her past but confirms instead his suspicion that she has inherited her mother's madness and promiscuity; she is wearing the white dress he liked so much, "but it ha[s] slipped untidily over one shoulder" (127). Antoinette herself is incapable of realizing that in Rochester's eyes, her attire actually associates her with (black) female sexual wantonness and prostitution since her only frame of reference is her favorite childhood picture she is striving to emulate, "'The Miller's Daughter,' a lovely English girl with brown curls and blue eyes and *a dress slipping off her shoulders*" (36; emphasis mine).

The discrepancy between Antoinette's (often unsuccessful) attempts at replicating dominant conceptual structures and her actual experience further demonstrates that Rhys is not identifying with so much as scrutinizing the position of the white Creole in post-emancipation Caribbean society.[13] For instance, despite Antoinette's desire to please her mother, stepfather, and later Rochester by behaving like a "lovely English girl," she is often presented as more in tune with black models than with the white standards to which she strives and is expected to adhere. On the one hand, she has—probably as a result of "Mr. Mason's lectures" (*Wide Sargasso Sea* 50)—no qualms uttering racialized and dismissive comments about black customs: "The girl was very black and wore no head handkerchief. Her hair had been plaited and I could smell the sickening oil she had daubed on it, from where I stood on the steps of Aunt Cora's dark, clean, friendly house" (49). On the other hand, her older self has adopted many of her black counterparts' practices and beliefs, and ironically, also incurs repulsion: "'Don't put any more scent on my hair. He doesn't like it.' The other: 'The man doesn't like scent? I never hear that before'" (79).[14] Antoinette's closeness to the black Creole culture becomes all the more evident when she actually expects to offend her stepfather by labeling him "white": "I thought that I would never like him very much. . . . 'Goodnight white pappy,' I said one evening and he was not vexed, he laughed'" (33–34).

In *Contradictory Omens,* the Barbadian writer and theorist Kamau Brathwaite discusses postslavery as the time when "creolization," that is, the process of "acculturation" of black to white norms, but also of a reciprocal and enriching "interculturation," was halted. He explains that the white Creoles' lack of cooperation with and degrading of the black labor force defeated the possibility of an alliance between the two as well as the completion of the creative process of creolization (24). Although Brathwaite goes on to castigate Rhys for her "neglect" of the black and poor West Indian people's experiences,[15] it is ironically his concept of "creolization" that I think best describes *Wide Sargasso Sea*'s racial/ textual politics. The novel, I argue, dramatizes the possibility of a mutual and creative "interculturation" between white and black Creoles, hints at ways in which this interaction could have been propitiously sustained, and foregrounds the reasons why it was stopped.

IN HER ESSAY "Problems in Current Theories of Colonial Discourse," Benita Parry points to Antoinette's black nurse Christophine as the rightful and defiantly resistant subaltern in Rhys's novel. In contrast to Spivak, who sees the same character as "inaccessible blankness circumscribed by an interpretable text" ("Three Women's Texts" 264), Parry describes Christophine as the text's female source of a counterdiscourse (38). Although Parry is (rightly) concerned that poststructuralist strategies of reading downgrade the historical evidence of the colonial subject's resistance, Spivak's point is not to devalue or deny the subaltern's resistance (she does not doubt its existence), but to question the possibility of an unmediated and disinterested access to these (hi)stories. She suggests that the Western analysis of the colonial subject's capacity for thought and action has typically resulted either in the denial of the external constraints that constitute the subaltern or in a naïve and unproblematical "nativist" position that sees colonized societies "as distant cultures, exploited but with rich intact heritages waiting to be recovered" ("The Rani" 247). I follow this model but also argue that *Wide Sargasso Sea*'s exploration of the different contexts and discourses in and through which colonial and racial subjects are constructed actually resists assigning to the subaltern the function of "a mere repository of Eurocentric assumptions." Although the black Creoles are indeed, in Spivak's words, "doubly silenced, doubly marginalized," their complex interplay with colonial strategies actualizes a resistance that effectively unsettles the colonizer's worldview and actions.

Once we realize that the text compels us to read against the grain of Antoinette's narrative, our understanding of the representation of the black characters necessarily changes as well. It no longer follows, as critics have argued, that Rhys is "naturalizing" the racist attitudes of the planter class and portraying the white Creoles as the innocent "victims" of a malevolent mob of black and mulatto people: "Still [the black Creoles] were quiet and there were so many of them I could hardly see any grass or trees. There must have been many of the bay people but I recognized no one. They all looked the same, it was the same face repeated over and over, eyes gleaming, mouth half open to shout" (*Wide Sargasso Sea* 42).

This scene follows the burning of the Coulibri estate and has often been objected to on the grounds that it depicts the black Creoles as an undifferentiated and unreasoning mass of hatred and betrayal (Gregg 94; Rody 307; Sagar 167). Taking this episode in isolation as representative of the text's ideology, however, signifies two things, both of which my argument contests: first, that Antoinette's voice represents Rhys's point of view, and second, that the absence of a straightforward narrativization of the island's abject slaveholding history is prejudicial to the perspectives of the black African Creoles. Indeed, the scene preceding Antoinette's depiction of the collective face helps elucidate the seemingly unjustified violence of the ex-slaves: one of the servants, Myra, overhears Mr. Mason's intention to "import labourers . . . from the East Indies" (35) and goes, Aunt Cora implies, to notify the others. It is left to the reader to infer that what Myra reports is that the "importation" and commodification of human beings, which to the ex-slaves would necessarily conjure up slavery, was to be resumed. Thus, rather than corroborating the white Creoles' stereotypical representation of their lower-class others, this episode also indirectly intimates the black Creoles' inflexible commitment to decolonization and freedom and recasts their "unreasoning and miasmic presence" as reasoned determination.[16]

Wide Sargasso Sea foregrounds black resistance without, however, offering unmediated access to alternative "negro traditions" or to a counter-discourse to an imperialist way of knowing. The novel neither celebrates an unproblematical articulation of the West Indian world from the black Creole point of view nor ascribes to the resilient obeah woman Christophine the role of the self-determining individualist that Antoinette has failed to become. Rather, it highlights the ways in which black Creole agency was primarily coded as criminal and affirmed not for its own sake so much as to justify subjugation and obscure white domination. Amélie and Christophine both know better, for instance, than to stay in Rochester's proximity once they have acted as agents by speaking their minds. Yet, at the same time as it foregrounds the historical and discursive processes that doubly silence the black subaltern, the text also denaturalizes these processes by exposing the racial contradictions embedded in the dominant imperial and patriarchal ideologies. In fact, it is paradoxically the formal disruptions and silences at the heart of colonialist and stereotypical discourses rather than the novel's reference to the historical and social reality of black resistance that allow for the perspectives and resistances of the subaltern to be recognized.

The practice of obeah, for instance, does not constitute an effective counterdiscourse in *Wide Sargasso Sea* on the basis of its historical function.[17] While I share Parry's desire to do justice to "the speaking position" and historical agency of the disempowered, I argue that her invocation of historical context to make sense of obeah in Rhys's fiction is problematic on two counts: first, because Rhys was not one to transcribe any event, whether it be historical or autobiographical, directly into writing. Form and imaginative intervention were foremost on her mind, so much so that even her autobiography, *Smile Please,* exemplifies the kind of highly structured and modernist piece of writing we associate with fiction. When it comes to her work's relation to history, however, this emphasis on creative transformation has less to do with a distortion of the historical truth than with her awareness that history too is a narrative told about oneself and others. It is therefore not surprising that obeah in *Wide Sargasso Sea* should give way not to a sense of anchored historicity but to a proliferation of narratives. What Rhys stated in reference to Antoinette's narrative is also true of the representation of obeah in the novel: "the story, if any, to be implied, [is] *never* told straight" (Wyndham 233). Second, a celebration of Rhysian obeah on the basis of its historical function overlooks the fact that the presence of obeah as a practice is in fact remarkably nondescript and intangible in her work.

Historically, obeah is a form of magic that, like its Haitian counterpart vodoun, uses charm fetishes and chants and derives from West African traditions.[18] The enslaved Africans brought the practice with them to the Caribbean during slavery. After its transplantation, obeah adapted to the new social and political context of the Caribbean and developed into a syncretic religion that incorporated and inflected Christian symbols. The practice survived in its hybrid form despite the slaveholders' repeated attempts at destroying what they knew to be a dangerous source of empowerment for the slaves. Indeed, on the plantation, obeah witch figures played a key role as go-betweens among the slaves. They were also believed to be the main instigators of slave revolt, inspiring both fear and awe among believers (Drake 110; Emery 44; Hall, "Religious Ideologies" 278).

As her autobiography, *Smile Please,* attests, Rhys was well aware of the staying power of obeah in Dominican society: "Our cook at Bona Vista was an obeah woman called Ann Tewitt. Obeah is a milder form of voodoo, and even in my time nobody was supposed to take it very seriously. Yet I was told about her in a respectful, almost awed tone" (15–16).[19] Yet, despite her knowledge and recognition of the redoubtable influence of obeah in Caribbean life, the black Creoles in her fiction are neither shown standing in fear of it, nor are they really shown practicing it. In fact, considering her forcefulness and appeal as a character, it is remarkable that *Wide Sargasso Sea*'s obeah woman should fail to incite the kind of respect among believers that obeah practitioners were known to inspire historically. When she discovers Amélie flirting with Antoinette's husband, for instance, Christophine's threat to use her magic against the black servant does not in the least dissuade the latter from sleeping with Rochester. Neither does Daniel Cosway seem to fear retaliation when he calls Christophine a liar and tells Rochester about her past troubles with the police. Baptiste, whom Christophine herself later echoes, calls obeah "foolishness" (106). In fact, the only time in the novel when Christophine is called upon to practice her art is when a desperate Antoinette asks her to concoct a love drink that would help her "charm" her husband. Christophine insists that obeah is not for *békés* yet gives her a potion that fails to achieve the desired effect. As Raiskin remarks, it is unclear "whether the hex fails because Obeah is essentially a practice of the black community . . . , or whether Christophine meant to poison the white master to free Antoinette" (139). *Wide Sargasso Sea* is thus consistently shown downplaying obeah despite its historical significance in black cultural traditions.

It is important to note that the attitude of disaffection reflected in her black characters' indifference cannot be attributed to Rhys herself since, in a letter she wrote to her editor, Francis Wyndham, she emphasized the central role obeah had played in her novel's genesis.[20] She explained that it was only after writing a poem entitled "Obeah Night" that "it clicked" for her, and that she managed to resume writing *Wide Sargasso Sea* after more than a decade-long interruption: "Even when I knew I had to write the book—still it did not click into place—that is one reason (though only one) why I was so long. It didn't click. It wasn't there. However I tried. Only when I wrote this poem ["Obeah Night"]—then it clicked—and all was there and always had been. The first clue is Obeah which I assure you existed, and still does, in Haiti, South America and of course in Africa— under different names. The others—sais pas. It was against the law in the 'English' islands" (262).

This excerpt reveals that obeah in *Wide Sargasso Sea* is pivotal to our understanding of the narrative even as it remains a nebulous presence in the characters' lives. The fact that this black cultural form is paradoxically both central to the text's meanings and intangible partly explains why critics have accounted for the references to obeah in *Wide Sargasso Sea* in terms of Rhys's *metaphorical* appropriation of Afro-Caribbean symbols. Because the material and political effects of obeah and zombiism are unclear,[21] critics who nonetheless feel and wish to account for its palimpsestic centrality to the narrative deduce that it must work as a metaphor of "white" alienation and oppression (by virtue of Rhys's subject position as a white Creole). According to Raiskin, for instance, Rhys appropriates the zombi as a metaphor for her heroines' social and sexual alienation and then extends this condition of "living death" to the dominant male characters. On the one hand, zombiism is seen as a strategy of self-protection that Rhys's white female characters deploy against British and European oppressive forces. On the other hand, it is a condition that affects the white masters as well, thus revealing them as victims of a "larger system that exploits all of the participants" (135). In other words, the white Creoles and the white British colonizers are both zombified, that is, victimized, and it is their "victimization," not obeah as a sign of black resistance, that takes center stage in this interpretation.

Raiskin supports these claims by listing instances in Rhys's novels when the female characters are in a so-called "zombilike state," including, for instance, when the heroine of *Voyage in the Dark*, Anna Morgan, is caught in self-denial ("a deadening attitude") or feels "like a ghost," and when Mrs. Heidler's eyes in *Quartet* have a "deadened look," or the protagonist, Marya, feels like a "sleepwalker." In *Wide Sargasso Sea*, Rochester is seen as a zombi for no other reason than that he remains nameless and that he denies his feelings of love. Mr. Mason, Antoinette's stepfather, is also a zombi, but in his case, it is because his wife claims that he is "less alive" than the island blacks (Raiskin 133–34). This interpretation of the alleged "zombi" imagery is troubling for two reasons: first, because it imputes to Rhys a metaphorics that, I contend, is a function of the critic's reading rather than of Rhys's writing.[22] Instead of seeing "this inappropriate focus on white victimization" as Rhys's (Raiskin 136), I argue that it is the result of reducing textual references to metaphors. Second, a reading that treats zombiism as a metaphor for the psychological effects of colonial relations on the whites effectively erases the black cultural tradition in which zombiism is grounded. Indeed, this interpretation does not, not even by extension, signify a black Creole historical agency, because the zombilike condition of the white rulers is consistently defined as a result of their colonizing impulses and not as a function of black resistance to imperialism. The white Creole is caught "in the limbo state of the zombi, fully alive in neither the English nor the black culture," while the white British is "deadened" by "a system that uses him as well as those whom he exploits" (Raiskin 135). Even when the black Creole Christophine is recognized as the actual agent behind the zombification, it is in the role of "good servant" and "black nanny," and not as a sign of the black community's punishment for the racism of the class of white rulers. As a result, the figure of the zombi is emptied of the political meanings it embodies in the specific context of Caribbean slavery.

By contrast, I argue that obeah in *Wide Sargasso Sea* is not about metaphors waiting to be read but about the *unreadability* of a potent black cultural tradition that destabilizes the white rulers' worldview. Critics have failed to comment on the extent to which it is precisely the unknowability of obeah that drives Rhys's narrative and where the answer to its role as black resistance lies. Rhys's own observations about this episode emphasize the impossibility of knowing what obeah and its effects ultimately consist of and suggest that the "altered state" that overtakes Rochester the night of his passionate lovemaking to Antoinette is induced not by obeah but by lust:

> The second clue was when Miss Anthill suggested a few weeks of happiness for the unfortunate couple—before he gets disturbing letters. As soon as I wrote that bit I realized that he must have fallen for her—and violently too. The black people have a good word for it—"she *magic* with him" or "he *magic* with her." Because you see, that is what it is—magic, intoxication. Not "Love" at all. . . . In obeah these drinks or sacrifices or whatever have this effect: The god himself enters the person who has drunk. Afterwards he (or she) faints, recovers, and remembers very little of what has happened (they say). I wouldn't know. Not Mr. R. he remembers *everything* including the fact that he has felt a bit uneasy in the early happy days and asked her to tell him what's wrong, promised to believe her, and stand by her, and she's always answered "Nothing is wrong." For, poor child, she is *afraid* to tell him, and cries if he insists. So he strides into her bedroom, not himself, but angry love and that is what the poem is about. Even when the love has gone, the anger is still there and remains. (No obeah needed for that!) And remains. (Wyndham 262–63)

In other words, the novel is not about obeah and what it does ("[Rhys] wouldn't know"). Instead of evoking black magic as a practice objectively determined from an underlying historical and social reality, *Wide Sargasso Sea* presents it as a discursive construct deployed by the colonizer as much as by the colonized. Rochester capitalizes on the love drink he was given (despite its failure at achieving any effect) because he needs to rationalize his overwhelming sexual desire for Antoinette and to displace its source on an external agent. He genuinely believes that only foul play and an intoxicating drug could possibly drive a respectable Victorian gentleman like him to feel love and sexual desire for a woman whose mixed blood (which the "disturbing letters" have exposed) mark her as belonging to an inferior species. Obeah is thus appropriated by the white colonizer as a way of preserving his sense of superiority within his purist and racist frame of reference.

Thus, even though the practice is historically embedded in black cosmology, the text does not try to account for its influence (whether nurturing or deterring) over the Afro-Caribbean community. In fact, its representation of the role of the practice among black Creoles remains cryptic. For example, we never know for sure whether Amélie ultimately leaves the estate, as Rochester suggests, for fear that Christophine might retaliate or whether, as she herself claims, she is simply carrying out a long-formed plan; whether Christophine's "powers" contribute to unifying the ex-slave community or to isolate her from it; whether the black Creoles qualify obeah as "foolishness" to mark their distance from the practice or to appease the British colonizer by dissimulating resistance behind a mask of docility. This ambiguity persists throughout the narrative and reflects the two narrators' inability to grasp a Caribbean experience whose opaqueness cannot be reconciled with their interpretive frameworks. In keeping with a narration that is split between Antoinette's and Rochester's focalizations, the explicit references to obeah thus tell us more about the Anglo-European stereotypical framework through which Afro-Caribbean traditions were given meaning in the nineteenth century than about the alternative Afro-Caribbean epistemology that the practice embodies. This is why obeah is not circumscribable in the narrative despite its centrality to the text's meanings. And this is why, throughout the novel, it is the two narrators, Antoinette and Rochester, rather than the black Creoles who repeatedly bring up its practice and its rituals.

A case in point is when the young Antoinette recalls how, after her mother's remarriage to Mr. Mason, it was the new servants' "talk about Christophine and obeah," "not the repairs or the new furniture or the strange faces," that changed Coulibri, her mother's estate:

I knew her room so well—the picture of the holy Family and the prayer for a happy death. She had a bright patchwork counterpane, a broken-down press for her clothes, and my mother had given her an old rocking-chair. Yet one day when I was waiting there I was suddenly very much afraid. The door was open to the sunlight, someone was whistling near the stables, but I was afraid. I was certain that hidden in the room (behind the old black press?) there was a dead man's dried hand, white chicken feathers, a cock with its throat cut, dying slowly, slowly. Drop by drop the blood was falling into a red basin and I imagined I could hear it. No one had ever spoken to me about obeah—but I knew what I would find if I dared to look. Then Christophine came in smiling and pleased to see me. Nothing alarming ever happened and I forgot, or told myself I had forgotten. (31)

Her characterization of obeah is necessarily articulated with prevalent stereotypes about the practice. Indeed, as Brathwaite points out, "obeah was associated in the [white] Jamaican/European mind with superstition, witchcraft, and poison . . . [whereas] in African/Caribbean folk practice, where religion had not been externalized and institutionalized as in Europe, the obeah-man [*sic*] was doctor, philosopher, and priest" (12). Similarly, Rochester's obsession with zombiism is derived from the stereotypical account of obeah he reads in an English text, *The Glittering Coronet of Isles*:

> "A zombi is a dead person who seems to be alive or a living person who is dead. A zombi can also be the spirit of a place, usually malignant but some-times to be propitiated with sacrifices or offerings of flowers and fruit." I thought at once of the bunches of flowers at the priest's ruined house. . . . negroes as a rule refuse to discuss the black magic in which so many believe. . . . They confuse matters by telling lies if pressed. The white people, sometimes credulous, pretend to dismiss the whole thing as nonsense. Cases of sudden or mysterious death are attributed to a poison known to the negroes which cannot be traced. (107)

Rochester's experience of the island and its inhabitants is in fact consistently and completely filtered through this English text. When he reads about Antoinette's past in the "disturbing letters" he has received, for instance, he interprets Daniel Cosway's words in the light of the British book's representation of black magic. Daniel keeps referring to Antoinette's and Annette's "madness" as just part of the problem: "madness *not being all either*" (97); "a crazy wife in your bed. Crazy *and worse besides*" (99; emphasis mine). He urges Rochester to find out about Antoinette's mother: "Is your wife's mother shut away, a raging lunatic and worse besides? *Dead or alive* I do not know" (98; emphasis mine). What determines Rochester's interpretation of "what's worse" than madness, however, is his newly acquired and stereotypical knowledge about the living dead, not Cosway's intended meaning. Indeed, Cosway attributes the "madness" to the white Creoles' historical participation in the history of slavery ("There is madness in that family. *Old Cosway* die raving like his father before him") and to their resulting collective guilt ("soon the madness that is in her, *and in all these white Creoles*, come out" [96; emphasis mine]). By contrast, what Rochester hears and remembers is "dead or alive I do not know," a characterization that his overworked imagination reads as zombiism. Similarly, when Antoinette does tell him about her mother's whereabouts, her ambiguous answer only further feeds his fear and paranoia by yet again summoning the image of a zombi: "why did you tell me that she died when you were a child? Because they told me to say so and because it is true. She did die when I was a child. There are always *two deaths, the real one and the one people know about*" (128; emphasis mine).

Rochester cannot help articulating the events that transpire around him through the same colonialist script. When Antoinette enlists Christophine's help to drug her husband and "make him love [her]," he wakes up the next day feeling giddy and nauseous and immediately relates his condition to a stereotypical understanding of zombiism. That he thinks, for instance, that Christophine is trying to turn him into a zombi ("I woke . . . after dreaming that I was buried alive" [137]) is confirmed when he rushes to the priest's ruined house in the forest (139) to counteract the effect of the "poison" Antoinette administered to him the previous night. Following the British text, he assumes that Christophine meant to cause his "sudden or mysterious death," and remembering that "sacrifices or offerings of flowers and fruit" can "propitiate" zombis, he rushes to the ruined house where he had noticed "bunches of flowers" and "a wild orange tree" (139). As he searches for an antidote, he thus literally "goes native" by engaging obeah on its own terms.

Although obeah's impact on the colonizer is circumscribed by the colonialist account of black magic, the practice still functions as a powerful site of disruption and resistance in the novel. When Rochester runs to the ruined house in search of an antidote, he has lost control. By engaging obeah on its own terms, he is in fact carrying out the colonizer's worst fear, namely that of "going native." What disarms him is thus not the obeah witch's "agency" but the stereotypical notions of a Eurocentric text he cannot question combined with and exacerbated by "native" silences he cannot interpret. Indeed, as long as he cannot determine with certainty whether the presence of obeah works against him or for him ("It's evidently useful to keep a Martinique obeah woman on the premises" [30]), whether it is "foolishness" and "nonsense" or subversive and dangerous practice, Rochester feels "half hypnotized" (158) and unable to take any punitive action against Christophine. Incapable of fixing obeah as an object of knowledge, he cannot control and appropriate it. He vacillates between interpreting the black Creoles' denials and silences as a sign of ignorance and lack of knowledge (their silence is the truth) or as evidence of their duplicity and underlying sinister intentions (their silence and denial hide the truth). The black Creoles' conspiracy of silence/ignorance thus enhances his feelings of paranoia by exploiting the dominant discourse's contradictory representation of its racial others (as both duplicitous and too stupid to plot, calculating and too simplistic to be so).[23] It is thus not *what obeah is* that overwhelms Rochester in *Wide Sargasso Sea* but rather the fear and anxiety produced in him by the articulation of his stereotypical notions with the natives' deliberate silences. In other words, it is paradoxically when the other's silence is articulated with the categories of imperial discourse that it has the potential to make visible and denaturalize the ambivalent modes of operation of colonial authority. The political effects of black magic need therefore to be examined in the context of the patchwork of ignorances/silences that ultimately constitutes the locus of black Creole resistance in the novel.

Wide Sargasso Sea recasts the black Creoles' silence in response to the legacy of colonialism as a strategy of power rather than as a reflection of weakness, and challenges in so doing the Western habit of associating speech with power. Indeed, the Afro-Caribbean characters' conspiracy of silence/ignorance surrounding the practice of black magic ultimately enhances Rochester's paranoia and undermines colonial authority from within in a way that their speaking up against injustice cannot. It is no coincidence that the few scenes that actually foreground a subaltern's "coming to voice" in the face of authority all result in the speaker losing rather than gaining power. No matter what Christophine or Antoinette *say,* their utterances are filtered through and consolidate a colonialist discourse whose premises and prescriptions Rochester cannot question. When Antoinette tells her husband "the truth" (what she calls "the other side" [128] of her mother's story), her impressionistic narrative only serves to confirm Rochester's preestablished views and the suspicions stimulated by Daniel Cosway's allegations. In the same way, when Daniel Cosway "comes to voice" in his first letter to Rochester, he is credulously addressing the British man as an ally who helped bring about "the glorious Emancipation Act" (96) and who would therefore share his aversion to the white Creoles' elitist attitudes. He mentions the "madness" that affected Antoinette's mother, but unlike Rochester, he is not attributing it to her sexual indulgence and racial "degeneration" but to the white Creoles' historical participation in slavery. He does not see madness as restricted to the Cosway women ("There is madness in that family. *Old Cosway* die raving like his father before him") and identifies it as induced by the white Creoles' collective guilt ("soon the madness that is in her, *and in all these white Creoles*, come out" [96; emphasis mine]). What Rochester hears, however, is not a critique of race relations in the Caribbean but a corroboration of his imperialist and patriarchal preconceptions.

Christophine's attempts to "reason" with Rochester by adopting his Anglo-European mode of communication lead to a similar impasse. When she tries to talk to him, he awakens from his zombilike stupor and threatens her with legal action. Critics have pointed to the "obeah scene"—the verbal confrontation between Rochester and Christophine in the former's interior dialogue—as central to the novel, because, they argue, the black nurse's intervention forces Rochester "to internalize her interpretation" (Emery 51) and constitutes a powerful countermeaning (Parry, "Problems" 38). This reading effectively ignores, however, the outcome of the confrontation that forces Christophine to leave the island and the property that Antoinette's mother had bequeathed her. That Rochester echoes Christophine's words during their talk does not signify that he is absorbing them or being invaded by her culture. Considering his expeditious dismissal of her, he rather seems to act as an obstructing surface from which Christophine's words bounce back unheeded. In fact, it is precisely when Christophine's free will and resiliency explode in Rochester's face that her powers are the most limited: he "no longer felt dazed, tired, half hypnotized, but alert and wary, ready to defend [him]self" (158), and he appeals to the "Letter of the Law" to subdue the black nurse he can at last clearly identify as an opponent. The moment she "explains" herself to him and appeals to his humanity on Antoinette's behalf, he sets in motion the hegemonic legal and medical systems that will allow him to successfully silence both her and Antoinette. Christophine "walk[s] away without looking back" (161) and disappears from the narrative altogether. Antoinette becomes a "marionette" and "silence itself" (168).

Thus, *Wide Sargasso Sea* "demonstrates that giving voice to oppressed peoples is more complicated than merely conferring narrative authority upon speakers" (Winterhalter 215). The novel deconstructs the opposition between silence and voice and, in so doing, questions the Western assumption that the speaker is always the one in power. Silences in the novel become a "way of speaking" insofar as they are examined in terms of their effects and not simply as effects of an oppressive power.[24] They are shown to operate alongside the things said as discursive elements that ensure effects of power and knowledge according to who is speaking, his/her context and position of power. For instance, even though both white and black Creoles in *Wide Sargasso Sea* tamper with the notion of a monolithic and linear History that is fundamental to Eurocentric ways of thinking, the narrative establishes a distinction between the effects of these different groups' denial or silencing of their past.

Before being reduced to silence by their British husbands, Annette and Antoinette obsessively silence their own implication in the island's historical and social relations. When her daughter asks her about Christophine, Old Cosway's "wedding present," Antoinette's mother does not want her to "pester and bother [her] about all these things that happened long ago" (21). Antoinette herself points out that "some things happen and are there for always *even though you forget why or when*" (*Wide Sargasso Sea* 82; emphasis mine). When their garden's state of abandon is positioned historically ("All Coulibri Estate had gone wild like the garden, gone to bush. No more slavery—why should anybody work?"), she does not remember and therefore does not oppose it to the pre-emancipation condition of the estate: "This never saddened me. I did not remember the place when it was prosperous" (19).[25] We discover that her British stepfather's "lectures" had indeed made her "shy about [her] coloured relatives" (50), since she refrains from telling us about her "affair" with Sandi until the very end of the novel. Rochester's inquiry about a village's appellation also confirms Antoinette's tendency to forgetfulness:

> "Massacre."
>
> "And who was massacred here? Slaves?"
>
> "Oh no." She sounded shocked. "Not slaves. Something must have happened a long time ago. Nobody remembers now." (65–66)

Although the white Creoles repeatedly deny their own historical and cultural participation in a colonizing process and their complicity with the master narrative, the text resists any facile equation of their situation with Antoinette's, which the reader might make because of her "forgetfulness." According to Mary Lou Emery, "By enduring sexual slaveries and identifying with native and black peoples, the protagonists of Rhys's novels share their histories and occupy their places or places similar to theirs" (178).[26] This occupation is precisely what the novel problematizes. Early in the novel, Antoinette turns to her childhood friend Tia to get her approval, thus seeking yet again to obliterate the difference history and culture has set up between them and to identify with black and mulatto female voices. Tia's reaction, however, prevents us from turning her into Antoinette's defining other. It forces, as it were, a recognition of the very difference that Antoinette is trying to ignore: "I saw Tia and her mother and I ran to her, for she was all that was left of my life as it had been. We had eaten the same food, slept side by side, bathed in the same river. As I ran, I thought, I will live with Tia and I will be like her. Not to leave Coulibri. Not to go. Not. When I was close I saw the jagged stone in her hand but I did not see her throw it. I did not feel it either, only something wet, running down my face. . . . We stared at each other, blood on my face, tears on hers. It was as if I saw myself. Like in a looking glass" (45).

One can now recognize the irony inherent in the old servant Godfrey's words at the beginning of the novel: "When the old time go, let it go. No use to grab at it." He is giving his white Creole employers some of their own medicine, coming up with clichés and denying differences ("The Lord make no distinction between black and white, black and white the same for Him" [18]) in order to evade responsibility for the horse's killing. By contrast to the white Creoles' attempts at silencing the past, the black characters' silences signify both their silencing by stereotype-informed discourses and their resistance to appropriation and misreading. Baptiste, another servant who was born on the island, refuses to recognize the existence of a French pavé road where Edward could actually see one with his own eyes: "I said, 'There was a road here once, where did it lead to?' 'No road,' he said. 'But I saw it. A pavé road like the French made in the islands.' 'No road'" (105–6).

By foregrounding "ignorance" while alluding to a deeper meaning, the black Creoles effect an opposing strategy using the same categories that constitute the discourses of nineteenth-century bourgeois society. They continuously shift from assuming an ignorant attitude that is in keeping with the way they are stereotyped by the dominant discourse ("Still I remain an ignorant man and I do not make up this story," Daniel says to Rochester [98]) to hinting at an underlying "truth" that Edward will necessarily read as a universal secret and an omnipresent cause. They turn ignorance, usually read as innocent passivity, into a potent and performative force, sending Edward on a wild goose chase for the truth to which he thinks their ignorance is pointing. They are thus largely responsible for maintaining his belief in a fundamental secret that the place and its inhabitants would be harboring and that he tries to attain through a wife he now clearly identifies as colored: "She had left me thirsty and all my life would be thirst and longing for what I had lost before I found it. . . . Very soon she'll join all the others who know the secret and will not tell it" (*Wide Sargasso Sea* 172). While the British silence alternative histories because they can only register the impact of an occurrence when it fits their prescribed values, the black Creoles' silences point to their resistance.

Similarly, racial stereotypes which typically construct the other as a "generalized" object of knowledge are, here as in *Windward Heights,* constantly manipulated to challenge such assumed position of knowing. Whereas stereotypes' claims to absolute knowledge usually aim to discourage one from any further inquiry about the stereotyped category, the question of who is speaking to whom in the novel reveals and unsettles the process by which stereotypes become loci of control and power. Mason's and Rochester's use of racial stereotypes exposes their arrogance and paternalism and shows that the abolition of slavery has far from eradicated the set of attitudes on which the concept of Englishness depends. The white Creoles are complicit in this hegemonic discourse insofar as they too rely on this type of gross generalization (although usually out of fear or anger). The black Creoles' use of stereotypes, however, requires us to shift the meaning from the content of the stereotype to its discursive context.

By juxtaposing the black and white Creoles' stereotyping, Rhys reminds us that blackness is not an essential identity but a discursive event. Although Edward uses clichés to establish commonalities between his wife and the black subaltern, the African Creoles resist this excision of the cultural, class, and historical contexts that are constitutive of their identity. Instead of emphasizing a shared identity with Antoinette on the grounds that she is "colored," Tia and later Amélie contest this essentializing move and dismiss any commonality by resorting to stereotypes such as "white nigger" and "white cockroach." This reversal makes impossible any facile identification that would allow Antoinette to evade her implication in the history of slavery. Antoinette thus remains caught between two ways of defining racial community, all the while continuing to deny her family's involvement in the history of slavery. She explains to Rochester that "[white cockroach] is what they call all of us who were here *before their own people in Africa sold them to the slave traders* [her own relatives had nothing to do with it]. . . . I often wonder who I am and where is my country and where do I belong and why I was ever born at all" (102; emphasis mine). Whereas the white Creoles are torn between a residual "white bias" and a vague feeling of guilt that makes them assume a paternalistic attitude toward the ex-African people, the language used by the black Creoles prevents their differences from the ex-planters from being subsumed.

Phrases such as "white nigger" or "black Englishman" also help refute the blood-based notion of racial identity that is rooted in British racial classifications by complicating the regime of visibility with which race is usually associated. As in *Windward Heights,* these apparent oxymorons emphasize the contingency of the racial meanings attached to "white" and "black" bodies so much that the very economy of the visible through which race comes to be is exposed and destabilized. This fluctuating process of signification affects "white" and "black" Creoles alike as their crossings of race through a "darkening" or "whitening" process reflects their transgression of other identity categories. For instance, in Rochester's narrative, his "white" fiancée gradually turns into a "black" character in a process that, I argue, has less to do with the suspected blood-mixing that occurred in her family than with her own crossing of gender boundaries. Significantly, it is after she blatantly transgresses the boundaries of the Victorian ideology of femininity that Rochester recognizes the signs of blackness in her physiognomy. It is her instigation of a night of passionate lovemaking and her uninhibited expression of sexual agency that drive him to comment on her possible kinship with the "black" servant Amélie. From seeing her as a "Creole of pure English descent" (67), he moves on to commenting on her now suspicious resemblance to the half-caste servant Amélie: "Perhaps they are related, I thought. It's possible, it's even probable in this damned place" (127). As Dalton points out in her psychoanalytic reading of the novel, "the motifs of racial impurity . . . and the impurity of the damaged female body are inextricably connected" in the novel (432). And indeed, Amélie's sexual forwardness results in her undergoing a similar process of racialization. When he wakes up next to her, Rochester remarks that "her skin was darker, her lips thicker than I had thought" (140). That both white and black Creoles are "darkened" in the narrative reveals the extent to which it is the feared and despised aspects of femininity that are projected onto corporeal signs of difference.

Instead of erasing the other's racial difference, the colonialist mode of representation in *Wide Sargasso Sea* ends up revealing its own constructedness. The process by which nineteenth-century symbolic practices aimed at fixing the meaning of "blackness" gets exposed precisely because its various categories of classification contradict each other. That blackness is an effect of the discursive context and not an essential identity is made clear by the various stages that Antoinette's racial identity goes through in Rochester's eyes or by the difference its intersection with class makes in the whites' perceptions (the colored Sandi is accepted among white people as one of their own; Daniel Cosway is not). As Hall explains (and the novel demonstrates): "The fact is that 'black' has never just been there. . . . It has always been an unstable identity, psychically, culturally

and politically. It, too, is a narrative, a story, a history. Something constructed, told, spoken, not simply found. . . . Of course Jamaica is a black
society, [people] say. In reality it is a society of black and brown people
who lived for three or four hundred years without ever being able to
speak of themselves as 'black'" ("New Ethnicities" 45).

The black Creoles' parodic "reverse" discourse offers a point of resistance that destabilizes the foundational categories on which the colonizers
construct their identity. They use the same categories as the speakers of
the dominant stereotype-informed discourse and yet do not reproduce the
same stereotypical and essentialist assumptions. Rather, these are rede-
ployed to make explicit the sociocultural constructions like "blackness"
or gender that could otherwise pass as prediscursive and establish a glo-
balizing subject. This reconceptualization challenges the tacit acceptance
of the anatomical as the foundation for difference in theoretical and
critical practice revealing instead the continuity between metaphorical
and literal meanings of race. It shows how tropes of racial, sexual, and
class difference are constantly informed by one another so much so that
an awareness of their inextricable intersections produces meanings that
resist hegemonic inscription. As Brathwaite points out, "it was in language that the slave was perhaps most successfully imprisoned by his
master, and it was in his (mis)use of it that he perhaps most effectively
rebelled" (*Folk Culture* 31).

THE INVESTIGATION of the historical contexts *in* and *about* which *Wide
Sargasso Sea* was written corroborates an interpretation that acknowledges
Rhys's insight into the workings of imperial and patriarchal ideologies.
The novel is about the post-emancipation period when "the legal castes
of slavery [were] replaced by the more complicated divisions of a class-
race-color system of stratification" (Hall 281) and the old slaves came to
form the landless rural proletariat. It was written, however, in a period
witnessing the ebbing of an old colonial order and the emergence of a
nationalist tradition.[27] Both contexts (*of* and *in* the novel) are often referred
to as "the best and worst of times" since they represented liberation,
hope, cultural and intellectual regeneration, as well as continued political
and economic dependence. As Christophine points out in the novel,
slave emancipation hardly meant that the British colonizers had relin-
quished control: "No more slavery! She had to laugh! These new ones
have Letter of the Law. Same thing. They got Magistrate. They got fine.
They got jail house and chain gang. They got tread machine to mash up
people's feet. New ones worse than old ones—more cunning, that's all"

(26). Similarly, the ending of colonial rule in the middle decades of the twentieth century gave way to a new manifestation of imperialism since the neocolonial societies' involvement in contemporary capitalism ensured the maintenance of an unequal international relation of economic and political power.

When she set out to rewrite *Jane Eyre,* Rhys deliberately shifted dates to write about post-emancipation times (Thomas 156); indeed, Jane Eyre's acquisition of the recently published *Marmion* locates the events occurring in Brontë's novel around 1808 and not after 1833 (Gregg 83). This change of dates—significant insofar as Rhys otherwise strictly respects the parameters set by Brontë's text—suggests that she had in mind the parallel between post-emancipation years and the independence period that I am establishing here. Besides, the sociopolitical context in which she was writing *Wide Sargasso Sea* makes it improbable that Rhys, whose insights into the workings of gender ideology have often been acclaimed, would be so unaware of the operations of racist ideology as to crudely reproduce racial stereotypes. *Wide Sargasso Sea* and its representation of black Creoles were bound to be informed by the process of decolonization and its attendant celebration of the black perspective that had been started in the 1930s. The decades during which Rhys was working on the novel witnessed the development of the (lower-class) black Creoles' challenge to the dominant cultural system of white bias and their increasing and positive identification with blackness. The movement, which was to culminate in Rastafarianism in post-independence Jamaica, eventually substituted "black roots" for the white models that had constituted cultural authority.[28] The novel was published just four years after Jamaica's independence and should also be placed in the context of the Caribbean artists movement in England, the Négritude movement in Paris in 1930, the Jamaican arts movement of the 1920s to 1940s, the Black Power movement of the 1960s, and, most significantly, the Frome "riots" and labor strikes of the 1930s. The 1930s social protests were later identified as catalyst for the decolonizing process and labeled "the second social revolution" (Parry, Sherlock, and Maingot 294; Marshall quoted in Gregg 25), the first revolution being of course the period of emancipation depicted in *Wide Sargasso Sea.*

Wide Sargasso Sea foregrounds the discursive frameworks that thwart an "authentic" knowledge of the black Creoles, but it does not do so by occluding Afro-Caribbean resistance. It highlights both the controlling processes that silence the black subaltern and the sites of resistance that undermine colonial authority from within. Although this paradox seems to point to a middle ground between the competing readings by Parry and Spivak that frame this essay, *Wide Sargasso Sea* does not exactly balance these polarized positions. Indeed, while Parry celebrates Christophine's defiance of the exigencies of colonialist discourses, *Wide Sargasso Sea* reveals the black nurse's articulatedness and "frontal assault against antagonists" as the very condition of possibility for the absolute exercise of colonial power. The "deliberated deafness to the native voice where it is to be heard" is not, as Parry contends, an attribute of Spivak's reading strategy but of the imperialist discourse that has already reappropriated Christophine's "counter-discourse" as criminality through a process Spivak has done much to expose. *Wide Sargasso Sea* reminds us that celebratory readings of obeah might actually obscure its appropriation by the dominant power as grounds for punishment. It foregrounds the reality of imperialist control by compelling us to question facile celebrations of "negro traditions" as authentic sources of subversion or alternative power. The novel's model of resistance challenges a conception of the "native as historical subject and agent of an oppositional discourse" insofar as it is precisely when the oppositionality of black cultural practices such as black magic is asserted in the British colonialist script but denied by the "natives" as "foolishness" that the colonizer is most threatened.

Although Spivak's ultimate answer to "Can the Subaltern Speak?" is "no," she points to ways in which the subaltern can speak with her body, as in the case, for instance, of the menstruating widow Bhaduri's suicide at the end of "Can the Subaltern Speak?" or of the heroine Dopdi's insistence at remaining publicly naked after being subjected to multiple rapes in Devi's story "Draupadi." As Spivak herself points out, these acts are not, however, highly subversive. They were not only seen in the immediate context as "absurd, a case of delirium rather than sanity," but they also failed to have any effect on the indigenous or colonial males whose constructions doubly marginalize the subaltern woman. Spivak consequently concludes that "the subaltern as female cannot be heard or read" ("Can the Subaltern Speak?" 308). In *Wide Sargasso Sea,* the subversive potential of alternative knowledges that Spivak recognizes here is taken further since it is presented as having potent effects on the British and Euro-Creole colonizers. Obeah is largely responsible, for instance, for sending Rochester packing home to England. In the section devoted to his narrative, Rochester does not once mention his father's and brother's deaths as the reasons for his departure but instead obsessively rehashes his discomfort vis-à-vis the Caribbean landscape and people. Unable to comprehend "the hidden place," he leaves behind "the secret he would never know" (172) and returns to his "cardboard house" in England where he can safely and unambiguously recast as madness his wife's association with the resisting opaqueness of the West Indies. Triggered by the black Creoles' own claims to "opaqueness" (to echo Glissant), the elite's paranoid reactions to the place and its people foreground and denaturalize the ambivalent modes of operation of colonialist discourse and succeed in making the white colonizers lose their bearings.

The Afro-Caribbean symbology of zombiism in *Wide Sargasso Sea* does not function as a metaphor for the exploited position of the white colonizers in an imperialist economy of their own creation. Far from thus erasing the significance of black cultural life, the novel uses zombi imagery to demonstrate the ways in which the colonizer's attempt at domesticating other cultures (through stereotypes) backfires. Obeah in the novel is neither exoticized (as black magic or sorcery), nor is it universalized (as Antoinette tries to do by appropriating its effects to rekindle her romance plot). It is a resisting principle of opaqueness that reminds us of what Glissant has called the "nonhistory" of the Caribbean people (224), that is, a history characterized by ruptures and that began with a brutal scission, slavery.

Wide Sargasso Sea's opacity, along with its shifting although not arbitrary racial/textual politics, is one reason why Rhys scholarship has traditionally had a difficult time identifying a stable ideological norm in the novel. While in *Jane Eyre,* the older narrating Jane, combined with the progressive narrative form of the *Bildungsroman,* provides a steady and trustworthy commentary on relationships and events, such identification is much more problematic in the Caribbean rewriting. The fluidity and polyphony of *Wide Sargasso Sea*'s narrative style, along with the "arrested development" of its traumatized female narrator, further complicate critical efforts to determine a stable ideological stance in the text. In fact, the resulting ambivalence echoes the effect of the Chinese-box structure of *Wuthering Heights,* a book Rhys deeply admired and that dominated her thoughts as she worked on her own novel.[29]

Rather than downplay Rhys's control over her material and see the novel as a mere reflection of her internally divided white colonial female subject position, I have argued that *Wide Sargasso Sea*'s narrative structure, its complexities of ethnicities and race, as well as the historical context in and about which it was written, attest to Rhys's understanding of white and black Creoles alike. By distancing herself from her white

Creole protagonist, Rhys challenges the realist conventions that identify the ideological position of the first-person narrator with the norms of the text and contradicts the contention that the narrative was "written in the interest of the white Creole." Like Condé, she radically reconceptualizes core concepts of postcolonialism such as race and agency by making visible the complexities of their deployment in culture.

3   Racial Vagaries in Emily Brontë's *Wuthering Heights*

> Cathy, Heathcliff, the fallen angels, the exiled lovers on the lonely
> moors, the woman and the man in whom I could recognize all the
> women and all the men uninvited to Jane Austen's tea parties or having
> to disguise themselves at a soirée at the Duchesse of Germanters'. . . .
> Let me put it to you that the role of the marginal cultures is that of the
> guardians of memory. A memory both of what the West sacrificed within
> its own culture and of what the West sacrificed in other cultures
> through its imperial expansion. Both aspects are intimately linked.
>
> Carlos Fuentes, "Central and Eccentric Writing"

IN THIS CHAPTER, I read Emily Brontë's *Wuthering Heights*
through the Caribbean lens of Maryse Condé's *Windward Heights*. As
mentioned in chapter 1, Condé's rewriting helps make visible patterns of
racial meaning that are embedded in the Victorian source-text and that
constitute a cultural ground common to both the Victorian and Caribbean
texts and contexts. Highlighting this shared source of narrative energy
brings about a renewed understanding of the shifting dynamics of race in
Victorian fiction. I argue that the racial logic at work in *Wuthering Heights*
resonates with *Windward Heights*'s racial/textual politics insofar as it
forces us to reconsider criticism's usual splitting of metaphorical from
literal meanings of race. References to a character's dark skin in Victorian fiction have traditionally been treated either as displacements of nonracial issues or as literal references to somatic racial difference, that is, as
belonging to dramatically opposed logics. This distinction underlies, for
instance, critical discussions of Heathcliff's and Cathy's racial identities as
discrete and stable categories of meaning. According to this perspective,
Bertha's racial alterity in *Jane Eyre* belongs to an altogether different logic
from Jane's identification as a rebel slave; the mulatto Miss Swartz's race
has no connection to Becky Sharpe's darkening in William Thackeray's
Vanity Fair; Maggie Tulliver's "dark skin" in George Eliot's *The Mill on
the Floss* should not be conflated with Heathcliff's metaphorical hybridity

in *Wuthering Heights,* and so on. These two instances of racialization are approached as two distinct phenomena that have no bearing on each other or, at best, as instances of a metaphorics of race that occurs at the expense of the "black" character's "greater-than-metaphorical status" (Meyer 103). By contrast, I argue that they should be understood as part of the same racial logic.

As Maryse Condé's rewriting shows, Heathcliff and Cathy's romance epitomizes not the coming together of discrete racial categories but the inseparability of discourses of race, gender, and class. *Windward Heights*'s recasting of race opens up a site where the multiple figurations of "difference" necessarily encounter their interdependence as one form of identity crossing is given meaning and contour through another. Characters' racial identifications change according to their shifting relation to other categories of identity, so much so that the very notion of race has to be reconceptualized as racial crossing rather than racial difference. If we reinterpret *Wuthering Heights* through such a model, we come to see that Heathcliff's and Cathy's racial identities too fluctuate as their relation to one another changes through their transgressions of socially prescribed (gender or class) roles. Throughout the narrative, their identification with a particular "race" is thus unstable, revealing that it was often through "racial hybridity" that the Victorian middle class configured and reconfigured the crossings of class, gender, and religious boundaries that they both feared and fetishized. In this symbolic economy, blackness—the epitome of racial difference—is no longer a minority identity so much as a category of knowledge that articulates other forms of alterity.

In other words, while postcolonial criticism typically foregrounds the English literary canon's investment in maintaining racial and cultural boundaries separate, Condé's reinterpretation of *Wuthering Heights* shows the racial logic of Victorian literature to be not a racial but an interracial problematic that reinscribes race as a set of crisscrossing categories. What is more, this figuration of crossing does not, as in other colonial texts, deploy racial otherness as a sign of contamination that the narrative needs to expel. Unlike *Jane Eyre,* which has been criticized so widely for harboring such a sacrificial logic, *Wuthering Heights* is too obviously preoccupied with the disruption of normative social values to reproduce fixed narratives of sexual and racial embodiment. Instead, the novel exposes the ideological process through which the inextricably imbricated categories of racial, sexual, and class difference get fixed in discourse as discrete categories of identity. Whereas identitarian approaches either examine identities in isolation from each other or, at best, account for their interaction *a posteriori*, this alternative model of identification represents their inter-action as the very condition of their constitution. Race, gender, and class are shown to be meaningful only in relation to one another, as the figura-tion of one identity is revealed as a double for another. This emphasis on the representational interconnections of norms of identity in *Wuthering Heights* challenges not only the separatism of identity-based interpreta-tions but also the simplified binaries of black/white and self/other through which we traditionally conceptualize the category of racial difference. To illustrate this radical reconfiguration of difference in the novel, I will begin by addressing the ways in which postcolonial criticism has heretofore dis-cussed *Wuthering Heights*'s racial/textual politics in relation to Heathcliff. I will then move to an examination of the implications of the relational paradigm outlined above for our analysis of both Heathcliff and Cathy.

Heathcliff's Race

Wuthering Heights abounds with descriptions of Heathcliff's dark com-plexion and moral depravity, so much so that the novel seems at first to exemplify Victorian culture's cathexis onto fixed narratives of racial and sexual embodiment. Earnshaw describes the boy as "as dark almost as if it came from the devil himself" (51), while other characters continue to comment on his dark features throughout the narrative. Yet, despite per-vasive and strikingly physicalist references to the character's "blackness," no cinematic or literary adaptation of the novel—until Maryse Condé's 1995 rewriting—has opted to represent him as "dark-skinned."[1] In fact, even Brontë criticism has traditionally interpreted Heathcliff's dark com-plexion as a metaphor for his moral baseness or lower-class background rather than as a signifier of his "visible" racial difference.

In contrast to this process of lactification (to borrow Fanon's term), the sparse postcolonial analyses of *Wuthering Heights* that emerged in the 1990s discuss Heathcliff's dark skin as evidence of a somatic and categor-ical racial difference. Von Sneidern and Meyer, for instance, argue that Heathcliff's appearance—as well as his provenance from Liverpool—evokes black slavery. Earnshaw found Heathcliff "in the streets of Liver-pool where he picked *it* up and inquired for its owner—Not a soul knew to whom it belonged" (51–52; emphasis mine). Liverpool was the first slaving port in Britain in the mid-1770s, that is, at the time when the events related in *Wuthering Heights* begin. And Heathcliff's status as black slave and commodity, these critics argue, is confirmed when Earnshaw brings not "him" but "it" back to Cathy and Hindley in replacement for the whip and the fiddle they had each requested as a gift.

I contend that neither reading, whether of the lactifying or the racializing kind, does justice to the novel's complex operations of difference. Both reproduce a splitting of the metaphorical and literal meanings of race that the novel challenges. I turn to Condé's rewriting to illuminate the racial logic that drives the original text but that is too often subsumed under these two interpretive poles. The edulcoration of Heathcliff's "blackness" is problematic because it reproduces the myth of ethnic purity promoted by hegemonic discourses in England and that the character's presence radically challenges. Victorian culture was invested in imagining the English nation as a white and homogeneous entity, and it proliferated images and representations that corroborated this fantasy. Specifically, Victorian gender and national ideologies depended on and strove to maintain a complete division between the (male) domain of the colonies and the idealized (female) sphere of domesticity at home. They consequently represented the home country as impervious to imperialism and its effects. As Stewart points out in *Domestic Realities and Imperial Fictions,* this separation "allowed for forms of domination in the distant reaches of empire not tolerable within the heart of the empire . . . , for forms of extralegal sexual arrangements that explicitly departed from the increasingly idealized domestic family of the metropolis [and that] became a particular focus of anxiety and ambivalence among contemporary observers" (106).

By wedding a nonwhite character (Heathcliff) to a gentried woman in rural England (Isabella Linton), *Wuthering Heights* makes these "intolerable" practices and "sexual arrangements" part and parcel of the domestic realm, the very space that was and still is typically considered most removed from the vicissitudes of empire and metropole. Whereas hegemonic discourse in England as elsewhere usually defined "the peasantry amongst whom [Emily Brontë] lived" by its adherence to traditional custom and "hereditary attachments," with "a settled existence" and an "unreasoning persistency" (Eliot 118),[2] *Wuthering Heights* depicts it as constituted not by a sedated and undisturbed veneration for tradition but rather by contradictions similar to those experienced in the colonies.[3] Heathcliff's involvement with the Heights's Cathy and Thrushcross Grange's Isabella epitomizes the "forms of extralegal sexual arrangements" about which the mid-Victorians were so anxious. A reading that erases Heathcliff's racial difference thus ignores one of Brontë's most radical interventions, namely, that she made racial mixing an incontrovertible and lived reality at home in England rather than just the result of questionable but distant sexual practices in the colonies.[4]

In 1848, a reviewer for the *Examiner* wrote that "it is with difficulty that we can prevail upon ourselves to believe in the appearance of such a phenomenon, so near our own dwellings as the summit of a Lancashire or Yorkshire moor" (Allott 40). Contemporary readings of *Wuthering Heights* seem to share the same difficulty when it comes to seeing racial crossing as a crucial aspect of the love story *Wuthering Heights* stages in rural England. That the idea that Heathcliff could be "black" continues to be treated as incongruous by contemporary critical, literary, and cinematic adaptations of the novel could arguably be seen as a legacy of Victorian ideology's investment in isolating domesticity from empire.[5]

Nevertheless, postcolonial readings that *do* racialize Heathcliff paradoxically prove to be as unsatisfactory as those that fail to do so. Indeed, capitalizing on Heathcliff's "blackness," these progressive readings fix the meanings of race in a way that fails to account for the temporalities of narrative. They interpret the tropes of race as a reflection of nineteenth-century theories of race and subsume the contradictory ways in which racial imagery is deployed through narrative form. In so doing, they obscure Heathcliff's racial indeterminacy and reinscribe a white/black binary that derives from a sociological study of extraliterary phenomena rather than from a serious engagement with *Wuthering Heights*'s complex narrative treatment of race. Postcolonial speculations are separated from the consideration of the literariness of the text, while the literary is subordinated to ideological, economic, and political issues rather than being examined in relation to them. That narrative form might give us a renewed understanding of the workings and instability of racial discourse is overlooked.

Certainly, as an icon of (post)coloniality, Heathcliff's character is unsettling because, like Condé's (anti-)heroes, he seems to reproduce the worst Victorian stereotypes of nonwhite people as uncivilized and animal-like. Hindley Earnshaw calls him "an imp of Satan" (54); Cathy describes him as "a fierce, pitiless, wolfish man" and warns Isabella Linton that he is "an unreclaimed creature, without refinement, without cultivation; an arid wilderness of furze and whinstone" (103); Nelly Dean, the narrator, often wonders if he is not some kind of demon, "a ghoul or a vampire" (279), and, witnessing his reunion with the dying Cathy, she adds: "I did not feel as if I were in the company of a creature of my own species" (149). Isabella comments on "his sharp cannibal teeth" (161) and tells Hindley: "His mouth watered to tear you with his teeth, because he's only half man— not so much—and the rest fiend" (164). According to Charlotte Brontë, Heathcliff "stands unredeemed; never once swerving in his arrow-straight course to perdition, from the time when 'the little black-haired, swarthy thing, as dark as if it came from the Devil,' was first unrolled out of the bundle and set on its feet in the farm-house kitchen, to the hour when Nelly Dean found the grim, stalwart corpse laid on its back in the panel-enclosed bed, with wide-gazing eyes that seemed 'to sneer at her attempt to close them, and parted lips and sharp white teeth that sneered too'" ("Preface" 23).

Heathcliff's "cannibalistic" countenance is compounded by his capacity for relentless mental and physical cruelty. Although readers have traditionally been reluctant to reduce his status to that of the narrative's ultimate villain,[6] the destructive effects of his ruthless brutality are described in elaborate detail. When he finally relents in the destruction of his "old enemies' . . . representatives" (273), it is out of mere exhaustion. And to make matters worse, he dies unremorseful: "as to repenting of my injustices, I've done no injustice, and I repent of nothing" (281). His love for Catherine might be glamorized and "transcendental," but his baseness certainly is not.[7] Emily Brontë's protagonist is an immoral being, and although the novel's emphasis on environmental influence partially explains his brutality, it does not seek to excuse it. Even critical readings confirm his characterization as inhuman since they have invariably described him as "a brute-demon" (Whipple 5); "a Ghoul—an Afreet" (Brontë, "Preface" 23); "a monster" (Ward 10); "a mean and sordid devil" (Sinclair 244); a "warning example of the self-destructiveness of the unregulated will" (Stone 42); a sadist (Miller 195); a "Gothic villain, a demonic, almost otherworldly figure" (Pykett 75). In light of his cruel treatment of friend and foe alike, Heathcliff's "humanity" is questionable to say the least.

Heathcliff's darker complexion thus appears to function as a marker of his savagery and absolute difference. His brutal actions evoke Victorian racialist ideologies according to which "the dark races of men" constituted another species altogether and were inherently inaccessible to reason. As a result, references to racial difference in the novel have been read as direct reflections of the most racist assumptions that were circulating in the mid-Victorian time. Von Sneidern offers such an interpretation in her essay "Wuthering Heights and the Liverpool Slave Trade." She argues that the black Heathcliff's offspring with the gentried Isabella Linton embodies "the corruption attributed to hybridization in mid-century racialist discourses" (184). Linton Heathcliff, she adds, "manifests most of the worst accidents and mistakes mixed blood could represent for mid-century England: disease, viciousness, treason, cowardice, duplicity, unmerited power, shiftlessness" (186). His characterization as effeminate, feeble, and morally depraved recalls the prevalent nineteenth-century stereotypes of hybrids as "vapid" and "distorted" so much so that he functions, according to Von Sneidern, as a warning for the degenerative effects of interbreeding among "distant" races.[8]

In the 1840s, the middle classes were indeed increasingly concerned about the hybrid forms of race that were threatening their self-proclaimed homogeneous cultural and national identity.[9] A major source of anxiety throughout the nineteenth century was the impossibility of ascertaining the separation of black and white strains in bloodlines and of tracing one's lineage back to an "origin." Heated ethnological debates ensued about the miscegenated foundations of Englishness and the heterogeneity of the Anglo-Saxon race historically.[10] Interracialism was all the more unsettling to the middle classes since race was the absolute form of difference on which they relied in order to curb the class and gender transgressions that threatened their authority. The ideological process of racializing human beings in cultural representations functioned primarily as a containment strategy. It imposed an indelible difference on social groups to distinguish them from each other at the precise moment when boundaries between them were menacing to dissolve. The working classes, for instance, were racialized because they were threatening to rise to power through the same means of aggressive individualism that had led to the dominance of the middle classes (Armstrong 52). Similarly, women whose overt sexual agency challenged the asexual ideal of the domestic woman were "blackened." And last but not least, racially distinct characters in fiction were consistently used to enhance the identity and superiority of the British as the privileged race.

This ideological work of race was in keeping with the old concept of the Great Chain of Being on which Victorians relied to determine the gradations of humankind. Racial traits—which, with the advent of evolutionary scientific doctrines, were increasingly linked to mental and moral character—were deployed to mark the position of various human groups on the evolutionary scale. Predictably, Caucasians occupied the top of the chain, while the darkest races remained in a state of arrested development at the bottom. There was a "short step from classifying races to describing them as unequal" (Biddiss 16), and as the century drew to a close, racial determination had become the order of the day. Robert Knox's ethnological writings best exemplified this shift. According to Knox: "That race in human affairs is everything is simply a fact, the most remarkable, the most comprehensive, which philosophy has ever announced. Race is everything: literature, science, art—in a word, civilization—depends on it" (v). Race is the attribute on which Victorians frequently relied to ascribe to darker races—but also white lesbians and prostitutes—an inferior disposition. Classifications based on comparative anatomy and craniometry increasingly provided a "scientific" explanation of social and moral development to justify British moral authority at home and abroad. In this relentless process of solidifying their superiority through racial discourse, the Victorians turned their backs on monogenist explanations of human origins. Polygenesis, the belief in different races as different species, was rapidly replacing the heretofore widely endorsed monogenist doctrine that saw the different races of humankind as varieties within the same species.[11] As the century progressed, racial ordering supplanted other types of political or civic groupings as the primary way of distinguishing between various groups, that is, of helping to legitimize human divisions along a double axis (West/East, Caucasian/Negro, Civilized/Savage) that grounded the myth of a unified nation. Race was a determining factor in producing a strict differentiation between the dominant culture and England's (external but also internal) others.

Yet, if the racialization of characters in mid-Victorian fiction does indeed function as a containment mechanism, that is, as a stabilizing because absolute figuration of difference that separates the normative self from threatening class or gender others, then Heathcliff's racial alterity miserably fails to perform its ideological work. Heathcliff epitomizes the constant transgression of boundaries of gender, race, and class in the novel. Brontë criticism over the years has powerfully illustrated this multiply transgressive logic since Heathcliff has been read alternatively as a representative of the working class (Eagleton's *Myths of Power*); of the Irish (Michie; Eagleton's *Heathcliff and the Great Hunger*); of "black" or "nonwhite" races (von Sneidern; Meyer); as well as of an androgynous being, "both masculine and feminine" (Gilbert and Gubar). What emerges from such proliferating violation of norms, however, is a condemnation not of Heathcliff's transgressive acts but of the norms themselves. At a time when the Victorian middle class consolidated their sense of superiority by mobilizing class and racial differences as signs of moral propensities,[12] Brontë's novel disarticulates morality from either class mobility or racial identity. As Mary Poovey points out, most novels of the 1840s condemn the aggressive individualism of the lower class as immoral, and in so doing mark the very class lines that the middle classes themselves had crossed to rise to power: "The same society that offers its blessings to everyone . . . sets limits to the achievements of all but a few. The same society that rewards the self-made David Copperfield punishes the self-made Uriah

Heep. The same society that proclaims the likeness of all humans institutes class difference and calls it moral character" (Poovey 120–21). Poovey examines Dickens's *David Copperfield,* whose representation of social climbers, she argues, powerfully articulates the middle classes' anxiety over the dissolution of class boundaries. David succeeds and Heep fails because only the middle-class penetration of landed property and rise to economic power can be justified in moral terms.

In contrast to Victorian fiction's duplicitous and parasitic social climbers such as Heep, Heathcliff remains "unpunished" at the end of the narrative. He is not "exploded" by anyone but himself. Although his appropriation of Hindley's and the second Cathy's entire inheritance certainly parallels Uriah Heep's underhanded manipulations and illegal acquisition of Mr. Wickfield's business assets, his ascent to power and wealth is neither challenged nor reversed, his moral corruption never publicly exposed. In fact, that he upholds his social status almost effortlessly becomes direct evidence that if such a villainous man as he could be accepted as a "born and bred gentleman," then social mobility and morality might not go hand in hand after all. His "passing" reveals that class distinctions are not difficult to perform and do not result from a system of ethics or, for that matter, genetics, but rather generate one to justify their existence. Heathcliff's success story exposes the absurdity of an ideology that yokes morality to social and racial status.

By showing that moral and personal character cannot function as an explanation for a person's social elevation or decline, Emily Brontë radically disrupts bourgeois ideology. While in *David Copperfield,* Dickens resorts to moral and racial difference to consolidate class difference, *Wuthering Heights* shows that moral corruption is not a function of the individual Heathcliff but is built into the fabric of class society and its rhetoric of economic individualism. The destructiveness that accompanies her protagonist's upward mobility is not, in other words, Emily Brontë's way of reestablishing the class distinctions that his rise to power had threatened to dissolve (Armstrong 52) since, in opposition to middle-class ideology, the novel highlights the independence of moral failure from material success. In *Wuthering Heights,* violence and oppression are shown to be a function of the system whose "morality" Heathcliff espouses.

At a time that was increasingly witnessing the yoking of racial "essence" with moral and intellectual character, Emily Brontë's novel disrupts the ideological and rhetorical equivalence of white/moral and immoral/non-white that constituted the bedrock of Victorian racialism, and in so doing it challenges the notion of race as the supreme determinant. Whereas

Charlotte Brontë claims that "carefully trained and kindly treated, the black gipsy-cub [Heathcliff] might possibly have been reared into a human being," Emily demonstrates that it is what counts as "human being" that needs to be scrutinized. Rather than provide an analysis of character in relation to the manners and morals of the period, an undertaking that constitutes "the main pattern of the nineteenth-century novel" (Ramchand 5), *Wuthering Heights* interrogates the supposedly higher moral order that Victorians saw manifest in the Anglo-Saxon race and nation. It is a novel in which "the center does not hold" since the distinctions between "civilized" and "savage" are evoked only to be exposed as artificialities.

It is significant in this respect that Lockwood—the delegate of the "artificial man of the city" and "one type of nineteenth-century reader" (Mayne 210)—is instrumental in sanctioning Heathcliff's brutalities. When he first visits Wuthering Heights, Lockwood is so immersed in the Victorian domestic ideology of female nature that he cannot imagine the household's deviation from the norm to be anything but unintentional.[13] He reads Heathcliff's anger and irritation at the second Catherine's "insubordination" as embarrassment vis-à-vis a guest for the household's failure to live up to the domestic ideal, that is, the foundation of the middle-class sense of self and respectability in the mid-nineteenth century. Convinced that he has "caused the cloud" by exposing Catherine's deficiencies as the "Angel in the House," he tries to dispel it by pretending that she does in fact fit the image of the "amiable lady as the presiding genius over [Heathcliff's] home and heart" (32). Despite Heathcliff's obvious mistreatment of the second Catherine, Lockwood persists in seeing his host's sullenness as the "exaggerated reserve" of "a pearl-containing oyster of a rustic" who "conceals depths of benevolence and affection beneath a stern exterior" (103). No matter how glaringly his understanding clashes with the violence he is witnessing, he remains constrained by his blind investment in the codes of middle-class domesticity. What shocks him is the "lack of decorum" of his hosts, not the violence that he pretends not to have noticed.[14] During his second visit to the Heights, he even confesses hearing "not altogether disapprovingly" (257) Hareton strike Catherine.

Nevertheless, Emily Brontë does not capitalize on Lockwood's far from innocent relationship to brutality in and for itself but uses it, along with his platitudes, to expose domestic ideology. By representing her controlling narrator as an almost invisible and ordinary observer who is vainly trying to make sense of extraordinary circumstances, she wants us to understand his attitude to violence as emerging from the social structure rather than from the depth of a psychologized individual. Lockwood's concern for saving appearances and his consequent indifference to brutality is a function of the ideology of the "polite society" he embodies. He is judging the situation by a Victorian domestic code whose very success depends on upholding the ideal irrespective of the underlying reality. *Wuthering Heights* thus highlights the distinction between ideology and practice. The incompatibility between his platitudinous comments and the violence he observes exposes the cost at which the domestic ideal, the foundation of middle-class ideology and power, is often upheld.

The novel juxtaposes to Heathcliff's brutality the violence perpetrated and perpetuated by the dominant cultural gaze. This is a gaze that obscures the oppressive effects of power in order to maintain its value system and that deploys sexual and racial alterity to establish an economy of differentiation and exclusion. For instance, when Heathcliff and Cathy are caught spying at Thrushcross Grange, the Lintons' disproportionate response to the two children's trespass demonstrates the force of this economy. According to Knoepflmacher, "the civilized Linton veneer merely disguises a brutality which the primitive Earnshaws openly acknowledge" (61). They construct Heathcliff as an outsider by interpellating him as a "gypsy . . . a little lascar, an American or Spanish castaway" (62), thus attempting to fix race as a meaningful category of difference. The "civilized" world of the Grange into which the infernal Heathcliff will eventually gain entry is based on a powerful system of exclusion that subjects him "to the potent gaze of a racial arrogance deriving from British imperialism" (Meyer 97).

The Lintons' effort at constructing Heathcliff as an outsider through racial interpolation reproduces the binary posited by the dominant symbolic structures between self and other, human and animal, black and white, etc. Yet the novel also resists the very hegemonic inscription it stages, since it denaturalizes the process through which racial alterity is produced in discourse to guarantee the normative Self. The Lintons and Lockwood cannot fix the meanings of race because there are too many racial categories generated in the narrative. Furthermore, they use familiar racial tropes that are consistently defamiliarized in the narrative, while the ground for their moral and social authority is derided. Brontë exposes the Grange's refinement as artificial, and its values as constructed conventionalities. Even education, which first defines the cultured Grange in opposition to the world of the Heights, is revealed as a double-edged sword linking rather than separating the two places. On the one hand, its transforming power is emphasized since its absence at the Heights is the cause of Heathcliff's downfall and its presence the key to the second generation's happiness.[15] On the other hand, its possession is also, however, represented as the very means of oppression and dominance. Heathcliff's acquisition of cultural capital during his exile, for instance, allows him to gain entry into the genteel world of the Grange, but only to co-opt the latter's "civilization" as a tool for dominance, not to benefit from education's transforming power. Significantly, Heathcliff performs his most horrendous acts after he has acquired the manners and resources of a "born and bred gentleman" (125). Similarly, attending college for three years does not prevent Hindley any more than Heathcliff from spiraling down the path of cruelty and baseness. Conventional education does not confer the Grange or Heights inhabitants any depth that would set them apart as "civilized" members of society, and it loses all credibility as the basis for any kind of "civilizing mission."

The racial interpellations that occur throughout the novel highlight not the fixed embodiment of racial and sexual otherness but rather the investment of the dominant discourse in producing narratives of alterity. When Lockwood describes Wuthering Heights as a "perfect misanthropist's Heaven" and Heathcliff as a "capital fellow [who] little imagined how my heart warmed towards him when I beheld his black eyes withdraw so suspiciously under their brows" (25), his reliance on configurations of racial difference to mediate and reflect upon his own identity is made visible. He further explains: "I know, by instinct, his reserve springs from an aversion to showy displays of feeling—to manifestations of mutual kindness. He'll love and hate, equally under cover, and esteem it a species of impertinence, to be loved or hated again—No, I'm running on too fast—I bestow my own attributes over-liberally on him" (27). Lockwood's own anxious emphasis on his use of Heathcliff as a screen to project his own attributes illuminates the process through which the dominant subject projects his colonial fantasies on figures of racial and sexual otherness. Because Lockwood's perspective frames the narrative, it sets the tone for the reader's relation to Heathcliff and highlights at the very outset his subjection to the imperial gaze. The text destabilizes the familiar racial tropes it evokes first by exposing the dominant subject's investment in representations of otherness and second by revealing the lack of fixity of the racial designations produced by the dominant cultural gaze.

Indeed, far from functioning as a categorical site of difference, Heathcliff's racial identity remains ambiguous throughout the narrative. The reader is at a loss to determine his specific ethnic or racial identity as racial determination is anything but absolute in *Wuthering Heights*. When the patriarch Earnshaw brings the little orphan boy back to the Heights, he describes him as being "as dark almost as if it came from the devil himself" (51). Heathcliff wishes he had "Edgar Linton's light hair and a fair skin . . . [his] great blue eyes and even forehead" (67). Years later, Nelly remembers him as "a gypsy brat . . . who kept repeating some gibberish nobody could understand" (51). Lockwood echoes the sentiment by referring to him as a "dark-skinned gypsy" (27), while Mr. Linton describes him as a "little lascar, an American or Spanish castaway." When Heathcliff is supplanted in Cathy's affections, Nelly comforts him through a fairy-tale suggestion that his father might be "Emperor of China, and [his] mother an Indian Queen" (67), thus implying that he is of mixed blood. Each of these representations evokes a very different visual image of "darkness" or skin color and introduces a gap between the materiality of race and its representation. The vocabulary that is used to describe Heathcliff is so unstable that it is, I argue, this instability—and not merely the effectivity of a residual conception of pure Englishness—that explains the lack of dark-skinned Heathcliffs in literary and cinematic adaptations of *Wuthering Heights*.

We are so accustomed to thinking of bodies as the referent and guarantee of racial identity—that is, of a stable "black" or "hybrid" identity—that the kind of fluctuating relationship between physical appearance and racial identity that Heathcliff embodies often justifies emptying textual meanings of their racial implications in critical analyses. Even when a character's racial indeterminacy is acknowledged, it is usually conceptualized as a less conspicuous "blackness" or hybridity that gets folded back into a form of fixed racial alterity. By contrast, I argue that Heathcliff's racial indeterminacy points to a racial logic in which hybridity designates a character's movement between identities. If discussions of Heathcliff's dark skin as a racial issue have been scarce, it is because the narrative's particular deployment of racial meanings as bound by social forces is incompatible with discourses of race as a stable site of difference. In the absence of the cultural logic of racial categories that we expect to find in nineteenth-century texts, the unstable meanings of Heathcliff's dark complexion are interpreted as displacements of other problematics rather than as exemplary of the relational workings of identity *tout court*.

But if Heathcliff's racialization in the narrative is not a stable and hence stabilizing site of difference that serves to guarantee the normative self, then what is its function? What are we to make of the references to his "blackness" and "dark skin" if they are not to be understood as mere metaphors for his putatively unparalleled moral depravity? Does race's lack of fixity in *Wuthering Heights* also function as a tool for maintaining the status quo in the face of the character's threatening ascension into the middle class? In their timely books, Susan Meyer and Elsie Michie answer these questions by discussing references to Heathcliff's skin color as displacements of nonracial (gender or class) issues. Their contribution to the study of race in the Victorian novel is important because they both speak to the inseparability of race from other categories of social identity such as gender (Meyer) and class (Michie), a pattern that informs my own analysis (via Condé's). At the same time, however, in singling out either gender or class as the ultimate determinant of racial meanings in the Victorian novel, these critics also circumscribe the workings of race in a way that fails to fully account for the intricacies of the text's symbolic economy. Indeed, they each represent either the "white" or "black" character's racial identity as unstable when, as I will show, the logic of racial crossing that permeates the narrative affects both characters in relation to each other.

In *Imperialism at Home,* Meyer highlights the ways in which Heathcliff, like other "nonwhite" characters in mid-Victorian fiction, is implicated in a symbolic economy that mobilizes racial oppression as a metaphor for gender oppression. She points to Cathy's famous declaration "Nelly, I *am* Heathcliff" as symptomatic of the Victorian habit of associating Englishwomen with nonwhite races. She writes, "Catherine Earnshaw's resistance to female acculturation, her 'half-savage' nature, is metaphorically represented not on her own body but associatively, in the companion from whom in her childhood she is inseparable: the dark-skinned gypsy Heathcliff" (104). Alternatively, in *Outside the Pale,* Michie explains the racialization of the male protagonists in the Brontë corpus in terms not of gender but of class. Michie identifies stereotypes of Irish national or racial behavior in the descriptions of Heathcliff and Rochester but argues that these racially indeterminate representations are replaced with absolute forms of racial difference once the two characters enact the Victorian fantasy of upward mobility. Whereas Rochester and Heathcliff are the embodiment of the Victorian stereotyped perceptions of the Irish when they are characterized as oppressed, "When they are in a position of dominance, they are characterized as 'oriental despots'" (16). Michie also traces the same pattern in the biographies of Charlotte and Emily's father, Patrick Brontë, who left an uneducated working-class background in Ireland to become an educated clergyman in England.[16] For Michie, these biographical and novelistic narratives both embody a colonialist wish to obscure the protagonist's Irishness, either by covering it up with a story of social elevation or by resorting to "images that suggest both more explicit 'racial' difference and distant colonies" (Michie 53). The stereotypes of the simianized Irish give way to images of Oriental despots for two reasons: first to suppress the Brontës' uneasiness about the Irish indeterminate racial difference and, second, to allow the novels' female narrators to participate vicariously in a narrative of social advancement from which Victorian domestic ideologies excluded them.

Meyer's and Michie's interventions reveal how intimately racial identifications are intertwined with the signifiers of gender (Meyer) and class (Michie), but each only goes part way in representing the complex dynamics of race in the mid-Victorian interracial narrative. Meyer's model, for instance, provides a truncated picture of the fluctuating but strikingly physicalist descriptions through which characters are racialized. Metaphor, Meyer argues, "refers both to yokings between white women characters and *actual characters of other races* and to references yoking them to races not actualized as characters in the novel but present only in its allusions, asides, and diction" (22; emphasis mine). This identification of the logic at play in the novel as a metaphorics of race fixes Heathcliff's "blackness" once and for all as one of the two terms of a recurrent metaphor. The yoking of "white woman" and "dark race" (that is, the differences between the two terms) is foregrounded, while the instability at the heart of at least one of the two categories (that is, the differences *within* each term) is subsumed so as not to threaten the logic of metaphor. For Meyer, Heathcliff functions as the "nonwhite" character through whose "actual" racial alterity Cathy realizes her own "white" identity. The category of "nonwhite" is posited as a constant throughout the narrative, while the "white" woman's "blackening" is seen as part of a metaphorical troping that belongs to an altogether different logic than Heathcliff's "greater-than-metaphorical status in the novel" (Meyer 103). This reading fails to explain the extremely physicalist nature of the racialization process to which "white women" are subjected in mid-Victorian fiction. It also overlooks the ways in which the representatives of the "dark races" (Meyer 104) in the Brontës are themselves associatively represented through metaphors of femininity for instance, their racial identity as unstable as that of the "white" woman to whom they are linked.[17]

By contrast, in *Outside the Pale*, Elsie Michie's postcolonial reading of the Brontë novels attends to the shifting meanings of race associated with racially marked characters such as Heathcliff. Michie argues that the racialist descriptions of the male protagonists in the Brontë corpus shift according to the changes in their class positioning. This reading avoids reducing Heathcliff to a representative of "actual . . . dark races" irrespective of his status in the narrative. At the same time, however, the pattern of development from racial indeterminacy to absolutized racial difference that

Michie identifies in *Wuthering Heights* is difficult to ascertain. Heathcliff's association with the Orient is limited to Nelly's fantasy of upward mobility and occurs in fact when he is in no condition to transgress class boundaries in the narrative. Trying to comfort a broken-hearted Heathcliff, Nelly's suggestion that his father might very well be "of China, and [his] mother an Indian Queen" (67) occurs when he is utterly dispossessed. Whereas Rochester in *Jane Eyre* is described as an Oriental despot when he is in a position of class and gender dominance, Heathcliff's association with this more absolute form of racial difference mainly occurs when he is an oppressed ploughboy at the narrative's beginning. In fact, the trajectory from indeterminacy to absolutized difference ironically unravels backward in *Wuthering Heights* since material references to Heathcliff's black countenance (that feel categorical because they are visible) give way to notions of Oriental despotism that seem indeterminate because they are not explicitly linked to physical differences. Furthermore, insofar as the only allusion to Oriental despotism in Emily Brontë's novel stages a hybrid alliance, it evokes, despite Michie's claim, the dissolution rather than consolidation of racial differences. *Outside the Pale* thus obscures the important differences that distinguish Rochester from Heathcliff, Jane Eyre from Nelly Dean,[18] and ultimately *Jane Eyre* from *Wuthering Heights*.[19] It also fails to recognize the extent to which fluctuations in Heathcliff's racial identity are intricately linked to the tropes of otherness that define the "white" Cathy's identity.

Cathy's Race

As Maryse Condé's rewriting highlights, Heathcliff and Cathy's romance epitomizes not the fusion of discrete racial categories but the inseparability of discourses of race and gender in the period. Both characters have shifting racial identities that fluctuate as their relation to socially prescribed roles and to each other changes. Catherine's assertion "I *am* Heathcliff" resonates with Heathcliff's own exclamation "I cannot live without my soul" to reveal just how symbolically inextricable their identities are. On the one hand, as Meyer convincingly shows, Catherine is configured in terms of the racial alterity Heathcliff embodies, while on the other, Heathcliff's identity is also constructed through his association with the metaphoric femininity Cathy represents. Their transgressions of class and gender boundaries in the narrative are configured through a figuration of racial crossing in relation to each other. Explicit references to Heathcliff's darker physiognomy are directly linked to his relationship with Cathy. This explains why there are hardly any references to an absolute form of racial reference when he is in fact enacting the Victorian fantasy of upward mobility. Alternatively, Cathy's darkening in the narrative also occurs in the context of her tumultuous relationship to Heathcliff.

Cathy's configuration in terms of racial alterity is consistent throughout the novel as evidenced, for instance, by the repeated references to her "half-savage" nature. Significantly, she undergoes a reverse racialization when she adopts a "proper" gender and class position by joining the gentried world of the Lintons. Her change in social status literally lightens her as her hands become "wonderfully whitened with doing nothing and staying indoors" in stark contrast to Heathcliff's "dusky fingers" (64). Her whitening occurs by virtue of her crossing of class and gender boundaries, a process that is reflected in the shifting racial signifiers that define Heathcliff's character as well. Just as her "white skin" is associated with indoor idleness, Heathcliff's "dark skin" is tellingly equated with dirt as well as with linguistic difference. In response to his lament that he does not and will never have his rival's "light hair and fair skin" (66), Nelly suggests that he wash and dress nicely. Her emphasis on ablutions as a means of redressing an identity that is supposedly fixed within visibility highlights yet again the interdependence of categories of identity such as race, class, and gender that are generated through their interrelations rather than through "real" or "natural" differences. Race is exposed as cultural. The characters' attempts to fix Heathcliff's racial alterity repeatedly slip into references to his slovenly appearance and incomprehensible speech. Unable to find a definitive racial designation for the boy, the Lintons resort to judging his language: "A wicked boy, at all events . . . and quite unfit for a decent house! Did you notice his language, Linton?" (62). Heathcliff is in fact introduced to the reader through the unintelligibility of his speech as his initial appearance in the narrative has him "repeat[ing] over and over again some gibberish that nobody could understand" (51). The "growling" and "snarling" boy epitomizes the process by which racial alterity is constructed not through its anchoring in "natural" difference but through its association with animality, dirt, and lack of language.

Heathcliff himself confirms the inextricable and sometimes unexpected entanglement of identities by explicitly linking race and class in his statement to Nelly: "I wish I had light hair and a fair skin, and was dressed and behaved well, and had a chance of being as rich as he will be" (*Wuthering Heights* 67). Later, when he tells his son, Linton Heathcliff, "Now, don't wince and colour up! Though it *is* something to see you have not white blood" (185), he establishes an equivalence between racial difference and his puny and effeminate son's passionate temper that introduces yet again a gap between racial traits and the materiality of the body. Far from being sites of stable and essentialized difference, class, gender, and race are thus revealed as inseparable complexes of social meanings that expose the symbolic nature of race and challenge the concept's yoking to the body. Race, in other words, is revealed as a product of language rather than of "visible" racial otherness.

This symbolic economy replaces the facile separatism of an identitarian approach and helps elucidate passages in the novel, which—although they occur at turning points in the book—have yet to be commented on, let alone analyzed by Victorian or postcolonial critics of the Brontës. One such puzzling moment occurs when Heathcliff returns from exile and when the representations of race, sex, and class are explicitly and incongruously linked in the narrative. Despite her husband's obvious displeasure at receiving Heathcliff at the Grange, an excited Cathy wakes a wary (and weary) Nelly in the middle of the night to share her happiness at being reunited with her soul mate and childhood love. Far from partaking of her joy, Nelly Dean advises her not to sing Heathcliff's praises to the jealous Edgar: "What use is it praising Heathcliff to him? . . . Let Mr. Linton alone about him, unless you would like an open quarrel between them." Cathy impatiently retorts: "But does it not show great weakness? . . . I am not envious—I never feel hurt at the brightness of Isabella's yellow hair and the whiteness of her skin; at her dainty elegance, and the fondness all the family exhibit for her" (100). Cathy contemptuously wonders how Edgar could possibly envy Heathcliff since she herself has never been jealous of Isabella's "whiteness." She uses the contrast between her own dark complexion and the "whiteness of [her sister-in-law Isabella's] skin" (100) to deride her husband's jealousy. What can her darker hue possibly have to do with her two lovers' sexual rivalry? How could Edgar shed his unseemly feelings by taking as a model her own lack of enviousness when it comes to Isabella's fair skin? What does sexual rivalry between the two men have to do with the difference in skin color of the two women?

Cathy's reaction is all the more confusing since Edgar's jealousy springs from anything but Heathcliff's darkened appearance. In fact, it is Heathcliff who had reasons in the past to envy Edgar's "light hair" and "fair skin" (*Wuthering Heights* 67). The parallelism is jarring unless we revise our understanding of the workings of race in narrative. The analogy between the two forms of jealousies only makes sense if we take seriously the contention that tropes of racial, sexual, and class difference are constantly informed by each other. The fact that the incongruity in this passage has never been noted points to the degree to which the imbrications of sexual, racial, and class configurations have been naturalized by post-Enlightenment discourses of race at the same time as, paradoxically, criticism persists in presenting identities as discrete categories of analysis. Yet the separation of gender, class, and race only serves to reproduce exclusionary configurations of difference that cannot account for passages such as the one above. Cathy's peculiar and unexpected focus on physical traits at this point in the narrative emphasizes the importance of reading the metaphoric operation of race in relation to the text's gender dynamics. It is significant in this respect that, separated from each other, Cathy and Heathcliff no longer function as transgressors and become "lightened" agents of racial and patriarchal oppression. Without Cathy, Heathcliff becomes an abusive husband and father, while without Heathcliff, Cathy turns into a spoiled upper-class Linton. In other words, racial identity is revealed as a fragmented, fluctuating, but no less significant category whose shifting patterns of meaning cannot be understood in isolation from other categories of identity.

Identity Crossing and Eccentric Writing

Critics have rightly noted that *Wuthering Heights* is constructed around the relationship between the two houses, Wuthering Heights and Thrushcross Grange, but they have typically emphasized the opposition between the two dwellings and their inhabitants and overlooked the ways in which the boundary between them is constantly blurred in the novel. Wuthering Heights has alternately been described as the symbol of savagery and inhumanity associated with Heathcliff, "the land of storm; high on the barren moorland, naked to the shock of the elements" (Cecil 137), or the site of a robust organic yeoman's lifeform (Eagleton, *Myths* 105).[20] As such, it has been opposed to the sheltered and civilized but artificial and pampered way of life of the gentry at Thrushcross Grange. As Tom Winnifrith notes, however:

> It is very easy to make too schematic a distinction and to maintain that all at Thrushcross Grange is peaceful, although the terrible scenes at Catherine's death occur there, or to maintain that all at Wuthering Heights is savage, although Heathcliff and Catherine enjoy happiness as children there, and Hareton and Cathy fall in love there before rather perversely moving house to Thrushcross Grange. . . . There are times, especially for Lockwood, when Thrushcross Grange provides a chilly welcome, and there are times, especially during Cathy's visits to Linton, when some added luxuries and even the weather contrive to make Wuthering Heights a haven of peace. (59)

What is even more striking than these periodic reversals is the constant shuttling back and forth of their inhabitants. In light of the apparent "opposition" between the two dwellings emphasized by both the novel's characters and readers alike, the incessant ambulation between the Heights and the Grange is, by contrast, all the more visible. The Lintons' determination to isolate themselves as much as possible from contact with the Earnshaws, for instance, ultimately highlights their obvious failure at avoiding "contamination" and at keeping the two dwellings and families separate. Thrushcross Grange, Wuthering Heights, and their inhabitants are shown to exist in an unresolved and ongoing articulation in relation to each other despite various attempts to avoid a "contact zone."

Before their respective marriages, both Catherines are forever travelling between the two houses to visit their future husbands. Catherine Earnshaw moves permanently to the Grange after her wedding to Edgar Linton but is transported back to the moors of the Heights to be buried. Heathcliff forces Catherine Linton to leave the Grange for the Heights to be with the dying Linton Heathcliff, but she ultimately returns to the Grange at the end of the narrative. Isabella Linton lives at the Heights after eloping with Heathcliff but briefly returns to the Grange before leaving these "infernal regions" (165) for her final exile near London. Nelly Dean, who is ironically one of the characters most intent on preserving the boundaries between the two worlds, is nonetheless herself constantly crossing them. She was raised at the Heights, where her mother, a local woman, nursed both her and Hindley Earnshaw. She becomes a housekeeper at Thrushcross Grange when the first Cathy moves there, and, despite her original ties to the Heights, quickly identifies with her new "master": when she speaks of "us" in her tale to Lockwood, she adds "I mean, of the Lintons" (50). Yet she continues to pay regular visits to the Heights, either to see her old foster brother Hindley whose "evil ways" worry her (108) or to accompany a disobedient young Catherine on her escapades. She is "summoned" back to live at the Heights after Lockwood's departure from the Grange, an order she "obeyed joyfully, for Catherine's sake" (263) but moves again to the Grange with the Hareton-Catherine pair following Heathcliff's death. Even animals cannot, it seems, be confined to one locale, since none other than the dog Skulker's offspring becomes the guard dog at the Heights. This constant border crossing in the novel explains why the first Catherine could literally not choose between Edgar Linton and Heathcliff as they both demanded that she do. In the context of the fluidity that characterizes the boundaries separating the two houses, a choice between opposed terms that cannot be kept apart becomes meaningless.

The polarity between the Grange and the Heights and by extension their representatives is constantly destabilized by the nonstop movement between them.

The spatial movement between the two dwellings mirrors and reinforces the proliferating crossings of race and class lines in the novel. The two protagonists' class transgressions are contagious since the other characters are similarly shown partaking of them. Both Catherine (Cathy's daughter) and Isabella are brought up as well-bred and wealthy Lintons but so radically fall in social standing and manners that it becomes impossible to distinguish between altered appearance and inner essence. After Isabella's wedding to Heathcliff, Nelly mistakes her ex-mistress for a servant, identifying her as a "thorough little slattern" (138). Isabella finally dies ruined and in exile, while the second Catherine inverts her mother's social trajectory, marrying beneath her class. At a time when the Victorian middle class was especially anxious to mark class boundaries (Armstrong 52) by appealing to categorical forms of difference, *Wuthering Heights* emphasizes the impossibility of naturalizing identity. High-bred characters are constantly mistaken for servants, while servants behave and speak like educated beings. The first time she meets Hareton, the second Catherine is shocked to find that he is no servant but her cousin. Edgar expects to see a "ploughboy" upon Heathcliff's return and is faced instead with a "born and bred gentleman" (138). Even Nelly, who does not literally transgress class lines, reinforces the Victorians' anxiety about their fluidity. Indeed, Nelly surprises Lockwood with the depth of her "reflective faculties." He cannot help but notice that she has "no marks of the manners which [he is] habituated to consider as peculiar to [her] class," and she confesses that she has "read more than [he] can fancy" and that he "could not open a book in this library that [she has] not looked into, and got something out of also" (71–72). Ironically, she is also more of a domestic woman than any of the female characters whom we would expect to fulfill that role in the novel. Nelly's first impulse at the Heights when she goes to investigate the battered Isabella's status is to blame the young bride's lack of domestic skills. Domestic duties are so sacred to the caretaker that she expects them to be fulfilled irrespectively of the domestic violence Isabella is enduring in this "inhospitable hearth" (132).

While other Victorian texts are aligned with a hegemonic logic that naturalizes identities and contains the intersections of race, sex, nation, and class, *Wuthering Heights* brings the logic of identity crossing center stage and defamiliarizes it. Instead of reifying the fixed narratives of racial and sexual difference that paradoxically both depend on and obscure the logic of crossing that defines identities, the novel makes visible the inextricable links between racial identifications and the signifiers of gender and class. Far from serving to maintain hierarchies of race, class, and gender, the novel stages and restages their undoing. It emblematizes endless proliferation rather than anxious containment. Furthermore, by virtue of its particularly modern form of narration, *Wuthering Heights* urges readers to establish a critical distance toward its structural meanings. Indeed, the story is told by narrators we cannot trust, about characters we cannot like, and through a Chinese-box structure that further obscures authorial intent. Such distancing mechanisms discourage readers from taking any interpretation for granted and prevent them from unproblematically attributing to the author a particular narrator's or character's deployment of racial tropes. This salutary invitation to interrogate the complexities of the text's meanings ultimately highlights the conflicting and fragmented identities that characterized the concept of race in nineteenth-century culture in a way that no other mid-Victorian novel does. What is more, *Wuthering Heights*'s "eccentric" relation to time and morality (to quote Fuentes) also singles it out as a narrative that highlights the tropic figurations of race, gender, class, and nation in Victorian literature rather than as one that merely reflects dominant cultural formations.

Race in literary studies is too often approached as a static aspect of characterization. Once the "blackness" of a character is ascertained (whether it is as a metaphorical or literal attribute), it becomes a fixed and indelible marker of his/her identity in the text, unproblematically serving as a basis of group distinction. Whether it is because it attributes somatic visibility to social and behavioral characteristics or vice versa, the concept is considered invariable in its function and effects. Racially marked characters are seen as different once and for all, all the more so since racial difference is usually associated with supposedly unshakeable corporeal signs and somatic visibility. The reconceptualization of race offered by Caribbean novelists like Maryse Condé proposes instead that we examine the shifting distribution of racial attributes in narrative as part of the same racial logic that links white and nonwhite characters. The physical descriptions of both sets of characters change throughout the text, and it is this shifting symbolic economy that is given analytical precedence over the black/white distinction through which critics often congeal the parameters of characterization. Condé's rereading helps highlight moments in the Victorian novel when a character's racial difference is invisible or, alternatively, when the invisible (because naturalized) white norm is rendered visible through a process of racialization. It emphasizes the symbolic nature of race and, by resisting the tendency to fix race to the body, reveals the importance of understanding the workings of race in relation to the construction of gender and class. This treatment of race has implications for postcolonial thinking about our contemporary world since it emphasizes the contingent ways in which a "visible" site of alterity like race or gender does or does not make a difference at certain times. Far from being a stable category whose ideological function transcends its imbrication with other identities, racial identity in Caribbean *and* Victorian literature is thus revealed as a fragmented, fluctuating, but no less meaningful category of meaning whose patterns can and should be traced.

4 Creolization and the Black Atlantic

Differentiated Aesthetics in Julia Alvarez's *Yo!* and Edwidge Danticat's *Breath, Eyes, Memory*

> The whole *notion* of authenticity, of the authentic migrant experience, is one that comes to us constructed by hegemonic voices; and so, what one has to tease out is what is *not* there.
>
> Gayatri Chakravorty Spivak, *The Postcolonial Critic*

OVER THE last decade or so, some exiled postcolonial writers have explicitly reconfigured their identity by rejecting the status of exile for that of migrant. Salman Rushdie and Bharati Mukherjee, for instance, have adopted the term "(im)migrant" to describe both their literary production and their personal experience of transculturation. Similarly, the new generation of diasporic Caribbean writers (Caryl Phillips, Fred D'Aguiar, Edwidge Danticat, Michelle Cliff, Jamaica Kincaid, Julia Alvarez), who are increasingly settling in the United States rather than in the "Mother Country," are no longer as consistently discussed in relation to the condition of exile as was the earlier generation (Samuel Selvon, George Lamming, V. S. Naipaul). Neither do they seem to thematize it as obsessively. This paradigmatic shift from exile to migrant has important implications for the representational politics of contemporary postcolonial writing insofar as it forces readers to reexamine the relationship between the experience of exile and the process of representing it. In light of this shift, it is no longer possible to assume that exile is just exile even when it is called something else, since the experience of exile (the referent) itself is necessarily affected by the change in signifiers. Writers might still be undeniably living "in exile" from their native land, but the transformation of exile into migrant literature challenges literary criticism's traditional reliance on that experience as the "basis" of explanation in criticism. Instead, it makes us look at exile as a condition that itself requires explanation and ideological analysis.

In this chapter, I examine the ways in which diasporic Caribbean women writers such as Julia Alvarez and Edwidge Danticat invoke and expose the opposition between the country of origin and the adopted country that typically structures interpretations of postcolonial fiction as an ideologically motivated configuration rather than as a representation of the "real." In its stead, their migrant aesthetic offers a transnational, cosmopolitan, multilingual, and hybrid map of the world that deconstructs the opposition between home and exile by building bridges between Third and First Worlds.[1] As Hamid Naficy explains in his study of Iranian immigrant communities in Los Angeles, this new migrancy is about "ambivalences, resistances, slippages, dissimulations, doubling, and even subversions of the cultural codes of *both* the home and host societies" (xvi). It moves away from a notion of national identity as an organic unity based on race and blood to advocate instead a model of identity that reconceptualizes the mutually constitutive concepts of self and other, foreigner and citizen as internally hybrid and relational categories.

Like other contemporary migrant Caribbean writers, Alvarez and Danticat display such a transnational and syncretic sensibility in their fiction, and more specifically in their autobiographical novels, *Yo!* and *Breath, Eyes, Memory,* respectively. In keeping with the critical shift from exile to migrant literature, it is no longer these writers' separation from their native land through exile so much as the coming together of cultures it occasions that matters. Their displacement itself is no longer seen as the basis for the alternative epistemology their fiction embodies and is downplayed in favor of their anchoring in the regional identity of the Americas. As a result, racial and cultural hybridity—which has long been recognized as a foundation of Caribbean identity[2]—provides the regenerative lens through which the notion of Americanness itself is rewritten as relational. The hackneyed notions of multiculturalism or the melting pot are retired once and for all as these writings offer a reconceptualization of identificatory structures that undoes the usual center/periphery binary through which nations such as North America and Canada have defined themselves historically.[3]

As Handley points out, during the period of greatest U.S. imperialism in the Caribbean, U.S. culture became particularly invested in distinguishing itself from the rest of the region. The United States "tried to shed its own miscegenated, Caribbean image of itself . . . to pretend to its whiteness and civilization against the background of a new, extranational 'barbaric' miscegenation" (Handley 6), while in response to the encroachment of this neocolonial power, Caribbean islands emphasized their own national autonomy. By contrast, contemporary Caribbean-American literature challenges rigid ideals about the purity of inherited cultures and dramatizes the interdependency of plantation cultures in the Americas. It thus has the potential of renovating North America's national self-image so that identity is no longer conceived as "only valuable and recognizable if it excludes the identity of every other being" (Glissant, *Introduction* 15). Instead, it becomes possible to replace the model of identity as root with that of identity as rhizome without thinking that opening up to the other means diluting and hence losing oneself (*Introduction* 23).

While this move toward a cross-cultural understanding of New World fiction is salutary and important, it can also, I argue, create its own constraining orthodoxies by obscuring important differences between various writers' representational politics. My comparative analysis of *Yo!* and *Breath, Eyes, Memory* reveals that immigrant New World writers are not all embracing a similar transnational aesthetic simply because they no longer envisage permanently returning to their native land. Despite the remarkable parallels that define Alvarez's and Danticat's as well as their protagonists' identities, each writer generates quite a different representation of identity and ambivalence resulting from cultural encounter. I show that whereas Julia Alvarez's *Yo!* embodies a syncretic and migrant aesthetic that dissolves exile literature's grounding in the binaries of self/other, here/there, etc., *Breath, Eyes, Memory* generates a "poetics of location" that complicates the Haitian writer's classification as "migrant."[4] The ethnic intricacies faced by Danticat and Alvarez in the contemporary United States translate into quite distinct narratives of legacy.

IT USED TO BE—and too often still is—the case that the mere mention of a writer's condition of exile was sufficient to imply certain foundational premises about his or her work. As Kaplan and Sugg argue, the experiences and aesthetics of many exiled postcolonial writers tend to be interpreted through the lens of a Euro-American conception of exile that is rooted in modernist and colonialist fantasies of unfettered mobility. The exiled (usually male) writer is seen as better equipped to provide an "objective" view of the two worlds he is straddling by virtue of his displacement. He is ascribed the status of neutral observer, a detachment on which his literary authority is partly based.[5] His "privileged" status as in-between, as a mediator between two cultures, thus often becomes the cue that grounds interpretation and constructs a binary logic between an alienating "here" and a romanticized "homeland" (or, as in the case of V. S. Naipaul, between a romanticized "here/England" and an alienating "there/Caribbean"). This high modernist conception of exile informs, for instance, the way the generation of Caribbean writers who moved to England in the 1950s and 1960s framed their own experiences and nationalist aspirations.[6]

The shift from exile to migrant challenges this binary logic by emphasizing movement, rootlessness, and the mixing of cultures, races, and languages. The world inhabited by the writers and their characters is no longer conceptualized as "here" and "there." Because of her displacement, the migrant's identity undergoes radical shifts that alter her self-perception and often result in her ambivalence toward both her old and new existence. She can no longer simply or nostalgically remember the past as a fixed and comforting anchor in her life since its contours move with the present rather than in opposition to it. Her identity is no longer a stable, fixed state of being but is in the process of becoming. Migration is thus

> not a mere interval between fixed points of departure and arrival, but a mode of being in the world—"migrancy." . . . The migrant voice tells us what it is like to feel a stranger and yet at home, to live simultaneously inside and outside one's immediate situation, to be permanently on the run, to think of returning but to realize at the same time the impossibility of doing so, since the past is not only another country but also another time, out of the present. It tells us what it is like to traverse borders like the Rio Grande, or "Fortress Europe," and by doing so suddenly become an illegal person, an "other." (King, Connell, and White xv)

In other words, rather than entrenching identities such as "illegal immigrant" in the very process of examining their effects, the shift from exile to migrant literature helps expose these identities as constructed by highlighting how they come into being in the first place.

Interestingly, this substitution of migrant for exile in academic discourse has not occurred without shifting the meaning of each away from its original connotation. For instance, whereas "exile" commonly suggested an unwilled expulsion from a nation, such that no return was possible unless it was under the shadow of imprisonment, execution, or some other coercive physical response, "migrant" suggested a relatively voluntary departure with the possibility of return. For instance, it was understood that migrant workers depart and typically move back and forth between two nations not through necessity but through a voluntary search for work, an improved life, and so on. By contrast, the contemporary configuration of migrant emphasizes the dynamic relationship between the past and present and the *impossibility of return,* while the discourse of exile tends to foreground what was left behind or the possibility of return (independently of how improbable that return is). This revised conceptualization thus downplays the relative freedom that accompanies migrancy to discuss the experience as a matter of the cultural construction by the migrant writer ("to think of returning but to realize at the same time the impossibility of doing so" [King, Connell, and White xv]). Inversely, the coercive circumstances that traditionally defined "exile" have also been deemphasized in favor or a view that foregrounds the renewed perspective and hope the experience brings the writer. It is therefore possible to argue that at the same time as the movement from "exile" to "migrant" literature has the potential to make us examine the assumptions that ground our critical practices, its particular reconfiguration of these metaphors of displacement also runs the risk of obscuring the change from the epoch of revolutionary nationalism and militant anticommunism that produced exiles to an epoch of capitalist triumphalism and globalization that makes various migrant experiences possible.

In Caribbean studies, the shift from exile to migrancy is exemplified by contemporary discussions of creolization as the constitutive principle of Caribbean identity. As discussed earlier, the term "creolization" refers to the processes of cultural, racial, and linguistic cross mixing and unrestricted mutation that define the New World experience. Its alternative epistemology has generated a new poetics that breaks away from notions of origins and rootedness to emphasize the unceasing and syncretic process that constantly reworks Caribbean cultural patterns. In Benítez-Rojo's words:

> Creolization is not merely a process (a word that implies forward movement) but a discontinuous series of recurrences, of happenings, whose sole law is change. It is the product of the plantation (the big bang of the Caribbean universe), whose slow explosion throughout modern history threw out billions and billions of cultural fragments in all directions—fragments of diverse kinds that, in their endless voyage, come together in an instant to form a dance step, a linguistic trope, the line of a poem, and afterward repel each other to re-form and pull apart once more, and so on. ("Three Words toward Creolization" 55)

According to Benítez-Rojo, creolization's "aesthetic of chaos" (or as Édouard Glissant calls it, "l'ésthetique du chaos-monde") is grounded in three words: plantation, rhythm, and performance—each of which exemplifies the history of cultural mixing and unceasing transformation that defines Caribbean identity. For Benítez-Rojo, the work of the new generation of Caribbean diasporic writers best embodies this new poetics. Specifically, he singles out the creolized aesthetics of Edwidge Danticat, Caryl Phillips, Fred D'Aguiar, and Robert Antoni as examples of Caribbean rhythm and performance. "Of course," Benítez-Rojo adds, he "could [also] use the works of Wilson Harris, Alejo Carpenter [*sic*], Gabriel Marquez [*sic*], or Maryse Condé" to illustrate his point (56). In other words, the poetics that results from creolization's cultural explosion defines Caribbean writing in a way that transcends ethnic, racial, linguistic, or national divisions. Like the Créoliste group before him, Benítez-Rojo urges us to "quit using the traditional raciological distinctions, and to start designating the people of our countries, regardless of their complexion, by the only suitable word: Creole" (Bernabé, Chamoiseau, and Confiant 90). According to this logic, Creole writers dramatize a common aesthetics of relationality irrespective of their socioethnic differences. Racial identities thus lose their conventional hold on the workings of culture in the Caribbean, all the more so since "no person with a truly Caribbean identity—carries his or her own true name, just as his or her skin pertains to no fixed race" ("Three Words" 58).

The instability of race that Benítez-Rojo sees as fundamental to Caribbeanness is particularly evident in the case of Julia Alvarez. The Dominican-American writer was shocked to find herself classified as a "woman of color" when she started her career as a writer in the United States, all the more so since her family had always identified with the dominant "white" caste in the Dominican Republic. The process of racialization she underwent powerfully illustrates that racial identity is indeed, to quote Henry Louis Gates Jr., "a fiction," or a contingent construction. That the same writer could be perceived as "white" in the Caribbean and as a "woman of color" in the United States powerfully demonstrates that the meanings of race shift according to the contexts in which it operates.

In the first two chapters of this book, I juxtaposed two Caribbean women writers whose textual politics similarly exemplify Benítez-Rojo's transracial model of creolization. Indeed, despite dramatically different ethnic, class, linguistic, and national backgrounds, the "black" Condé and "white" Rhys nonetheless generate a common poetics of relationality in their novels. Both of their rewritings illustrate how race, ethnicity, and postcolonial nationality crisscross with other configurations of difference such as gender and sexuality so much so that this condition of relationality is itself shown to be constitutive rather than derivative of identity. They thus expose the constitutional segregation of sexual and racial difference as an impossibility, and in so doing challenge the core concepts of earlier postcolonialism. Their shared poetics embodies, in other words, the "seal of common creoleness" (Bernabé, Chamoiseau, and Confiant 90) that unifies Caribbean writers from diverse national, racial, and linguistic backgrounds in the regional context of the Americas.

While the first half of the project thus focuses on two writers whose fiction corroborates the assumptions underlying the emerging field of New World studies, I now turn to another pair of Caribbean migrant women writers whose aesthetics complicates and extends this paradigm. In *Yo!* and *Breath, Eyes, Memory,* respectively, the Dominican-American Julia Alvarez and Haitian-American Edwidge Danticat highlight the very different modalities that a hybridizing impulse can take in the writings produced by the members of the new Caribbean diaspora. In contrast to the Condé/Rhys juxtaposition, the Alvarez/Danticat pairing shows that postcolonialism's recent preoccupation with the supplanting of nationalist by postnationalist representations risks obscuring important differences within the new postnationalist paradigm.[7] The terms "creolization" and "hybridity" have gained such currency in Western academic circles that they are often indiscriminately applied to works whose authors share a common experience of exile in the Americas. By contrast, the juxtaposition of Alvarez's and Danticat's autobiographical novels allows us to produce a more differentiated account of the transnational ethos that defines New World fiction.

Yo! and *Breath, Eyes, Memory* help distinguish between the various expressions of a creolized postnationalism all the more so since there are remarkable commonalities between the two authors' and their protagonists' exilic experiences. Both writers are Caribbean-American writers whose identity is situated in the hyphen rather than on either side of their hyphenated identities.[8] Both of their novels are fictional autobiographies that draw on the authors' own experiences of migrancy to depict the heroines' tribulations. They center around girls who moved from their native island of Hispaniola to the United States at a relatively young age. *Breath, Eyes, Memory* begins in Haiti, which through the young protagonist Sophie Caco's eyes appears as a paradise of colorful flowers, warmth, and the loving care of her Tante Atie. The story unravels as the twelve-year-old Sophie is sent for from New York City by a mother she only knows from a photograph and tape recordings. Similarly, *Yo!*'s protagonist Yolanda Garcia is taken to Queens, New York, when she is ten years old. Her immediate family had to leave the Dominican Republic to escape the tyrannical regime in place. For both characters, Yolanda and Sophie, the transplantation to North America and immersion in a completely new language leads to a sense of dislocation and identity anxieties that land them in therapy. Both of them are haunted by ghosts from the past and have to return to their homeland as adults in order to cope with them. Both of them have problems with sexuality and intimacy and must confront aspects of their past sexual identity to integrate them with the present. And last but not least, the individual circumstances of the protagonist in each novel function as an allegory for the racial and gender dislocations attendant on the migrant condition.

In many postcolonial novels today, the country of destination to which the protagonist moves is no longer, as it used to be, the old colonial metropole (London or Paris) but the new world power, the United States. This is especially true for West Indian immigrants who, in the post–World War II era, went to England or France (the "mother country") in search of a better life, education, or publication opportunities, but who are now migrating to the United States. As Belinda Edmondson points out, this difference in destination is precisely what distinguishes the first generation of predominantly male Caribbean writers "in exile" from the second generation of predominantly female "immigrant" writers. The prior generation, she argues, migrated to England in search of the kind of literary authority associated with Cambridge and Oxford, while the heavily female contemporary migration to the United States is economically motivated, "associated with physical, not intellectual, labor" (13). It is then the conditions of women writers' journey to the United States rather than "the fact of actually being there" (141) that ultimately leads them to revise the opposition between modernization and tradition that animated the first generation's writings: "while [Paule] Marshall's text traverses the route first established by Bita Plant in McKay's folk romance, she does not finally renounce modernity altogether. Instead, the folk and the modern become mutually constituting categories. The ideal of modernization is effectively deconstructed as a masculine act and reconstructed as something that can encompass a black, female, immigrant experience without a corollary rejection of folk origins" (166).

In other words, women writers stage a dissolution of the opposition between the cultural remnants of the Afro-Caribbean space on the one hand, and the industrialization and cultural changes that define contemporary Western society on the other. Since the authors themselves migrated to the States to better their lives, it makes sense that they should depict characters who succeed in preserving their cultural heritage without sacrificing the economic aspirations that are associated with modernization. These female protagonists carve out a space that successfully renegotiates the relationship between progress and tradition, written and oral modes, individualism and communitarianism. Edmondson's model thus reverses postcolonial criticism's usual association of the migrant aesthetic with its writers' economic and social privilege.[9] It also emphasizes the Caribbean writer's positionality in a way that contrasts with the call for a "seal of common creoleness" (Bernabé, Chamoiseau, and Confiant 90) that plays down the effects of gender, race, and class differences on New World aesthetics.

Edmondson limits her analysis to the anglophone tradition of Caribbean writing. Yet in light of the historical parallels between the ex-British colonies and the territories appropriated by other colonial powers, it is important to investigate the ways in which her paradigm resonates with the experiences of the recent waves of migrants from the hispanophone and francophone Caribbean as well. Like their younger anglophone counterparts in Edmondson's model, Danticat and Alvarez developed literary aspirations subsequent to rather than as a condition for their migration to the States. Their families, which belong to very different class and ethnic backgrounds, also moved to North America in search of a "better" life, although in Alvarez's case, the move was made to escape political repression and entailed loss of status and privilege. Both writers evoke Edmondson's model insofar as they represent "the folk and the modern [as] mutually constituting categories" (166), but each of them does so in a radically different way.

I ARGUE that Alvarez's mode of representation in *Yo!* embodies a migrant aesthetics insofar as it challenges the kind of opposition between the modern and the traditional, the country of destination and the country of origin, that motivates the discourse of exile. The protagonist Yolanda Garcia's relation to both the Dominican Republic (her "homeland") and the host country (the States) is characterized by ambivalence. She belongs neither here nor there. She is perceived as "Americanized" by her island relatives and as a "Latin lady" by her American boyfriend. The model of identity that emerges is a hybrid one in which the protagonist occupies the position of the "in-between." Despite her repeated efforts at belonging, she never manages to feel rooted in any culture. She is alienated from the island she left behind as evidenced by her repeated and vain attempts at retracing her lost roots.[10] And although she now lives in the States, the legacy of her island's culture prevents her from ever quite feeling at home away from the Dominican Republic. Her conception of home never matches her actual experience of it.

Throughout the narrative, the static definitions of home and belonging as either/or that had previously driven Yo's actions are thus reconfigured as dynamic and vital. The novel reconceptualizes the notion of "home" from the preexisting meanings it represents in the discourse of exile (stability, comfort, identity, or inversely, oppression, poverty, and so on) to a trans-formative site of constant renegotiation of the migrant's identity. In this context, the act of returning to the Caribbean does not produce a fixed outcome, since the migrant's re-experience of home is defined by her fluc-tuating idea of it. The origin community is revealed as a dynamic and changing world that cannot be reclaimed intact but can only be envi-sioned through a fragmented memory.[11] Alternatively, the host country also fails to function as a new or substitute "home," whether it is because of the racism that migrants to the United States encounter or because of the cultural baggage they bring with them. Both countries are thus represented as dynamic entities, while the traditional notion of "home" as belonging and community is exposed as a myth. If the Dominican Republic continues to be referred to as "home" in the novel, it is only with the understanding that the reader's conventional idea of home needs to be revised to include a more complex conceptualization, one that emphasizes ambivalence, fragmentation, and plurality as a new way of thinking about space and identity.

North American students are often inclined to read the migrant pro-tagonist's arrival in the States as a narrative of progress from oppression to freedom. This reading is enhanced by their knowledge of the sexual oppressiveness and the volatile political situation that immigrant authors often leave behind in their home country. Inevitably, then, the writings of the new Caribbean diaspora—and *Yo!* is no exception—run the risk of turning the West Indies into the alter ego against which Americanness is measured and unconditionally valorized.[12] In Alvarez's novel, the tempta-tion to associate the Caribbean with repressive sexual mores and North America with a liberating narrative is checked through the ways in which the various sections dynamically comment on each other. In part 1 of the novel, a Dominican peasant woman's internalization of patriarchal values as she is shown justifying her daughter's victimization echoes a North American landlady's resignation to oppressive gender norms and domestic violence in part 2. Conversely, the liberated sexual behavior of American women is exposed as a fear of intimacy with men, that is, as merely another form of enslavement rather than as a genuine sign of freedom. Yo forces her "promiscuous" best friend, Maria, to recognize this paradox: "You're running away from men just as fast as I am" (141). This kind of deconstructive gesture in the novel is reminiscent of Gayatri Spivak's striking conclusion in "French Feminism in an International Frame," which juxtaposes the practice of clitoridectomy in non-Western countries with women's "sexual liberation" in the West to "promote a sense of our common yet history-specific lot." Spivak's analysis ties together "the terrified child held down by her grand-mother as the blood runs down her groin and the 'liberated' heterosexual woman who, in spite of Mary Jane Sherfey and . . . *Our Bodies, Ourselves,* in bed with a casual lover—engaged, in other words, in the 'freest' of 'free' activities—confronts, at worst, the 'shame' of admitting to the 'abnormality' of her orgasm: at best, the acceptance of such a 'special' need" (153). Free bodies do not amount to free minds.

In *Yo!,* the supposed repressiveness of Yolanda's Dominican island relatives that prompts her to hide her sexual relationship from them is blown out of the water when her boyfriend comes out to her uncle as her companero and is met not with rage but with a sympathetic chuckle. Dominican male characters whom we might expect to be representatives of the kind of rigid patriarchal framework that is supposedly absent in the States are instead shown undergoing a transformation that challenges any simplified interpretation of that country's sexual politics. In the last section of the novel, Yolanda's repentant father embraces her daughter's storytelling as crucial to the future generations of the Garcia family. Furthermore, the fact that his conciliatory words are juxtaposed to the point of view of Yolanda's American stalker reminds us that sexism is no one nation's prerogative. At the conclusion of the narrative, we are actually left wondering whether Yolanda has survived her American stalker's attack.

Significantly, the younger Yolanda's condescending attempts to raise the consciousness of her less fortunate island relatives are never left unchallenged. Cousin Lucinda, for example, exposes the paternalism that her American cousins claim with their questions: "How could I let the maids make my bed? How could I let my novio push me around? How could I put fake eyelashes on top of my real ones? . . . How could I live in a country where everyone wasn't guaranteed life, liberty, and the pursuit of happiness?" (37). "Yo," she adds, "would be hammering away about some book she'd read on the third world. . . . Third world to whom?" (37). Throughout the narrative, this conflict of ideologies and nations not only reveals the larger dynamics that affect interpersonal relationships, but it also emphasizes the material conditions that create and maintain hierarchies of material and symbolic power.

In keeping with the migrant aesthetics' dissolution of boundaries, the alternative to oppressive norms in *Yo!* is neither associated with one space nor the other. Rather, it is a function of a syncretism that derives from both Caribbean and North American values. It is, for example, through the empowering combination of written language and oral culture that gender violence is effectively countered in the narrative. In the section entitled "The Stranger," Yo (who is "the stranger") meets Consuelo, the illiterate Dominican peasant woman who—loyal to the cultural tradition that preaches women's subservience to their husband—sees the domestic violence that victimizes her daughter as the abuser's prerogative. Yolanda agrees to write the letter Consuelo wants to send her battered daughter concerning this matter. When she transcribes into writing the peasant woman's words, however, she leads the old woman to condemn rather than rationalize domestic violence and to write an empowering rather than an accusatory letter to her daughter. Yet the feminist rephrasing of the old woman's initial message is not merely an outcome of Yolanda's persuasiveness since, as the peasant woman tells us, it actually represents the dream she had been trying to remember all along: "As the lady spoke and wrote these words, Consuelo could feel her dream rising to the surface of her memory. And it seemed to her that these were the very words she had spoken that Ruth had been so moved to hear. 'Yes,' she kept urging the lady, 'Yes, that is so.'" (109).

Yolanda's influence is thus represented as catalytic. She is not imposing her Euro-American interpretive grid on the illiterate woman's values so much as helping release the message of Consuelo's "secret heart." Ironically, rather than implying heroism, Yolanda's repeated interventions as a feminist crusader in lower-class Dominican women's lives ultimately highlight her blindness to the gender dynamics that underlie her own identity crisis. She is unable to locate the source of her own problems as a writer and as a woman. The very patriarchal violence that, in her case, takes the shape of a severe beating by her father for telling stories/storytelling is also responsible for her fractured identity and tortured relationship to writing. Yet, she is as unaware of the legacy of violence that defines her relation to her origins as she is lucid about it in other women's lives. It is only the concluding section devoted to her father's testimony that retrospectively clarifies the reasons behind her inability to write or her insistence on becoming celibate: "As my wife held her, I brought down that belt over and over, not with all my strength or I could have killed her, but with enough force to leave marks on her backside and legs. It was as if I had forgotten that she was a child, my child, and all I could think was that I had to silence our betrayer. 'This should teach you a lesson,' I kept saying. 'You must never ever tell stories!'" (307).

We are thus far from the model of identity offered by autobiographical novels of exile in which the protagonist's (re)constitution of a coherent sense of self takes center stage. Although the title *Yo!* is both the name of the central character and an exclamation of selfhood ("I!"), the process of making the self in the novel gives way to fragmentation and ambivalence, all the more so since the protagonist's uneven development is related by others, never by herself. Yo herself never gets to tell her story in her own voice, an absence that is all the more remarkable in a narrative so unequivocally centered around the protagonist's struggle at "finding her voice." Our only access to her voice is in fact through the narratives of relatives, friends, acquaintances, servants, and even enemies (for example, her stalker) who relate their conflicting impressions and give us insight into Yo's character, either directly focalized through their individual consciousness or indirectly through the third-person narration of the implied author. In thus circling a central character we never hear from directly, the novel offers a portrait of the self as constructed within a countless number of interlocking identities. It challenges the possibility of any totalizing picture as the self is continually situated in relation to the histories and perspectives of others. The layering of perspectives emphasizes how the character or story changes each time a narrator modifies, adds to, or contests another's assessments. Meaning is endlessly remade as Yo's self is inscribed and reinscribed by her complex and conflicted social environment. Identity is thus reconfigured as an intersubjective and collective process insofar as the constitution of the self occurs in its reflection through others rather than in opposition to them.

Remarkably, however, that this constant reinvention of the self is located in Yo's encounter with others does not in the least result in the reader's inability to determine who Yo *really* is. The novel's protagonist is no amorphous or diluted character about whom we are unable to develop an opinion. As the narrators succeed one another, a highly defined image of her identity and life force takes shape and is sustained throughout the novel. To borrow Braidotti's formulation, Yo "endures" as a subject even as she is in-between. Her intensive encounters with others do not make her any less of an embodied and recognizable subject. She is "a folding-in of external influences and a simultaneous unfolding-outward of affects . . . , in-process but . . . also capable of lasting through sets of discontinuous variations, while remaining extraordinarily faithful to [herself]" (Braidotti, "Becoming-Woman" 396). The interdependence of self and other entails, then, "affirmative not dissipative processes of becoming" (397). Identity's relationality leads to empowering transformation and definition, not to dilution or dissolution.

Through this representation of the "nomadic" self, *Yo!* subverts the traditional form of the *Bildungsroman,* which relates the protagonist's process of achieving a coherent sense of self in her own voice. Gone is the familiar *telos* that determines the development of a unique individual. Instead, we find an enfleshed self that becomes itself through its encounters with others and that "lies at the intersections with external, relational forces . . . [in] a constant unfolding" (Braidotti, "Becoming-Woman" 397). The novel's relentless challenge to traditional notions of form, identity, home, and nationalism associates it with a relational migrant aesthetic that is, I further argue, significantly different from *Breath, Eyes, Memory*'s representational politics.

EDWIDGE DANTICAT'S revision of nationalist narratives of legacy in *Breath, Eyes, Memory* offers a contrasting alternative to the dynamics of identity Alvarez dramatizes in her tale of transplantation. In contrast to *Yo!*, *Breath, Eyes, Memory* arrives at a final point of rest in Haiti with the triumph of the central narrating subject. In this context, narrative voice becomes a trope of individuality and power, and the first-person narration converges with the feminist emphasis on narrative voice as a metaphor for female agency and "coming to voice." The process through which Sophie Caco undergoes an inner transformation ultimately culminates in her achieving self-understanding and full autonomous subjectivity. The older narrating Sophie unequivocally represents the ideological norm of the text, and her linear account contrasts with the cacophony of testimonies and orbital perspectives that circle Yolanda Garcia. Furthermore, the opposition between tradition and modernization, between the country of origin and the country of destination that resonates with the exile paradigm is paradoxically upheld and revalorized in a way that is reminiscent of the nationalist writings of the first generation of Caribbean exiles like Claude McKay. Indeed, whether the opposition is consolidated (by Caribbean writers from McKay's generation) or reconfigured (as it is by diaspora writers like Danticat), the side of the binary tradition/modernity that undeniably assumes a positive valence is "tradition" and the values associated with it. What distinguishes Danticat is that her celebration of the Haitian cultural heritage foregrounds its creolized and transformative nature rather than its invariable "authenticity."

That Danticat honors and revises Caribbean (folk) tradition is not to say, however, that the values associated with it are unproblematically embraced in the novel. In fact, aspects of the Haitian cultural heritage depicted in *Breath, Eyes, Memory* are represented as unequivocally oppressive, so much so that they caused a major controversy in the Haitian-American community. Specifically, Haitian-American women strongly disapproved of the novel's representation of the practice of "testing," a cultural practice they have for the most part abandoned and that consists of probing the vagina to check that the hymen is still intact. It is performed by the mother to ensure that her daughter's chastity is preserved before marriage, often leaving indelible emotional and psychological scars as its victim can no longer distinguish between maternal nurture and torture. In the novel, this aspect of the "virginity cult" is passed on "like heirlooms" (233) through the generations of women who, having intensely suffered from it themselves, go on nonetheless performing it on their own daughters. Martine does it to Sophie even though testing was such a source of self-loathing and shame to her that she could not help but see her rape experience as a nightmare that freed her from it. Testing is also deeply damaging to Sophie, who finds herself unable to have a healthy sexual relationship with her husband. When years later, Sophie confronts her mother about the practice, Martine simply retorts: "Because my mother had done it to me. I have no other excuse" (170). Grandma's response is no less frustrating: "You must know that everything a mother does, she does for her child's own good. . . . My heart, it weeps like a river . . . for the pain we have caused you" (157).

The violation perpetrated against women's bodies through testing in the novel highlights, however, not only the negative valence assumed by certain traditional practices in Haitian society but also their constitutive syncretism. In an interview with Vintage Books, Danticat explained that the source of testing virginity can be traced back to the Virgin Mary: "If you look at the apocryphal gospels, after the Virgin Mary gives birth to the Christ child, a midwife comes and tries to test her virginity by insertion, if you can imagine. The family in [*Breath, Eyes, Memory*] was never meant to be a 'typical' Haitian family, if there is ever a typical family in any culture. The family is very much Haitian, but they live their own internal and individual matriarchal reality and they worship the Virgin Mary and the Haitian goddess Erzulie in many interesting forms" ("Conversation"). As in *Yo!*, this emphasis of the convergence of Christian and Afro-Caribbean practices checks any attempt at opposing or ranking the two traditions. Throughout the novel, the two remain imbricated as, for instance, when the use of doubling is represented both in the language of the folk tale of the *Marassas* and in biblical terms.

Both Martine and Sophie resort to "doubling" as a defense mechanism for self-preservation in relation to the trauma of testing. As she tests Sophie for the first time, Martine explains that in checking her daughter's virginity as her own mother did before her, Sophie and she will become "the same person, duplicated in two":

> The *Marassas* were two inseparable lovers. They were the same person, dupli-
> cated in two. They looked the same, talked the same, walked the same. When
> they laughed, they even laughed the same and when they cried, their tears were
> identical. When one went to the stream, the other rushed under the water to
> get a better look. When one looked in the mirror, the other walked behind the
> glass to mimic her. What vain lovers they were, those *Marassas*. Admiring one
> another for being so much alike, for being copies. . . . You and I we could be
> like *Marassas*. (85)

The theme of the double in this passage is represented by reflections in mirrors and in water, which evoke the myth of Narcissus. In the myth, Narcissus, who pines away in love for his own image in a pool of water, finally falls in the pool and drowns. Although Martine (who has already been linked to Narcissus through her love for daffodils, a common species of narcissus) condemns the vanity that undergirds such a relation to the self, she nonetheless shares Narcissus's yearning for a reflection or identity that will restore her sense of wholeness. She recreates such a reflection in Sophie by subjecting her to the same form of abuse she herself experienced as a young girl and by turning her daughter into her *Marassas*. Similarly, "following in the *vaudou* tradition" (156), Sophie learns "to double," that is, to have her mind leave her body during painful episodes such as testing or sex. She too generates a split identity in order to cope with trauma, creating "an imaginary figure, which, just like the soul, the shadow, the mirror image, haunts the subjects like its other, which makes it so that subject is simultaneously itself and never resembles itself again" (Baudrillard 95). Later, she literally becomes Martine's *Marassas*: "Her nightmares had somehow become my own, so much so that I would wonder if we hadn't both spent the night dreaming about the same thing" (193). Her use of doubling also comes to define her sexual relationships with the man she loves and ultimately manifests itself through bulimia. Unable to cope with her own appearance (a reflection and constant reminder of her mother's rapist), she refuses to look at herself by becoming instead her mother's Marassas, so much so that her deliverance will ultimately depend upon revisiting the spot where her mother was raped and confronting the "shadow" (209) of the man Martine could never face.

Throughout the novel, the practice of doubling is also overlaid, however, with biblical imagery, yet again emphasizing the syncretism of the cultural forces at work in the Haitian context. When Sophie asks why she has a mother and no father, Tante Atie provides her with a tale of Immaculate Conception according to which she was born out of "rose petals, the stream, and the sky" (47). This image, which identifies Martine with the Virgin Mary, is then sustained in the rest of the narrative. When Sophie is tested for the first time, she combines the vaudou tradition of doubling with prayers to the Virgin mother, thus again invoking her own mother's spirit through a hybrid religious form. Later, when she resorts to doubling during sex, it is again to return to her mother as "a shadow on the wall" (200). As Martine's *Marassas,* she in turn becomes identified with the Virgin Mary, as confirmed by her husband's name: Joseph.

Paradoxically, the perpetrators of the sexually abusive practice of testing in the novel are also the most lucid as to its destructive effects in their daughters' lives. When Grandma learns about Sophie's lack of sexual desire, she immediately (and unprompted) links her granddaughter's "trouble with marital duties" with "testing." "Your mother?" she asks, "Did she ever test you?" (123). Similarly, Martine cannot help but subject her own daughter to testing, even though she is ultra-aware of the suffering it causes. This self-consciousness has the interesting effect of separating the agent from the disturbing act they are performing in the novel. It is as if the characters are watching themselves perpetuate a cultural practice they know to be problematic and can comment on it but not stop it. They are cultural transmitters independently of their own volition, victims of their own unconscious yearnings.

At the same time, the protagonist's resistance to the sexual oppressiveness of testing emerges in very much the same way in the novel. It too is found in the traditional way of life represented and transmitted by the matriarchal line. It is indeed Grandma's folk tales of the "bleeding woman," "the lark," and the "flying woman" that ultimately provide the narrator-protagonist with models of resistance to patriarchal ideology (rather than, for instance, Sophie's assimilation of more modern or so-called rational values). Significantly, when Sophie breaks her hymen with a pestle to put an end to her mother's tests, she endures this symbolic rape by remembering and relating the first tale she heard her grandmother Ifé tell. The story is about a "bleeding woman" who chose to become a butterfly rather than go on bleeding "out of her unbroken skin, sometimes from her arms, sometimes from her legs, sometimes from her face and chest . . . soaking her clothes a bright red on very special occasions—weddings and funerals" (87). The blood embodies Haitian culture's obsession with female virginity. Sophie recalls the liberating conclusion of the tale: "The woman was transformed [into a butterfly] and never bled again" even as she tears apart her vaginal skin in a symbolic break from her colonized gender identity: "My flesh ripped apart as I pressed the pestle into it. I could see the blood slowly dripping onto the bed sheet" (88). This act frees her from the history of violence passed on by her mother by invoking the very cultural heritage from which testing derives. Sophie's resistance is thus ironically grounded in the empowering tales told by Grandma Ifé, the very same woman with whom testing originates in the narrative. As the tale reaches its apotheosis, the reader realizes that Sophie will not carry on the tradition of testing with her own daughter, Brigitte. Haiti and its cultural traditions thus become both a site of oppression and freedom in the novel.

Significantly, notwithstanding the history of violence with which Haitian culture is associated, the narrative ends with a sense of cultural wholeness and celebration. At her mother's funeral in Haiti, we watch as Sophie reconstitutes her sense of self by unearthing the buried cultural language her grandmother embodies and that, the novel suggests, still animates the Haitian consciousness. *Breath, Eyes, Memory* ultimately celebrates the storyteller Grandma Ifé, the repository of Haitian culture and the link to the ancestral home of Africa, who fittingly also gets the last word in the narrative: "I come from a place where breath, eyes, memory are one, a place from which you carry your past like the hair on your head. Where women return to their children as butterflies or as tears in the eyes of the statues that their daughters pray to. My mother was as brave as stars at dawn. She too was from this place. My mother was like that woman who could never bleed and then could never stop bleeding, the one who gave in to her pain, to live as a butterfly. Yes, my mother was like me. . . . My grandmother walked over and put her hand on my shoulder" (234).

Sophie's tribute to the women in her family echoes Danticat's own words in a note distributed by her publisher: "I look to the past—to Haiti—hoping that the extraordinary female storytellers I grew up with—the ones that have passed on—will choose to tell their story through my voice. For those of us who have a voice must speak to the present and to the past. For we may very well be Haiti's last surviving breath, eyes, and memory" (quoted in Casey 527). Danticat's nostalgia for the Haitian past can thus also be seen as a yearning for an African past Sophie repeatedly evokes when she speaks of Guinea as the "place where all the women in my family hoped to eventually meet one another, at the very end of each of our journeys" (174); it is where her dead mother "is going to be a star . . . a butterfly or a lark in a tree . . . free" (228).

In her celebration of Haitian indigenous practices and storytelling, Danticat reveals herself the heir of black consciousness movements whose genesis can be traced back to movements like Négritude and Haitian "Indigenism." Indigenism emerged in reaction to the American occupation of 1915, when in a spirit of resistance, Haitian intellectuals turned to folk culture and native traditions to instigate a literary renewal. They championed this ancestral heritage as Haiti's rediscovered national culture and foregrounded their African origins as the bedrock of Haitian identity. Belinda Jack's definition of Indigenism strongly resonates with the novel's textual politics:

> Responding to a sense of rootlessness, dislocation, loss of identity, and absence of cultural homogeneity, Indigenism involved a "rooting" of consciousness and an attempt to reinstate the potential of art by reestablishing the artist as the voice of the community. . . . The Indigenists presented Africa as the embodiment of a quintessential cultural wholeness and authenticity. [Carl] Brouard was one of the first to celebrate his Africanness and to advocate a return to the freedom of African traditions, traces of which remained in Haitian culture. The obvious corollary of this was, of course, opposition to European tradition and the rejection of rationalism, in particular. (36)

The representation of Haitianness in *Breath, Eyes, Memory* offers a similar reevaluation of Haitian identity even as it corrects the Indigenous movement's masculinist focus by making visible women's contributions to the heritage and traditions of the nation's culture. In "hoping that the extraordinary female storytellers [she] grew up with . . . will choose to tell their story through [her] voice," Danticat similarly seeks to play the role of artist as "the voice of the community." She champions the cultural inheritance of the past, and her concern for cultural identity entails a rejection of rationalism. (Sophie's self-awareness and understanding of the causes of her psychological problems does not help her overcome them; only her intuitive mobilization of inherited culture does.)

The Haitian island's centrality to Danticat's narrative is another aspect that associates it with black nationalist movements. Haiti is the setting for the longest of the four sections in the novel, even though it covers only a few days in a story that spans years. The section is tellingly filled with a joyful imagery of daffodils, sunshine, vibrant colors, and bright yellows that sharply contrast with the deep reds with which Sophie and her mother are surrounded in New York: "The tablecloth was shielded with a red plastic cover, the same blush red as the sofa in the living room" (44). On the one hand, the image of the daffodil associated with the island is that of a flower that was successfully transplanted from Europe to a new land by adapting through a darker hue. On the other hand, the red imagery associated with New York anticipates Martine's failed transplantation and her gruesome suicide at the end of the narrative.

Although the novel's plot is about Sophie's exile to North America, the United States—or the fact that her exile is set in the States—is remarkably inconsequential to the story. What matters is not America but rather Haiti's absence. What grounds Sophie's and her mother's identity crisis is the country and traditions they left behind. Where they landed plays only a secondary role as the opposite term in the Haiti/United States dyad. New York is where the lasting effects of oppressive cultural and social pressures (such as Martine's testing and rape) that originated in Haiti become visible. Thus, far from representing liberation from oppressive Haitian practices, it is actually the site where abuse and death converge. Unlike Haiti, it is also a world in which boundaries between black and white remain impregnable and where Sophie's interactions remain limited to the members of the black diaspora. Interestingly, the African Americans Sophie encounters (Joseph, the therapist Rena) are represented not as Americans but as extensions of the black world that characterizes Haiti. Joseph, a "Creole" from Louisiana (70), insists that he is "not American" but "African-American" (72); Rena is "a gorgeous black woman who was an initiated Santeria priestess . . . [and] had done two years in the Dominican Republic" (206). She is the person who suggests that to feel whole again, Sophie should go back to Haiti and confront the ghosts of her mother's past. In other words, the novel encourages us to see African American culture within the context of a worldwide black ethos rather than as the sign of a larger intermixed and hybridized (North) America. It constructs a diasporic black identity based on a common link to Africa and the history of slavery and opposes this inclusive notion of blackness to white America's racist and purist ways. This model of identity thus ultimately works to reproduce a Caribbean/United States binary, albeit in a revised form.

Indeed, the novel reifies the opposition between the modern and the traditional even as it paradoxically revises the concept of Haitian tradition to signify a hybrid and changing space that is open to incorporating aspects of the other culture. For instance, red, which is first overwhelmingly associated with the oppressiveness of North American culture and with Martine's gruesome suicide, is also the color that, when transposed to the island, turns from a symbol of isolation and self-immolation into one of survival and creolization. After all, Sophie's own family name,

Caco, "is the name of a scarlet bird. A bird so crimson, it makes the reddest hibiscus or the brightest flame trees seem white" (150), as well as a reference to the "Caco Wars" of 1915–16 and 1919–20, which were both revolts against the U.S.-led occupation. The First Caco War began after the United States selected Philippe Sudre Dartiguenave as the president of Haiti, ignoring the people's choice (Dr. Rosalvo Bobo). The *cacos* (Haitian peasants) revolted with a revolutionary fervor fueled by their growing nationalism, but the coup was suppressed by the U.S. presence. The second Caco War erupted when Charlemagne Massena Péralte, a former general in the Haitian army and supporter of Dr. Bobo who was imprisoned by Dartiguenave, escaped to become general-in-chief of the revolution. He organized more than a thousand *cacos,* or armed guerrillas, to oppose the Marines and their brutal extraction of forced road, or *corvée,* labor from the Haitians. Péralte's assassination would later give him a heroic status among the Haitian peasantry who nonetheless continued to rebel. In what they would come to refer to as the "caco hunt," the American Marines were given orders to "kill all Cacos and Voodoes" (*sic*) (Renda 41).

In *Breath, Eyes, Memory,* Haiti is also the space where in assuming a darker reddish coloration, the European yellow daffodil signifies the flower's successful adaptation to its tropical surroundings. It is the place where Sophie can dress her mother's corpse in red, even though, in the traditional context of Haiti, it is considered "too loud a color for burial" (227). And while Sophie's transgressive act initially makes Grandma almost "fall down, in shock" (231), it is soon recuperated by the matriarch herself as a sign of Haitian female rebelliousness, which she proceeds to transmit to the younger generation through her storytelling: "There is a place where women are buried in clothes in the color of flames, where we drop coffee on the ground for those who went ahead, where the daughter is never fully a woman until her mother has passed on before her. There is always a place where, if you listen closely in the night, you will hear your mother telling a story and at the end of the tale, she will ask you this question: 'Ou libéré?' Are you free, my daughter?" (234).

In other words, the novel represents the traditional culture of the past as open to reinterpretation rather than as an inert and immutable condition waiting to be unearthed. It is in this sense reminiscent of Frantz Fanon's conception of national culture according to which oral traditions should be dynamic in order to ground a successful national consciousness: "On another level, the oral tradition—stories, epics, and songs of the people— which formerly were filed away as set pieces are now beginning to change.

The storytellers who used to relate inert episodes now bring them alive and introduce into them modifications which are increasingly fundamental. There is a tendency to bring conflicts up to date and to modernise the kinds of struggle which the stories evoke" (240).[13]

Breath, Eyes, Memory thus revises decolonizing nationalisms' typical alignment of women with a pure and stable precolonial past. In her study of race and gender in colonial contexts, Anne McClintock writes that most nationalist discourses equate women with an "authentic body of national tradition (inert, backward-looking, and natural), embodying nationalism's conservative principle of continuity," and identify men as "the progressive agent[s] of national modernity (forward-thrusting, potent, and historic)" (359). By contrast, in *Breath, Eyes, Memory*, women and their storytelling practices embody a more transitional space between change and stability. Grandma Ifé herself, the repository of the traditional past, is aligned with the nation's "betweenness" vis-à-vis modernity and tradition. Cultural heritage thus becomes a site of interaction between cultures that cannot be accounted for in simple terms.

Nevertheless, while reworking *Haitian* cultural patterns, this syncretic process does not ultimately threaten the oppositional stance of the text. In fact, the dissolution of boundaries in the Haitian context paradoxically becomes fodder for upholding the opposition between a fluid and spiritual Caribbean and an alienating because hermetic United States. While Haiti is characterized by a vital and dynamic culture, North America remains the impervious and static site where the characters' struggle with their Haitian identity is enacted. *Breath, Eyes, Memory* thus maintains a strict opposition between the country of origin and the country of destination. The values associated with modernity and Americanness are opposed to the dynamic traditions of the heroine's native island. Even education— which Sophie, Martine, and Tante Atie embrace at various points and which was a source of syncretism in *Yo!*—fails to become the site of cultural mixing in the States. In New York, Sophie goes to a Haitian Adventist school where all the lessons are in French. It was, she comments, "as if I had never left Haiti" (66). The two worlds between which Sophie is divided thus remain separate, and as a result, she does not share migrant literature's ambivalence about the protagonist's relation to the two countries. Haiti is unequivocally the place where the heroine needs to return both physically and spiritually in order to find and empower herself.[14] Haiti is where both Sophie and the novel as a whole achieve closure as she learns to acknowledge and come to terms with the contradictions of her cultural heritage. It is "home," the cultural place where she really belongs, and the refuge that gives her stability and to which she will always return when she needs to recollect herself.

IN HIS *Introduction à une Poétique du Divers,* Édouard Glissant distinguishes between the three kinds of Americas that constitute the New World: Meso-America, which includes the indigenous people of the Americas; Euro-America, which consists of European immigrants who preserved the customs and traditions of their home country; and last but not least, Neo-America, which is the site of creolization.[15] Like Benítez-Rojo, Glissant celebrates the fact that Neo-America is increasingly influencing the rest of the Americas. What is more, he adds, "the whole world is creolizing itself" (15). Nevertheless, despite such hopeful declarations, Glissant is also careful to identify the conditions in which creolization might occur in an unsuccessful or unproductive manner. Creolization, he explains, "presupposes that the cultural elements that are put into contact be necessarily 'equivalent in value' so that creolization can take place successfully. That is to say that if some of the cultural elements that are put in relation are seen as inferior to others, creolization does not really occur. It happens but in a bastard and unfair way. In countries of creolization like the Caribbean or Brazil, where cultural elements came into contact as a result of the slave trade, the African and black constituents were consistently denigrated. Under these circumstances, creolization still takes place but leaves a bitter and uncontrollable residue" (*Introduction* 18). This is why, Glissant argues, intellectual movements like Négritude and Indigenism are such crucial and unavoidable stages in (and of) the creolization process. Without the revalorization of blackness generated by these interventions, creolization as a balanced process that incorporates cultures on an equal footing would not be possible. It took such ethnocentric movements for the right balance between the cultural entities that were meeting in the contact zone to be reestablished. "Creolization demands that the heterogeneous elements that are in relation 'intervalorize' each other, i.e. there be no denigration or diminution of being, either from within or without, in this contact and intermixing" (18).

Danticat's portrayal of the Haitian cultural heritage in *Breath, Eyes, Memory* revalorizes the black diasporic experience as an inherent aspect of the authentic and productive kind of creolization process that Glissant highlights in his essay. Like Glissant, she highlights the predominance of the African element in the people that constitute Neo-America's creolization: "And what is interesting in the creolization phenomenon, in the phenomenon that constitutes Neo-America, is that the people of this

Neo-America are very special. In it, Africa prevails" (Glissant, *Introduction* 14). She also goes further, however, to suggest that the "special" place the descendants of the ex-slaves occupy in Neo-America is a function not only of their numbers but also of their unique and exemplary relation to creolization. This openness to the process of unceasing transformation that Glissant calls Relation derives, however, not from an inherent or essential condition of blackness but from the experiences of slavery and oppression that define black history and (collective) memory. Danticat's focus on a regenerative black ethos implies that the dominant Euro-American culture has yet to engage in the kind of intervalorization of cultures that the African diaspora embodies in her work. Her reconceptualization of creolization also echoes, in this respect, Kamau Brathwaite's valorization of the African legacy in his discussions of Caribbean cultural identity.[16]

In his study of colonial Jamaica, Brathwaite defines creolization as "a way of seeing Jamaican society" and the Caribbean islands generally, "not in terms of black and white, master and slave, in separate nuclear units, but as contributory parts of a whole" (307). Yet even as he defends the idea of a Caribbean culture for which creolization in its "infinite possibilities" (310) is "the tentative cultural norm of society" (*Contradictory Omens* 6), he also emphasizes that "for the Caribbean islands to attain (regain) cultural wholeness," the culture of the ex-African majority has to be accepted "as the paradigm and norm for the entire society" (*Contradictory Omens* 30). Evoking Glissant and the Créolistes' recognition that black consciousness movements like Négritude were the condition of possibility of creolization and creoleness, Brathwaite stresses the need to privilege the African over the European connection as a necessary step toward the completion of the creolizing process. Similarly, Danticat's model of cultural integration maintains a strong sense of the cultural differences that separate the fluid cultural heritage of the black Atlantic from the dominant U.S. culture. In *Breath, Eyes, Memory,* Joseph's protestation that he is "not American" but "African-American" privileges his link to the African diaspora because unlike the term "American," he believes it to be inclusive of difference. To Sophie's question "What is the difference?" he retorts: "The African. It means that you and I, we are already part of each other" (72). This divided consciousness in the novel is ultimately not that surprising in light of the historical relationship between Americans and Haitians, which, as Michael Dash explained in his 1988 book on the subject, grew particularly intense with the fall of the Duvalier dynasty.

Danticat's alternative brand of transnationalism has important implications for our conceptualizations of identity in general and of American identity in particular. Whereas some contemporary hyphenated American writers prefer being identified as American rather than as Indian-American, Asian-American, and so on, Danticat belongs to a group of postcolonial authors who remain invested in the hyphen and its emphasis on cultural difference. On the one hand, writers like Bharati Mukherjee claim that the label "American" is more likely to bring about a reconceptualization of Americanness as plural than are hyphenated categories, which, she claims, only perpetuate a bankrupt multicultural model. On the other hand, writers such as Danticat and Alvarez reclaim the spaces opened up by the hyphen as important disruptions in an otherwise homogeneous narrative of national identity. Alvarez identifies herself as a "mixed breed" (*Something to Declare* 173), a "pan-American, gringa-dominicana, a synthesizing consciousness" (175), while Danticat confesses to "relishing the role of permanent outsider" with which her fragmented identity endows her ("AHA!" 44). In a recent essay, the Haitian-American author even went so far as to add a hyphen to her already hyphenated identity by temporarily endorsing the label of "AHA, African-Haitian-American." This term, she explains, has "the following elements: African to acknowledge our ancestral roots deep in the African continent; Haitian, because of course most of us were either born in Haiti or were first generation born of Haitian parents; and American because we were from the Americas, living in the other 'America,' the United States of America" (39–40).

Joseph's rejection of a blanket American identity in *Breath, Eyes, Memory* thus resonates with Danticat's own investment in the Afro-Creole dimensions of her identity. Her endorsement of a doubly hyphenated identity reflects but also diverges from other Caribbean writers' emphasis on the fragmented nature of their cultural heritage. Whereas Alvarez, for instance, argues that in calling herself neither Dominican nor *una norteamericana,* she is "mapping a country that's not on the map" (*Something to Declare* 173), Danticat makes no excuses for reclaiming a country that is on the map, namely Haiti, as the cultural space through which she reenvisions a regenerative and relational model of identity. Throughout her writings, Haiti remains her chosen foundation in this "equally a-geographical and poly-geographical" world ("AHA!" 44). On the one hand, she claims that, "These days, I feel less like an immigrant and more like a nomad," and that there is "no longer a singular harbor" to which people's bodies and shadows can be anchored exclusively in our interdependent world, while on the other, she paradoxically affirms that, "The more cultures I experience, the more Haitian I feel" (44). Like Glissant, she develops a poetics of location in which one's privileging of a particular cultural space not only does not hinder Relation but provides the very condition for it.

As a result, the postnationalist paradigm that roots/routes Sophie Caco in her homeland Haiti differs from as much as it evokes Yolanda's transnational identity. The difference is nowhere more salient than in two episodes whose functions mirror each other in the two novels: Martine's funeral in *Breath, Eyes, Memory* and Yolanda's wedding in *Yo!*. At the end of *Breath, Eyes, Memory,* the transformative site for Sophie Caco's self-constitution is her mother's funeral, a ceremony whose cultural function is similar to that of a wedding, namely to bring the community together. In *Yo!,* her wedding is the site where Yolanda comes to terms with her fragmented identity. Although these social events are both turning points in the formation of these two women's sense of self, each has very different implications in terms of the model of identity it propounds.

The funeral is where Sophie's concept of self is finally reconciled with her public identity as she confronts the past by yanking the cane that concealed her mother's rape. Significantly, it takes place in Haiti and among Haitians (despite the fact that Martine had been living in the States for over ten years). By contrast, Yolanda's wedding is set in New Hampshire among an eclectic group of Dominican and North American guests. Unlike Sophie, Yolanda does not go home to liberate herself by hacking down the past and immersing herself in traditional culture. In fact, far from being the apotheosis Sophie's return to Haiti becomes at the end of *Breath, Eyes, Memory,* Yolanda's trips to the Dominican Republic are only stages in her negotiations of migrant identity. Her experiences do not result in the reconstitution of a coherent sense of self but in the acceptance of fragmentation as a constitutive part of the self. Similarly, when she starts referring to her island as "home," the reader knows better than to read her claim as the epiphanic moment that the same speech act becomes for Sophie. Whereas "home" for Sophie is associated with the feelings of belonging and rootedness that the word maybe more traditionally invokes, the notion of "home" in *Yo!* forces us to radically reevaluate our conventional understanding of the term and its meanings.

Like Yolanda Garcia, Sophie Caco only begins to think and speak of her native country as "home" as an adult, when she goes back to the Caribbean after many years away. In both novels, each woman's boyfriend remarks on the shift in the way she relates to geographical space. In *Yo!*, an annoyed Dexter ridicules Yolanda's sentimental reference to the Dominican Republic as home: "She hasn't lived there for a quarter of a century. She works here, makes love here, has her friends here, pays taxes here, will probably die here. Seems to him all she goes down there for is to get confessed or disowned. Still, when she talks about the D.R., she gets all dewy-eyed as if she were crocheting a little sweater and booties for that island, as if she had given birth to it herself out of the womb of her memory" (193), while in *Breath, Eyes, Memory,* a surprised Joseph tells Sophie: "You have never called [Haiti] that since we've been together. Home has always been your mother's house, that you could never go back to" (195). While these passages both highlight the concept's constructedness, Danticat's novel nonetheless reifies the model of home as belonging and rootedness. Indeed, the sense of dislocation and fragmentation resulting from migrancy is only a temporary setback that Sophie overcomes as she rediscovers the alternative systems of knowledge that ground Haitian cultural identity. In *Yo!,* however, the sense of displacement that defines the heroine's relation to "home" remains no matter where Yolanda is. And unlike Sophie Caco's, Yolanda Garcia's displaced position never gives way to restored wholeness and cultural rootedness.

Julia Alvarez and Edwidge Danticat are two contemporary Caribbean-American authors living in the United States and writing in English, a language they have both identified as their "home." Both of them subvert existing notions of identity and citizenship by opting for alternative rewritings of the narrative of legacy. Insofar as both authors replace traditional paradigms of identity with transnational and cross-cultural models, the theories of creolization and migrancy provide crucial and illuminating frameworks through which to understand their fiction. The members of the new Caribbean diaspora are mapping new literary and cultural spaces that cannot be fully accounted for outside the regional context of the Americas. At the same time, even as a transnational and cross-cultural ethos certainly does unite these two writers, it is important to recognize the differences that distinguish their creolized sensibilities. In scrutinizing the distinct models of identity and place offered by Alvarez and Danticat respectively, I have sought to show that although related, their refashionings of communal and individual identities do not exemplify a homogeneous creolized aesthetics. Their novels show us that in stories of cultural encounter, difference and the will to change are wrongly assumed to result either in assimilation to the new home or to the vestiges of the other cultural space (tradition). This chapter has made visible the seemingly inexistent and relational space between two cultures where, as Danticat's and Alvarez's novels reveal, resistance and becoming are often located.

Postscript

In no way should I derive my basic purpose from the past of the peoples of colour. In no way should I dedicate myself to the revival of an unjustly unrecognized Negro civilization. I will not make myself the man of any past. I do not want to exalt the past at the expense of my present and my future.

Frantz Fanon, *Black Skin, White Masks*

AFTER HAVING repetitively written about her protagonists' angered relationship to their mothers in her previous fiction, the Antiguan novelist Jamaica Kincaid turns in her autobiographical novel, *Mr. Potter,* to her absentee father, a man with whom she came face to face only once, when she was thirty-three years old. It is one thing to negotiate one's relation to one's homeland through a maternal figure whose imposing presence and familiarity warrants the level of mediation she is granted in *Lucy, Annie John,* and *The Autobiography of My Mother.*[1] It is quite another to examine one's island's history and society through a paternal figure whose defining relation to the protagonist (and the author) is paradoxically one of absence and outright indifference. Kincaid's reliance on an absent but no less haunting figure to rewrite her relation to Caribbean identity in *Mr. Potter* offers a powerful metaphor for Caribbean migrant women authors' mediated relation to their homeland. Like Kincaid, these writers use their contradictory position vis-à-vis their native soil—"[they] are rooted, but [they] flow" (Woolf 69)—to rewrite themselves and their mix of cultures with an imaginative eye. For Kincaid, remembering and transcribing her relationship to her father entails the memory of events that she neither directly experienced nor witnessed, let alone documented. Similarly, Caribbean and postcolonial writers today write in response to the legacies of a history of slavery and violence that left no records other than the colonial chronicle, a history, to borrow Glissant's formulation, of *raturage,* or erasure. Their novels record the process involved in the confrontation and negotiation of a past they can only partly imagine and whose meanings cannot be stabilized in the present. This intangible reality is manifest only through the protean but indelible traces it has left behind and needs to be reimagined over and over again. History in Caribbean women's aesthetic constructions might then, like memory, be best described as "the land of the almost" (*Mr. Potter* 107), as a fluid and flowing process that does not necessarily derive from real experience even though it retains the importance of the event itself.

Mr. Potter abandoned the narrator's mother when his daughter was not yet born, and like his own father before him, never so much as wonders about the existence of the many offspring who periodically cross his path on the island. As Kincaid emphatically states, "Not only did he ignore me, he made sure that until the day he died, I did not exist at all" (126). The very title of the book *Mr. Potter* powerfully illustrates the formal but emotionally fraught distance that separates the heroine from her biological father, a man whose centrality in the narrative paradoxically entails no depth. Indeed, to the narrator, Mr. Potter might best be described as a surface, a blank screen she has to inscribe with meaning based on snippets of memory, a couple of photographs, and her own mother's resentful account of him. She further reminisces: "his presence was a shadow and that shadow had more substance than any real person I actually knew, and a real person was made up of blood and tissue and veins and arteries and organs and soft matter, but in my life Mr. Potter was a shadow, a shadow more important than any person I might know, a shadow more important than any apparition I would ever come to know. And then I became myself and Mr. Potter remained himself" (154).

In other words, it is not the protagonist or his life experiences that matter to the author so much as her own ability to (re)write the past in order to reinvent her future through the changing present. Her novel is the story of a specter ("my specter" [138]), a revenant that keeps recurring in and haunting the present, shaping it through the feelings of repression, loss, and mourning it evokes. Mr. Potter, Kincaid confesses, "has been a central figure in my life without either of us knowing it" (153). The narrator is learning to live with such ghosts, which, as Wendy Brown argues, "means living with the permanent disruption of the usual oppositions that render our world coherent—between the material and the ideal, the past and the present, the real and the fictive, the true and the false. Ghosts are what . . . figure the impossibility of mastering, through either knowledge or action, the past or the present. They figure the necessity of grasping certain implications of the past for the present only as traces or effects . . . and of grasping even these as protean" (*Politics* 146). This means learning to live with the irreducible character of a past that can paradoxically exist only through a shifting present and whose effects are no less real for being uncategorizable.

The migrant aesthetic discussed in *Reclaiming Difference* evokes Brown's definition of ghostliness as disruptive of binaries since it too treats the past not as an immutable given but as a construction that must constantly be updated to speak to the present and reimagine the future. Indeed, these writers not only engage in an "aesthetic reconstruction of historical experience" (Nesbitt xiv), but they also, as *Reclaiming Difference* testifies, radically reformulate the old categories of identity and knowledge through which postcolonialism has been configuring difference in the name of an immutable historical past. Their transformative aesthetic disengages memory from its putative mooring in fixed and invariable identities. It reveals history's inseparable dependence on the imagination or rather on an imaginative process of recollection that opens up "spaces of movement— of de-territorialization—that actualize virtual possibilities that had been frozen in the image of the past" (Braidotti, "Becoming-Woman" 399). And it is, *Reclaiming Difference* demonstrates, in light of such a radically reconfigured relation to the past that the scope of Caribbean migrant women's intervention is to be understood.

Through their intertextual and transnational forays, the Caribbean women writers of this study create a new paradigm for the study of literature and culture that revises conventional models of identity and relationality. Their creolized aesthetic challenges identitarian approaches that, in freezing difference, fail to do justice to the deep interconnectedness of today's global world. As Condé puts it, "we live in a world where . . . frontiers have ceased to exist" ("Order" 130). At a time when the United States' tentacular and imperialist omnipresence in the Middle East so transparently echoes the colonial relations of the nineteenth century and when cultural difference is exoticized and commodified at will, a renewed understanding of difference as a contingent and shifting ground of positive identification might be the only path to a genuinely ethical and noncoercive form of human relatedness. Caribbean women writers offer, I argue, such a transformative view of the lines of power and development that define the globe's growing transnationalism by recasting identity as a site of crossing and relationality rather than of separatism. Their emphasis on Relation revises figurations of the other as a site of categorical (and hence expulsable) difference into a representation of alterity that recognizes it as an inherent aspect of the self. This is a model of identification rather than identity since the self's transformation is shown to occur through "an active reflection of the self through the other" (Nesbitt 214). In reinscribing identity as Relation, it offers a renewed understanding of difference as becoming, a process that, far from implying dilution or dissolution, signifies cross-cultural enrichment and affirmative transfiguration.

Critics who, like me, highlight women writers' diasporic status as an integral aspect of their Caribbean identity do not necessarily make this paradox grounds for redefining conventional norms of identity such as race or nation. In her analysis of Caribbean migrant women's writing, for instance, Hoving deploys the category of blackness without considering its radical reformulation by the authors she examines. *In Praise of New Travelers* opens with epigraphs by an Egyptian and a South African writer who, the author claims, elucidate how and why Caribbean women write. "Black" in this model of reading serves as an umbrella term for everyone who is not identified as "white." It subsumes cultural, historical, geographical, and ethnic differences and reproduces the very white/black binary that underlies colonialist perspectives. Even Michelle Cliff's challenge to the notion of blackness as a stable identity is folded back into a conventional racial categorization. Cliff's statement that "many of us became light-skinned very fast" (Hoving 248) leads not to the discussion of the shifting and contingent nature of race that the Jamaican writer promotes but to a warning that "light-skinned" and "black" should not be conflated. This admonition reproduces a naturalizing discourse of the body that is based in Western "economies of visibility" (Wiegman 4) and cannot help but reinscribe that mode's logic of bodily essence. That different racial labels have real material effects need not lead to a reification of racial categories. Dividing the world into "black" and "white" readers as Hoving does necessarily reinscribes the logic of the very system one wants to defeat lest one addresses the limits and contingency of race as a social category of belonging. This lack of theorization of the concept is all the more disturbing in a field like Caribbean studies that has been at the forefront of postcolonial challenges to the racial dichotomies that ground colonialist discourse.

The women writers examined here exemplify a new postcolonialism that resists evoking unproblematized labels such as race, whose genesis in nineteenth-century racist discourses necessarily renders their use dubious. They offer instead new articulations of the ties that link race and nation to gender and class, and subject these articulations to constant scrutiny and contextual analysis. Their writings challenge the kind of sociology of race relations that has been dominating literary criticism and expose the forms of identity politics that such sociology runs the risk of reproducing.

Their reinscription of identity as a complex set of crossing categories (gender, but also class, ethnicity, and nationality) radically revises readings of difference in terms of blood or filiation. It urges us instead to rethink the binaries of black/white and self/other through which difference has been traditionally conceptualized, and to see identifications based on race or gender as a function of culture rather than of phenotypical or biological ab/errancy. It emphasizes the interdependence of identities "as a necessary [step] prior to the creation of noncoercive relations of global dependency and ecological consciousness" (Nesbitt 214), and through its tales of cultural and national crisscrossings, sets an empowering new agenda for the new millennium: "the point is not to know who we are, but rather what, at last, we want to become, how to represent mutations, changes and transformations, rather than Being in its classical modes . . . to provide illustrations for new figurations, for alternative representations and social locations for the kind of hybrid mix we are in the process of becoming" (Braidotti, *Metamorphoses* 2).

Notes

Introduction

1. See Boehmer's *Colonial and Postcolonial Literature,* especially chapter 3, "The Stirrings of New Nationalism" (98–138); Eagleton, Jameson, and Said's *Nationalism, Colonialism, and Literature;* Hutchinson and Smith's anthology *Nationalism;* and Young's recent *Postcolonialism: An Historical Introduction.*

2. See Benedict Anderson's *Imagined Communities* and Ernest Gellner's *Nations and Nationalism* for a study of the Western origins of the ideas of nation and nationalism.

3. In *Postcolonial Paradoxes in French Caribbean Writing,* Jeannie Suk similarly focuses on Caribbean literature to examine paradoxes that are endemic to the field of postcolonialism. Her book "explores the ways in which Antillean literature bears multiple allegorical burdens, unveiling paradoxes of postcoloniality and post-structuralism while recounting the failure of such referential relationships" (2).

4. Said's *Orientalism* (1978) is credited with instigating this turn since it radically questioned the humanist approaches of 1970s Commonwealth criticism. Its publication is also linked to the splitting of postcolonial studies into theory and literature that has "accompanied the emergence of postcolonial studies as an institutionalized field" (Huggan 255). In discussing how Caribbean women's fiction helps us theorize anew, *Reclaiming Difference* seeks to challenge this theory/textual criticism opposition.

5. Helen Tiffin, for instance, argues that postcolonial literature is inevitably "informed by the imperial vision" ("Post-colonialism" 172). Hutcheon shares this view in "Circling the Downspout of Empire."

6. See Duara's *Rescuing History from the Nation.* In the first theoretical part of the book, Duara argues that history needs rescuing because post-Enlightenment thinking has turned history into "History," that is, into a narrative that privileges the nation-state and represses or even decimates alternative histories that are anti-modern, antilinear, or show the nation-state to be divided and contested. As an alternative approach, Duara suggests a bifurcated history that "denies that the

movement of history is causally linear . . . [and] views history as transactional, where the present, by appropriating, repressing and reconstituting dispersed meanings of the past, also reproduces the past" (233).

7. Bongie has coined the term "post/colonial" to refer to this process of rewriting the colonial/postcolonial relationship in terms of both continuity and discontinuity.

8. John Thieme's *Postcolonial Con-Texts: Writing Back to the Canon* exemplifies this transformed writing and reading practice. Thieme argues that "writing back" today operates along a continuum between complicity and oppositionality and can no longer be assumed to be adversarial. He also suggests that postcolonial appropriations of canonical texts often generate rereadings of the source-texts themselves.

9. In his essay, Fuentes draws an explicit connection between Emily Brontë's and Faulkner's aesthetics. Faulkner too, he argues, "is both yours and ours" and "creates another time, a past that is a constant present in memory" (215). See Harris (*Womb of Space*); Glissant (*Faulkner, Mississippi*); and Handley for critical/theoretical rereadings of novels by Faulkner in a New World context.

10. Such excellent overviews of the field already exist. See Robert Young (*Postcolonialism*); John McLeod; Bart Moore-Gilbert; and Elleke Boehmer.

11. I am indebted to John McLeod's introduction to postcolonialism for this account of the forms of textual analysis that developed in the wake of Said's *Orientalism*.

12. See, for instance, Brathwaite's *Contradictory Omens*; Ferguson; Gardiner; Gregg; Handley; Hulme; O'Connor; Rody; and Savory.

13. In her essay, McDowell revisits the commonplace assumption that feminist theory is what white middle-class feminists do, while African American feminists are more interested in less abstract thought and remain on the side of practice. She argues that it is the way black feminist thought has been represented, not the work itself, that explains its exclusion from theoretical thought.

14. Caribbean women writers cannot be claimed to be marginalized in relation to fiction since, as Maes-Jelinek and Ledent have pointed out in a recent survey of Caribbean literature, until the appearance of Caryl Phillips and Fred D'Aguiar on the literary scene in the 1990s, the new generation of diasporic Caribbean writers seemed to consist primarily of women (149). Similarly, according to Belinda Edmondson, the new "migrant literature" today is produced primarily by female writers who, in contrast to the previous generation of predominantly male exiles, left the Caribbean out of economic necessity rather than for educational purposes. Caribbean women writers are in the limelight when it comes to fiction and the observation that "as with most other literary and accompanying critical traditions, the principal writers and critics of the Caribbean remain male" (Davies and Savory xviii) can no longer be unproblematically maintained at the beginning of the twenty-first century.

15. Interestingly, *Against Race* was published in England under a far less con-

troversial and sensationalistic title: *Between Camps: Nations, Cultures, and the Allure of Race.*

16. I am indebted to Linda Nicholson's "Interpreting Gender" for the "coat rack" metaphor I am using here. In her essay, Nicholson provides an extremely lucid and compelling account, in relation to gender, of the distinction between biological determinism and biological foundationalism.

17. Louise Yelin's essay "In Another Place" documents this hypothesis.

18. It is telling, for instance, that in her overview of the three different modalities of hybridity, Susan Friedman provides examples only for the first two. The lack of illustration when it comes to the third postmodern kind of mixing and radical unforeseeability reveals the difficulty of imagining the endless mutations and play of relations that this last form of hybridity represents: "Language as both medium and site of cultural commerce provides ready examples of these three types. Within the terms of hybridity as fusion, the blending of many different distinct languages results in the formation of a new language like English (made up of Saxon, French, Latin, Greek, etc.) or Yiddish (German, Hebrew, Slavic mixture). Within the framework of hybridity as intermingling, different parts of distinct languages (e.g. grammar, vocabulary, syntax) combine to produce a creole language in which the original languages remain recognizable, as in Spanglish, Tex-Mex, or Hawaiian and Jamaican pidgin. The third approach would stress that any given language is always in the process of hybridic formation through borrowings and adaptations of linguistic traditions with which it comes into contact—whether or not the speakers are aware of or resistant to such syncretism" (84–85). Friedman significantly uses the conditional tense as soon as she moves on to the third form of hybridity. The tense shift compounded by the lack of a concrete example emphasizes the difficulty of distinguishing this state of constant flux from the first and second types of hybridity. Indeed, if a language's constant borrowings from and adaptations of other traditions are visible, then it is unclear why it is different from a creole language "in which the original elements remain recognizable." Is it that the patterns of borrowings are untraceable? If so, how can we know that there were borrowings at all? The proliferation of differences, in other words, cannot so easily do away with concepts of difference and identity no matter how endless the diffraction, how shifting the elements that come into contact.

19. See Firdous Azim for a genealogy of the relation between narrativity and subjectivity. Her book *The Colonial Rise of the Novel* traces the development of the historically shifting correspondences between author/text/experience since the emergence of the novel form. One of the main formal properties of the novel is the central narrating subject.

20. See Lanser's *Fictions of Authority.*

21. See Bongie's essay "Exiles on Main Stream" about the tensions between cultural studies and postcolonial studies that explain why postcolonial novels that are best sellers (especially in the Caribbean) do not usually join the postcolonial academic canon.

22. The location of the postcolonial within the privileged and hypocritical space of the Western academy is one of the paradoxes Jeannie Suk engages in her book *Postcolonial Paradoxes*.

23. Friedman coined the term "relational positionality" to refer to scripts that "regard identity as situationally constructed and defined and at the crossroads of different systems of alterity and stratification" (47).

24. See my essay "Toward a New Feminist Theory of Rape" for an elaboration of this point in relation to the discourse of rape.

25. For a trenchant feminist critique of the mystification of voice that intersects with my own analysis, see Carla Kaplan's *The Erotics of Talk*.

26. Similarly, in his book *Creole Identity in the French Caribbean Novel*, Adlai Murdoch reminds us that even as it constitutes a "particularization of global patterns of creolization," "the ethnocultural heterogeneity" of the Caribbean "is not in and of itself a monolithic construct" (2).

1. Maryse Condé's *Windward Heights*

1. Similarly, in Condé's first novel *Hérémakhonon*, her heroine Veronica's quest exposes the idealized "Mother Africa" championed by the Négritude thinkers as a romantic illusion "because material political realities forestall any such construction of a totalizing entity named 'Africa'" (Lionnet, *Autobiographical Voices* 181). In *Traversée de la Mangrove*, it is the Créolité writers' precepts that Condé challenges in light of Caribbean realities. For instance, Kathleen M. Balutansky shows how *Traversée* problematizes Bernabé, Chamoiseau, and Confiant's injunction that Caribbean literary production be about the recovery of a collective consciousness by accumulating fragmented perceptions that disrupt the possibility of a collective experience.

2. Strikingly, Jean Rhys shared Maryse Condé's admiration for Emily Brontë. Indeed, while her letters reveal an intensely critical attitude toward *Jane Eyre* (she could not believe that someone as sensitive as Charlotte Brontë could be so blind to human misery), she eagerly admired Emily Brontë's only novel. In fact, *Wuthering Heights* absorbed her thoughts while she worked on *Wide Sargasso Sea;* and she particularly admired the character of Heathcliff who, she explained, was not "whitewashed" like Rochester. See Joan Givner's "Charlotte Brontë, Emily Brontë, and Jean Rhys: What Rhys's Letters Show about That Relationship."

3. Maryse Condé has herself repeatedly objected to the use of the term "postcolonial" in an Antillean context. Indeed, the French Caribbean islands never gained their independence and, as overseas departments, have never entered a postcolonial era. I nonetheless persist in calling her fiction "postcolonial" because I use the term to refer to discursive practices that are defined by a resistance to colonialist ideologies rather than to texts written by the ex-colonized after independence.

4. As Eagleton argues in *Myths of Power*, the Brontë novels are a fictional version of the struggle between the landed gentry and the industrial bourgeoisie at

the end of the eighteenth century, with the Earnshaws representing the yeomen, the disappearing class of small freeholding farmers. In *Windward Heights*, a similar class structure places the vicissitudes of history in the foreground.

5. In contemporary Guadeloupe, the top positions in society and public service are still predominantly held by whites, and social relations between the various categories of the population remain a rarity. The overwhelming majority of the population is of unmixed, black ancestry, and the racial contrast is starker than in the other French islands.

6. Mary Louise Pratt's term "contact zone" refers to the cultures on both sides of the colonial divide, be it Victorian or Caribbean, which absorb aspects of the "other" culture, generating new identities and ideas in the process.

7. While the Senegalese Senghor, however, perceived black culture and solidarity as rooted in biology and nature, the Martinican Césaire saw it as determined by geography and a common history of suffering and survival.

8. See Patrick Taylor's analysis of *Cahier d'un Retour Au Pays Natal* in chapter 5 of his book for how this opposition structures Césaire's long poem.

9. "La Civilisation du Bossale" refers to the oral culture of the first generation of slaves who arrived in the New World on slave ships. In her book, Maryse Condé examines the distinction between this culture and the folktales of future generations of slaves.

10. See her "Notes on a Return to the Native Land" in *Conjonction: Revue Franco-Haïtienne*.

11. Lionnet's *Autobiographical Voices* and Rosello's two essays cited in the bibliography elaborate on these points in relation to Condé's previous novels.

12. See Glissant's *Le Discours Antillais* for the distinction between "retour" and "détour" (40–57).

13. This is also true incidentally of these writers' respective approach to the cultural dynamics of the creole language. Although Condé shares Bernabé, Chamoiseau, and Confiant's emphasis on multilingualism, or "polysonic vertigo," as constitutive of creoleness (Bernabé, Chamoiseau, and Confiant 108), she distances herself from their attempts at codifying which creole words exactly are suited to Créolité's "open specificity." See Chamoiseau's essay "Reflections on Maryse Condé's *Traversée de la Mangrove*" for an example of such codification.

14. According to Dash, while Créolité is indeed "tempted to produce its own rhetoric, its own approved texts . . . and a new heroic of marronage," Glissant's thought is characterized by an "ironic self-scrutiny" and an "insistence on process ('creolisation' and not 'créolité')" that preserves its integrity as a relational model of analysis. Dash adds that "despite its avowed debt to Glissant, *Éloge de la Créolité* risks undoing the epistemological break with essentialist thinking that he has always striven to conceptualise" (Dash, *Édouard Glissant* 23).

15. Also see Condé's essay "Chercher Nos Vérités."

16. As Thomas Spear has shown, this exaggerated sexuality is characteristic of francophone Caribbean fiction in general. Spear argues that male writers tend

to emphasize male conquest and virility, while women writers focus on the violent nature of Caribbean machismo (Spear 139). I argue that Condé does both.

17. Note that the idea of crossing is already included in the Greek roots of the term "metaphor," which means to carry (phoro) across or between (meta).

18. That, as Ralph Ellison's *Invisible Man* so powerfully demonstrates, visible racial difference does not preclude one from being "invisible" exemplifies the kind of questioning of the visible that emerges from Condé's reworking of race.

19. My essay "Rewriting the Postcolonial: Maryse Condé's *Windward Heights*" provides a more elaborate interpretation of the novel in light of this debate and of the history of Guadeloupe in 1899.

20. In *Ségou* (*Segu*, 1987), the characterization of Tiékoro, a Bambara who converts to Islam despite his family's wishes, undergoes a similar treatment. While his murder turns him into a martyr and a hero in his own people's eyes, readers have a hard time sharing such feeling of awe for someone to whose personal motivations and doubts they had access.

21. Although Endomius is not Légitimus in the novel, he assumes a lot of the qualities of the real life Légitimus, whose speeches were known for their eloquence and whose "Parti Noir" emerged in May 1898. Légitimus was elected president of the regional council (Conseil Général) of La Guadeloupe. His fiery injunctions were often condemned in the press as powerful incitations to violent action.

22. For a critique of identity politics, see Lawrence Grossberg's *We Gotta Get Out of This Place* (364–96). As Grossberg points out, the problem with identity politics is its rationalist assumption that "people act based on a calculation of their interests, which are rooted in their experiences, which are determined by their identity, which is an expression or representation of their place within a system of social differences" (376). This model "effectively erases affective subjectivity and has no theory of political commitment" (379). Also see Parmar's "Other Kinds of Dreams," and Wendy Brown's "Feminist Hesitations, Postmodern Exposures."

23. See Nyatetu-Waigwa's essay for an elaboration of this point in relation to Condé's earlier novels.

24. I use "subaltern" here as a general term to designate the groups who have no access to hegemonic power rather than in its original Gramscian sense.

25. For instance, in *The Myth of Aunt Jemima: Representations of Race and Region*, Diane Roberts identifies two poles in white representations of black women: the sexless Aunt Jemima who feeds and nurtures, and the sexy Jezebel who entices and gets pregnant (2). In *Imperial Eyes*, Mary Louise Pratt also points to the "nurturing native" as a key figure in sentimental travel writing (96).

26. See Homi Bhabha's essay "Of Mimicry and Man."

27. See George Lamming's *The Pleasures of Exile* and Retamar's *Caliban* for a discussion of the ways in which Shakespeare's characters in *The Tempest* function as paradigmatic figures of postcoloniality.

28. Caryl Phillips, whose most famous novel to date is *Cambridge*, was asked

to edit the English translation of Condé's *La Migration des Coeurs* (*Windward Heights*). The translation's title in English is no doubt an editorial choice that ties it to the nineteenth-century original, but it betrays the rewriting's scope by anchoring it in a definite space.

29. According to Bénédicte Ledent, Phillips's characters in *Crossing the River* "do not fit traditional stereotypes. Nash, the educated slave turned colonizer and missionary; Edward, the liberal-minded and homosexual master; Martha, the black settler and frontierswoman; and even Joyce the color-blind outcast, are nonconformist pioneer figures most often excluded from traditional historiography and literature" (290).

30. At a public lecture she gave at the University of Oklahoma in March 1993, Condé went back to talk about *Tree of Life*: "Even now," she explained, "this book is my forgotten novel. At colloquia scholars like to give papers on *Hérémakhonon* or *I, Tituba, Black Witch of Salem* or *Traversée de La Mangrove* (Crossing the Mangrove). . . . But *Tree of Life* raises too many embarrassing questions" ("Role of the Writer" 698). Condé is clearly revisiting her "forgotten book" and its concerns in *Windward Heights*.

31. It is significant in this respect that Condé moved the time frame of the Brontë story to the postslavery period. This choice prevents readers from safely compartmentalizing the experience of slavery into a bygone and hermetic era. Instead of representing emancipation as a genuine shift in political and economic reality, the novel demonstrates that its potential as a revolutionary experience was blocked "once measures to curb the freedom of blacks by retaining control of government proved effective" (Beckles and Shepherd ix). As *Windward Heights*'s dispossessed characters repeatedly point out, the forms of domination that derived from slavery did not end with it. Nelly Raboteur, for instance, explains with a perceptiveness that emulates Christophine's lucidity in *Wide Sargasso Sea*: "The abolition of slavery hadn't changed anything at all, you know. It was still the rich white planters who laid down the law and the blacks who lived from hand to mouth" (19). Lucinda Lucius, her successor at Belles-Feuilles (Thrushcross Grange), echoes her comment almost word for word: "For my generation, the end of slavery means nothing. It's the same sadness, the same wretchedness we've been chewing on for as long as we can remember" (67). Sandrine, the second Cathy's *mabo*, also remembers that for all his abolitionist ideals, Aymeric de Linsseuil had no qualms keeping on her mother as his live-in laundress with, twice a year, new garments for her children as her only payment.

32. Similarly, whereas Heathcliff lets Isabella escape and live in exile, Razyé goes to fetch Irmine from her old *mabo*'s house where she had taken refuge, marries her to seal his domination, and abuses her until his death. Irmine's nostalgic reminiscences later reveal that besides battering her, he also forced her to sleep with the drunken and debauched Justin: "Perhaps if there was one thing she could reproach Razyé for, it was having forced her to share Justin's bed, that rum-soaked wreck drifting on a sea of regret for his beloved" (279).

33. Condé identifies three parts in Césaire's *Notebook:* the first part denounces the misery and degradation the poet faces in Martinique when he returns; the second relates these conditions to the history of slavery and European colonialism; and the third valorizes blackness and points to the beginning of revolt.

34. See Condé's analysis of *Notebook:* "la grande valeur nègre/africaine, c'est la capacité à souffrir. C'est la capacité à survivre à la souffrance. . . . Vivre, survivre pour le peuple antillais sont déjà victoire" (49).

35. As Arnold points out, "the suffering male hero of négritude must transcend . . . representations of feminine weakness in order to realize his salvatory maleness in the radiant future that beckons beyond his present sacrifice of self" (23). Condé also mentions the Haitian Jacques Roumain's *Masters of the Dew* as the novel that contributed, along with Négritude, to establishing the "model which is still largely undisputed to this day" ("Order" 156) and whose principles are: that the setting be the native land, the hero male and peasant, the woman a mere accessory to his struggles, and that sexuality be exclusively heterosexual.

36. See Césaire's celebratory conclusion to his *Notebook:*

And the nigger scum is on its feet

the seated nigger scum
unexpectedly standing
standing in the hold
standing in the cabins
standing on deck
standing in the wind
standing under the sun
standing in the blood
     standing
     and
          free
               (Césaire 81)

37. There are many *Jane Eyre* derivatives and imitations, that is, novels with striking plot similarities (Stoneman 254–92) or fictional works that include explicit references to *Jane Eyre,* but what I have in mind are sequels that, like *Wide Sargasso Sea,* directly engage and rewrite, correct, reproduce (with more or less variation), extend or critique the nineteenth-century perspective of the original text. In the realm of fiction, it is *Wuthering Heights,* not *Jane Eyre,* that has sparked writers' imagination (albeit not from a postcolonial perspective): Jeffrey Caine's *Heathcliff* and Lin Haire-Sargeant's *H.* tell the story of Heathcliff's missing years. John Wheatcroft's *Catherine, Her Book* focuses on the first Catherine's perspective through her diary notes, while Anna L'Estrange's *Return to Wuthering Heights* writes "beyond the ending" to tell the story of the second generation. Alice Hoffman's *Here on Earth* and Jane Urquhart's *Away* are more recent rewritings of Emily

Brontë's novel. See Patsy Stoneman's impressive study of the Brontë novels' cultural dissemination.

38. Indeed, the same neglect also characterizes the novel's postcolonial criticism. A study of the contrasting genres to which the rejoinders to these two Brontë novels belong is yet to be written. While *Wuthering Heights* provides much fodder for creative rewriters but not for postcolonial critics, *Jane Eyre* has occasioned a proliferation of feminist and postcolonial readings but not of literary rewritings. These differences alone show why postcolonial critics' tendency to discuss the "Brontë novels" as part of the same corpus is problematic if not utterly misguided.

·2. Shutting Up the Subaltern

1. As the postcolonial critic Gayatri Spivak explained in her influential 1985 essay, in glorifying Jane, they conveniently forgot that Rochester's West Indian wife had to "act out the transformation of her 'self' into that fictive Other, set fire to the house and kill herself so that Jane Eyre [could] become the feminist individualist heroine of British fiction" ("Three Women's Texts" 270). Also see my essay "Double (De)colonization" for a survey of feminist and postcolonial criticism of *Wide Sargasso Sea*.

2. This chapter's title references Gayatri Spivak's essay "Can the Subaltern Speak?" as well as the plot of *Jane Eyre* in which the subaltern is literally "shut up" in the attic. My combination of Spivak's essay with *Jane Eyre* is meant to provide a grounding for an examination of speech and silence in relation to both physical and textual space.

3. Gregg makes a more nuanced claim when she identifies a dialectical tension between the text's recruitment/obliteration of blacks and Rhys's acute critical awareness of the workings of colonialist discourse (38): "both the deployment and the unmasking of the colonialist discourse help to forge Jean Rhys's 'truth'" (39). Nonetheless, when she discusses Rhys's representation of black and mulatto people, we lose all sense of the ambivalence or tension she had previously identified in Rhys's textual politics: "The racialist usurpation of the voices, acts, and identities of 'black people,' so central to Rhys's writing as a whole, is the psychological cement in the architecture of this novel: Tia as cheating, hostile nigger and container for the self; Amélie as the lusty mulatto wench who hates the Creole; Daniel as the hateful mulatto and mirror image for the husband; Christophine as nurse, black mammy, and obeah woman who privileges the white child's needs over her own and, at times, infantilizes the Creole woman; the deletion of any autonomous 'life' for the black and mulatto characters" (Gregg 114–15).

4. According to the influential Caribbean critic Brathwaite, Rhys's "sociocultural background and orientation" makes it impossible for her to grasp the experience of the primarily black and poor West Indian people (*Contradictory Omens* 35). He later changed his mind about Rhys (see note 15 below). For Moira Ferguson, "the text favors Jean Rhys's class—the former white planter class" and "does not allow the implied victors [Christophine] . . . to be articulated

as victors" (115). Veronica Gregg objects to Rhys's representation of black and mulatto people and sees her insight into the workings of power as restricted to the British colonialist's discursive constructions of his female Other (Antoinette). Aparajita Sagar's interpretation is similar to Gregg's; Sagar recognizes in the novel an antilinear narrative (that resists conventional history and epistemology) but also, however, "a corrected and single-minded Caribbean history" that compromises the first project in its racism toward the black and colored characters (159). Judith Gardiner and Theresa O'Connor identify a racist ideology in Rhys's writing (Gardiner 48; O'Connor 36), and Caroline Rody agrees that the text's evocation of racial history (or lack thereof) might be read as complicit with colonialist discourse (307). George Handley's reading "agrees with that of Peter Hulme who asserts that Rhys is 'fundamentally sympathetic to the planter class ruined by Emancipation'" (Hulme 73; Handley 151). According to Elayne Savory, "Rhys certainly reflects the prejudices of her time, race and class, but . . . she was in many ways ahead of her time in that willingness to deal with race" (134–35).

5. For critics who, beside Parry, praise Rhys's treatment of black subjectivities, see Lucy Wilson and Elaine Campbell. Their readings of the novel stress the astuteness and resiliency of Rhys's black characters whose significance they see as "Rhys's legacy" (Wilson 73), that is, as the result of her conscious manipulation of the text's ideology. In "'Women Must Have Spunks': Jean Rhys's West Indian Outcasts," Lucy Wilson states that Rhys's black characters "thrive on adversity and draw strength from their opposition to the prevailing power structures" (67). She focuses on two of Rhys's strongest black characters (Christophine and Selina from the short story "Let Them Call It Jazz") and, like Parry, sees them as endowed with what Antoinette lacks, that is, an insight into the workings of power in postslavery society. She reads Antoinette's suicide as the logical outcome of her passivity and defeat, which, she emphasizes, it is futile to try and present as a positive and self-determining gesture (69). Ramchand and Hearne, two other West Indian critics, also foreground the collision between black and white Creole values in the novel. Ramchand borrows Fanon's phrase "terrified consciousness" to describe the white Creoles' "shock and disorientation as a massive and smouldering Black population is released into an awareness of its power" (Ramchand 225), but like Hearne, he sees the "terrified consciousness" of the white West Indian as "a universal heritage" (Ramchand 236), as part of "the human condition" and its search for love (Hearne 192). Elaine Campbell's perspective, on the other hand, is less disheartening since she argues that Rhys managed in literature what she could not achieve in real life, namely "an erasure of racial barriers with a resultant free flow between black and white identities" (63). Following the Guyanese critic Wilson Harris, who, in his influential article "Carnival of Psyche," identifies Rhys's creative insights as both "white" and "black" (129), Campbell argues that Antoinette's internalization of Dominican black magic/obeah (the African religion of the slaves) is what enables her to unite herself with her black friend Tia (65). Campbell's analysis parallels the Australian Helen Tiffin's insofar as the latter

emphasizes Antoinette's identification with the black Creole community (339). Unlike Campbell, however, Tiffin sees this identification as resulting from Antoinette's sexual enslavement.

6. See Parry's influential "Problems in Current Theories of Colonial Discourse," an essay that "remains 'required reading' for any student of postcolonialism" (McLeod 265).

7. Spivak discusses the colonialist perspectives of these two approaches respectively in "A Literary Representation of the Subaltern: A Woman's Text from the Third World" and in "Can the Subaltern Speak? Speculations on Widow Sacrifice." This thesis is derived from a study of indigenous and imperialist historical archives documenting the practice of sati in nineteenth-century India, which shows that the widow's voice is caught between indigenous patriarchal and colonial constructions and can therefore not be heard (see "The Rani of Sirmur"). Feminists who have taken up Spivak's views in their own work on colonialism are Firdous Azim in *The Colonial Rise of the Novel,* Jenny Sharpe in *Allegories of Empire,* and Rey Chow in *Writing Diaspora.*

8. See Bhabha's "The Other Question" in *The Location of Culture.*

9. My use of the term "patchwork" is not incidental here: Antoinette's two mother substitutes, Christophine and Aunt Cora—who are also the two most resolute and astute characters in the novel—are associated with this motif. Christophine had a patchwork counterpane in her room, and Aunt Cora's patchwork is one of the last things she remembers about "home" before her suicide (189). I read the term not only as a metaphor for Antoinette's divided self but as a metaphor for my own act of reading, that is, of patching together this polyphonic narrative's scattered meanings and voices.

10. An interesting narrative about Sass emerges when we patch together all the fragments of information that are scattered through Antoinette's often imperceptive account: his mother, Annette explains, "pranced off and left him" when "he was a little skeleton" (22); his name derives from "Disastrous" (131), which implies that he might be one of Old Cosway's illegitimate children ("And all those women! . . . Presents and smiles for the bastards every Christmas" [29]).

11. Following Genette and Rimmon-Kenan, I am using the term "focalization" to distinguish the person who does the seeing (in an ideological as well as perceptual sense) from the person who does the speaking (narrator). This helps distinguish between the terms "perspective" and "narration," which tend to get conflated when we use the phrase "point of view" (Genette 206; Rimmon-Kenan 71–86). When the adult narrator tells us about herself as a child in *Wide Sargasso Sea,* we talk of "external" focalization when the language is that of the narrator at the time of narration and of internal focalization when the perceptions of the experiencing child "color" the narrator's language (Rimmon-Kenan 83–85). Rimmon-Kenan explains that "the overall language of a text is that of the narrator, but focalization can 'colour' it in a way which makes it appear as a transposition of the perceptions of a separate agent" (82).

12. Later, he reiterates the trope of the infantile black and of the isolated, unmarried woman who suffers from delusions and paranoia: "They are children—they wouldn't hurt flies" (35).

13. This discrepancy is also largely responsible for the ambivalent critical response to the novel's final scene: the ending is either interpreted as triumphantly asserting Antoinette's identification with the black Creole community (Campbell 63; Emery 59; James, "Sun Fire" 127; Tiffin 339) or, inversely, as reinforcing the impossibility of transcending racial barriers (Brathwaite, *Contradictory Omens* 36; Wilson 69). Both of these responses, however, have generally assumed an unproblematical equivalence between Rhys's stance and her protagonist's at the expense of the black Creole perspective and need to be challenged insofar as such identification does not do justice to the thoughtful and complex representation of the black characters in the novel.

14. See Brathwaite's *Contradictory Omens* for examples of black influence on the dominant sections of the society: "Many white creole ladies, for instance, were using the kind of headties worn by the African slave women and cleaned their teeth with 'chaw-stick[s]'" (18).

15. In a more recent article written for *Wasafiri* in response to Peter Hulme's review of Rhys criticism in the same journal, Brathwaite powerfully reiterates his criticism of the appropriation of racial difference, but he now discusses it as "something that does not apply willy-nilly to Jean Rhys but to those who now seek to use her in their Caribbean &/or postcolonial &/or womanist &/or wonderland paradigms" ("A Post-Cautionary Tale" 76).

16. The critic Louis James refers us to the "Guerre Nègre" in Dominica to elucidate this scene. The taking of census in 1844, that is, "of names," misled the freed population into believing that slavery was going to be reinstated and generated riots and incidents similar to the burning of Coulibri (*Jean Rhys* 47). That the very idea of "taking census" could cause such unrest and violent reaction is explained by M. G. Lewis in his *Journal of a West Indian Proprietor* (1834): "They find no change produced in them [by Christianity], except the alteration of their name, and hence they conclude that his name contains in it some secret power" (290–91).

17. See Mary Lou Emery's book *Jean Rhys at "World's End"* for an account of the historical significance of Caribbean cultural practices such as obeah.

18. Anthropologists have started using terms like "vodoun," "vodun," "vodu," or "voudoun" to describe this traditional religion in an effort to avoid the stereotype of black magic and sorcery which the conventional appellation *voodoo* has come to represent (Davis 11).

19. In presenting obeah as a "milder form of voodoo," Rhys highlights the way in which the two creole religions are historically and culturally associated. Yet it is important to acknowledge the differences between the two given that they are practiced in such different locations, with different histories, and under different European cultural influences. Rhys critics often also conflate obeah and

vodoun. See, for instance, Judith Raiskin and Thomas Loe, whose analyses of the patterns of zombification in *Wide Sargasso Sea* are based on Wade Davis's study of Haitian vodoun. For the distinction between the various African-derived religions that developed in the Caribbean region, see Olmos and Paravisini-Gilbert's *Sacred Possessions: Vodou, Santeria, Obeah, and the Caribbean.*

20. In her essay, Elaine Campbell also shows that obeah is deeply embedded in the white Creole consciousness (44).

21. According to legend, zombis are bodies without will or, as Rhys puts it in her autobiography, "black shapeless things" (*Smile Please* 23) whose deadened condition is attributed to a poison administered by the obeah sorcerer; the victims are said to be buried alive until the sorcerer raises them from their graves in order either to sell them as slaves or to sentence them to aimless and memoryless wandering. When directed at the dominant classes, this process of "zombification" can also embody the possibility of subverting social hierarchies insofar as it results in their loss of influence and material privilege (Raiskin 131).

22. This analysis implies that the white Creole Antoinette's voice represents Rhys's point of view, an assumption that I challenge at the beginning of this chapter.

23. See Homi Bhabha's "The Other Question" for a discussion of the stereotype as a site of destabilizing ambivalence.

24. Similarly, in her essay "Women's Silence as a Ritual of Truth," Patricia Laurence argues that the silences of the female characters in the fiction of Austen, Brontë, and Woolf should not be read as a sign of passivity and submission but as a discourse of enlightened interiority and an alternative way of knowing. In his *History of Sexuality*, vol. 1, Foucault also warns us against reducing silence to a prohibitive device: "There is no binary division to be made between what one says and what one does not say; we must try to determine the different ways of not saying such things, how those who can and those who cannot speak of them are distributed, which type of discourse is authorized, or which form of discretion is required in either case. There is not one but many silences, and they are an integral part of the strategies that underlie and permeate discourses" (27).

25. Antoinette is seventeen when she leaves the convent in 1839. Emancipation was implemented in 1834. That she does not remember the place when it was prosperous but does remember its being safe ("My father, visitors, horses, feeling safe in bed—all belonged to the past" [17]) not only situates the crumbling of the plantation system before emancipation (wouldn't she recall being prosperous since she was twelve when she experienced it?) but also recalls a time when whiteness did not require economic solvency to be considered a privilege.

26. In "Mirror and Mask," Helen Tiffin also sees Antoinette as "finally sharing the history that apparently divided her from the Blacks" (338).

27. The break-up of the British empire took place between the mid-1940s and the mid-1960s, and even though Rhys completed *Wide Sargasso Sea* in 1966, it was partly written by 1945.

28. See Stuart Hall's "Religious Ideologies": "This 'reversal' was cultural and ideological rather than political or economic. But its consequences were nevertheless profound. Jamaica became, for the first time in its history, *culturally* black" (288).

29. Joan Givner reveals Rhys's fascination with *Wuthering Heights* in "Charlotte Brontë, Emily Brontë, and Jean Rhys: What Rhys's Letters Show about That Relationship" (106). She focuses, however, on the correspondences of incident, phrase, and imagery that link *Wuthering Heights* and *Wide Sargasso Sea* and omits to comment on the remarkable parallels in narrative technique between the two works. Like *Wuthering Heights, Wide Sargasso Sea* has two major narrators whose unreliable and often naïve narration filters others' or each other's voices, and as in *Wuthering Heights,* this structure has the effect of obscuring authorial intent. Rhys thus rewrote one Brontë sister's masterpiece by emulating the other's method of presentation, and this proliferating intertextuality further increases the difficulty of determining a stable ideological stance in her novel.

3. Racial Vagaries in Emily Brontë's *Wuthering Heights*

1. Maryse Condé does not, however, single him out as a black character since she relocates the story in turn-of-the-century Guadeloupe and racializes not only Heathcliff but also the Earnshaws and Nelly. The Lintons remain "white" insofar as they are part of the planter class, or *békés.*

2. Criticism often contributes to reinforcing the image of the serenity of the rustic background by representing Heathcliff as the alien element and "destructive principle" whose arrival disrupts the "working of the natural order" in *Wuthering Heights* (Cecil 137–38; Keith Sagar 145) and family stability at Thrushcross Grange (Pykett 75). By contrast, Winnifrith argues that it is Heathcliff and Catherine who embody a "complete harmony" constantly broken by intruders (51). Although others such as Mrs. Humphry Ward have described "the solitudes of the moors and the ruggedness of Yorkshire life" as the source of the novel's "wildness" and "perpetual state of personal violence" (Ward, quoted in Bloom 9), their reading does not necessarily challenge the first one since if the rustic adherence to custom is "unreasoning," it is also always one step away from chaos. In the preface to *Wuthering Heights,* Charlotte exemplifies this view by representing Emily as a "homebred country girl" and her work as "rustic," "simple," and "homely" whose "wild" and offensive elements are only the result of an "uncultivated" mind and would have been taken away with maturation and education.

3. In *Half Savage and Hardy and Free: Women and Rural Radicalism in the Nineteenth-Century Novel,* Judith Weissman takes issue with the characterization of rural life in Victorian novels and contemporary criticism as at best "scenery in a literary text, not the stuff of literary, intellectual, and political meaning" and at worst the site of "idiocy" (3). She concentrates on a group of writers (Wordsworth, Austen, Emily Brontë, Hawthorne, Trollope, Hardy, and Forster) who "were in a tradition of radical protest . . . [and] saw agricultural communities as a place to take a stand for economic and social justice" (5). In chapter 3, she contrasts Charlotte

Brontë's aborted (because asocial) Romantic radicalism derived from Shelley with Emily's powerful vision of radical politics originated in Wordsworth. Her analysis of *Wuthering Heights*'s radicalism does not include, however, the politics of race in the novel.

4. Her choice of the Yorkshire setting in *Wuthering Heights* becomes all the more meaningful when we remember that in contrast to Charlotte and Branwell, who placed their juvenilia's Glasstown in West Africa and had their heroes engage in wars with an (existing) Ashantee tribe, Emily located her and her sister Anne's juvenilia conquest stories in Gondal, an island in the North Pacific resembling Emily's native Yorkshire.

5. The persistence of this ideal of Englishness is all the more remarkable since, as Meyer points out, thousands of black slaves lived in England at the end of the eighteenth century (98).

6. Some see Heathcliff and his love as the embodiments of cosmic forces (Cecil 140), of "an inhuman world of pure energy" (Van Ghent 182) that is "no more ethically relevant than is flood or earthquake or whirlwind" (Van Ghent 181). Others argue that Emily Brontë's reluctance at judging a character "it is fairly clear that [she] admires" and finds "rather magnificent" (Wilson 228) can be ascertained from the authorial detachment and the lack of moral direction generated by the layering of unreliable narrative voices in the novel. Others attribute Heathcliff's "attractiveness" to a late-Romantic legacy that celebrates intensity of emotion for the sake of intensity, independently of the morality or immorality of that emotion.

7. According to Pete Miles, the interpretation of *Wuthering Heights* as cosmic myth might in fact have more to do with its "moral censors'" attempt to explain away a disturbing sympathy for an immoral character than about Emily Brontë's desire to transcend social relations (36). Heathcliff is not either portrayed as a "nobly satanic" Byronic figure "flirting with [a] glamorized wickedness" whose consequences readers are never really shown (Ewbank 99–100). There is none of the ambiguity and vague suggestiveness of Romantic tales. Heathcliff's cruel treatment of foe and friend alike makes his humanity questionable to say the least, and the reader is even left wondering if he did not actually murder Cathy's brother, Hindley, when they were left alone together. See Sutherland's *Is Heathcliff a Murderer?*

8. In his infamous journals (published in 1834 and re-edited in 1845), the planter Monk Lewis described mulattos as "almost universally weak and effeminate persons," whose children, he added, "are difficult to rear" (55). In fact, while blacks were seen as "brutish, ignorant, idle, crafty, treacherous, bloody, thievish, mistrustful, and superstitious" (Long 354), Lewis indicates that "on a sugar-estate, one black [was] considered as more than equal to two mulattoes" (55). Three decades later, Lewis's observations were echoed by a member of the Commission whom President Abraham Lincoln had appointed to examine the situation of the newly emancipated slaves in America: "The mixed race are the most unhealthy,

and the pure blacks the least so. The disease they suffer most from is pulmonary. Where there is not real tubercular affection of the lungs, there are bronchitis and pulmonary affections. I have the idea that they die out when mixed" (quoted in Young, *Colonial Desire* 148).

9. See Robert Young's *Colonial Desire: Hybridity in Theory, Culture, and Race* and Biddiss's *Images of Race* for an account of the ways in which the Victorians were obsessed with "miscegenation" and its implications for the origins of the Anglo-Saxon race.

10. Biddiss's *Images of Race* brings together lectures given by Victorian naturalists and ethnologists about these very issues. For instance, Darwin's disciple Huxley delivered a talk in which he explained that, due to the degree of racial mixing that the "races of mankind" had undergone over the centuries, it was no longer possible to distinguish between European stocks. Although Huxley never went so far as to question that "physical, mental, and moral peculiarities go with blood," he claimed nonetheless that "blood infusions" had made it impossible to separate an Irishman from a "Devonshire man" and that "the sooner we leave off drawing political distinctions between Celts and Saxons the better" (Biddiss 165). Similarly, the historian Edward Augustus Freeman, a champion of Anglo-Saxonism, qualified his racial determinism by agreeing that language could only be a "presumption" not a "test" of race. He wrote that in fact:

> It is certain that there can be no positive proof of real community of blood, even among those groups of mankind which we instinctively speak of as families and races. It is not merely that the blood has been mingled in after times; there is no positive proof that there was any community of blood in the beginning. No Englishman can prove with absolute certainty that he comes in the male line of any of the Teutonic settlers in Britain in the fifth and sixth centuries. . . . If direct evidence is demanded, we must give up the whole doctrine of families and races, as far as we take language, manners, institutions, anything but physical conformation, as the distinguishing marks of races and families. . . . We may thus be landed in a howling wilderness of scientific uncertainty. (Biddiss 216–19)

11. Evangelical and abolitionist groups had fostered monogenesis, which upheld the biblical narrative of the descent of all humankind from Adam and Eve. With the decline in prestige of the antislavery movement, however, monogenesis was supplanted by the racial doctrine of polygenesis, which relied on "hybridity" as the ultimate test for species: if the merging of races produced fertile offspring, then humans were all one species and the different races were merely subgroups; if the product of the union between black and white was sterile, however, then the races were taken to be different species. By 1850, the British were so invested in denying their common humanity with the Negro that despite the obvious fertility of the large and growing mixed-raced population of the West Indies, they kept thinking of new ways of justifying the polygenist thesis.

12. See Mary Poovey's *Uneven Developments* and Deirdre David's *Rule Britannia* for an elaboration of the ways in which middle-class Victorians solidified their difference from other classes and races by calling it moral character.

13. The Victorian domestic angel was to make her exertions look effortless and selfless regardless of the amount of work involved in superintending the household (Armstrong 78–79); she had to ration the victuals so as to create the impression of bounty irrespective of the income level of the family provider (Armstrong 81–88); and last but not least, she had to exert her power of moral influence and self-denying love to compensate for the debasing effects of the competitive public sphere on the head of the household, no matter how much physical or mental harm such abnegation entailed.

14. Similarly, when Nelly visits the Heights after reading Isabella's letter about the abuse she daily endures at the Heights, her first comments upon entering the "dreary" house concern Isabella's unfulfilled domestic duties, not the young girl's miserable circumstances: "I must confess that, if I had been in the young lady's place, I would, at least, have swept the hearth, and wiped the tables with a duster. But she already partook of the pervading spirit of neglect which encompassed her" (*Wuthering Heights* 138).

15. Maryanne C. Ward argues that education in *Wuthering Heights* "provides the basis for the next generation's equality. Catherine begins to educate Hareton, whom Heathcliff has done his best to turn into a brute. When Heathcliff comes home to find Hareton and Catherine reading together and Hareton transformed 'because his senses were alert, and his mental faculties wakened to unwonted activity,' Heathcliff announces his inability or unwillingness to complete his revenge. . . . Heathcliff recognizes that Hareton has found the means of escape" (23–24).

16. See Winifred Gérin's *Emily Brontë* (225–26) and Eagleton's introduction to the second edition of his *Myths of Power: A Marxist Study of the Brontës* for similar intimations that Heathcliff's background, like the Brontës', is Irish. Eagleton wrote the preface in order to acknowledge and make up for the exclusions in his study and in so doing alludes to the possibility of Heathcliff's Irishness. In *Heathcliff and the Great Hunger*, an investigation of Irish culture and history, he goes on to develop an allegorical reading of the novel in terms of the Irish/British conflict but acknowledges that he can do so only by disregarding chronology. Indeed, Emily started writing *Wuthering Heights* at about the same time the famine struck in Ireland (autumn 1845); she could not, therefore, as Gérin and Michie suggest, have been drawing on her brother Branwell's account of "the Irish children that were pouring into England in the late 1840s as a result of the potato famine" (Michie 54) since his visit to Liverpool took place in August 1845, that is, before the Famine.

17. That Meyer's model cannot contain the complex and contradictory meanings of race is all the more evident in her analysis of *The Mill on the Floss*, where she falls back on a literal interpretation of race to make sense of Eliot's insistence

on Maggie's physical darkness. Maggie's skin color, according to Meyer, is evidence of the repressed heterogeneity of the Anglo-Saxon race. The character who otherwise functions as the term "white woman" in the metaphorical troping Meyer identifies in Victorian women's writings thus becomes both white and nonwhite, a contradiction Meyer notes but cannot explain. Similarly, in *Jane Eyre,* the white woman is paradoxically a site of convergence for both anti-imperialist and racist discourses. The process of likening them to "inferior races" indirectly challenges race hierarchies (as when Jane, for instance, identifies with rebellious black slaves), but the very same metaphorization also reproduces racial hierarchies (this identification subsumes race oppressions under gender oppression).

18. Jane's deployment of racial tropes is characterized by a level of self-consciousness about their rhetorical and figurative function that is missing from the unreliable Nellie's use of the same imagery. See my postcolonial reading of Charlotte Brontë's novel, "Suspect Listener and Unsuspected Storyteller: A Postcolonial Reading of Charlotte Brontë's *Jane Eyre.*"

19. In fact, Heathcliff's counterpart in *Jane Eyre* is Bertha rather than Rochester. Both have ambiguous racial identities. In *Wuthering Heights,* the question of Heathcliff's origins never gets elucidated. In *Jane Eyre,* Bertha Mason's origins are disclosed but remain nonetheless ambiguous. As the West Indian daughter of "Jonas Mason, merchant, and of Antoinetta, his wife, a Creole," and as the sister of "the yellow-skinned yet socially white" Richard Mason (Meyer 67), she is automatically suspected of having black blood in her veins. They are also both perceived as "a ghoul" and "a vampire" by the respective narrators of the novels.

20. Q. D. Leavis describes it as "a wholesome primitive and natural unit of a healthy society" (99).

4. Creolization and the Black Atlantic

1. For a lucid account of how this intensively hybridized and transnational aesthetic has achieved a position of prominence in Western literary circles and universities, see Boehmer (233–43). As Boehmer points out, migrant writings are increasingly hailed as *the* model of anti-imperialist literature, and their tales of straddling different cultural worlds as the culmination of the postcolonial. Recently, however, some critics have argued that the success of migrant literature is not a sign of the West's increasing engagement with alternative perspectives and aesthetic criteria so much as a celebration of cultural forms that come closest to Western ideas of high art (see Ahmad and Dane Johnson).

2. As Newson and Strong-Leek point out, "With the exception of native populations (Arawaks and Caribs, whose history is much longer than those of the groups presently predominating in the region), inhabitants of the Caribbean—historically from another place and another culture—were compelled to adjust to new environments and societies outside of their ancestral milieu" (79).

3. See Bharati Mukherjee's essay "Beyond Multiculturalism: Surviving the Nineties" for a critique of these two notions. As Mukherjee points out, "The sinister

fallout of official multiculturalism and of professional multiculturalists is the estab-
lishment of one culture as the norm and the rest as aberrations" (135), while the
"failed nineteenth-century model of 'melting pot'" could only lead to "coerced
acceptance" (135).

4. I use the phrase to evoke the "politics of location" that Adrienne Rich discusses in *Blood, Bread, and Poetry* to advocate for a responsible kind of feminist
criticism. This approach, she argues, means "recognizing our location, having to
name the ground we're coming from, the conditions we have taken for granted"
(129). It emphasizes the importance of examining our investments in geopolitics
rather than assuming the vision of a unitary world. In her essay on the politics of
experience, Chandra Mohanty integrates Rich's politics of location into her feminist, anti-imperialist cultural criticism.

5. See Edmondson's "Return of the Native" for a discussion of the coincidence between the ideal of objectivity in the literature of exile and the rise of modernism in early-twentieth-century England. See Kaplan's *Questions of Travel* for
an elaboration of Euro-American tropes of exile.

6. George Lamming's *The Pleasures of Exile,* for instance, relates his experiences as a West Indian in London through a discussion of issues such as canonic-
ity, exile, center-periphery relations, and the effects of Shakespeare's *The Tempest*
in the postcolonial world.

7. See Kutzinski (*Sugar's Secrets*); Handley; and Dash (*The Other America*) for
accounts of the development from the nation as a unified "imaginary community"
to the interrogation of the concept.

8. In his essay "Three Words toward Creolization," Antonio Benitez-Rojo
states that "according to the silly labels that we use in the United States, Danticat is
a Haitian-American; in fact, her identity is in the hyphen, that is, in neither place:
Danticat is a Caribbean writer" (60). By contrast, I argue that while her personal
identity might very well be located in the hyphen, this does not justify eliding the
very important differences between her representation of Caribbean difference
and that of other Caribbean writers. At the same time, to observe that her black
diasporic status is important to Danticat's particular formulation of creolization
is not to say that all "black" Caribbean writers will write in the same vein as she
does. Caryl Phillips's poetics, for instance, is remarkably different from Danticat's.

9. In her discussion of migrant literature, for instance, Boehmer states that
"in making this move [to less repressive and richer places in the world], writers
have been much advantaged by the class, political, and educational connections
with Europe and America which in many cases they enjoyed. They have developed
what was anyway a cosmopolitan tendency, often picked up as part of an élite
upbringing in their home countries. . . . But as the compounded privilege, if nothing else, of the writers suggests, their work remains a part and also an expression
of the neo-colonial world" (238).

10. *How the Garcia Girls Lost Their Accents,* the prequel to *Yo!,* opens with
Yolanda Garcia's decision to move back to the island: "Let this turn out to be my

home" (11). The novel then proceeds to go backward in time and to narrate the events that preceded this day. Thus, Yolanda's "permanent" return is chronologically what we were left with when we begin the sequel *Yo!*. Insofar as *Yo!,* however, reopens in the States years after the attempt to go back "home" obviously failed, it ironically and retroactively redefines its prequel as a migrant novel that also highlights the difficulty of determining where home is as well as the impossibility of return.

11. In his essay "Imaginary Homelands," Salman Rushdie similarly explains that Indian migrants' "physical alienation from India almost inevitably means that we will not be capable of reclaiming precisely the thing that was lost; that we will, in short, create fictions, not actual cities or villages, but invisible ones, imaginary homelands, Indias of the mind" (10). Also see Madan Sarup's discussion of the politics of place and the shifting meanings of home in his book *Identity, Culture, and the Postmodern World.*

12. What is deeply ironic about this response is of course that it engages in a fierce critique of the legacy of Spanish or French imperialism depicted in these novels, yet, in emphasizing American superiority, it unwittingly reproduces the same patterns of perception it condemns. Odile Ferly's essay "'Giving Birth to the Island'" similarly represents Yo's trajectory from the Dominican Republic to the United States as an unproblematized "journey to freedom" from gender constraints (3).

13. In her essay "Resistance Theory/Theorizing Resistance, or Two Cheers for Nativism," Benita Parry similarly discusses contemporary writers such as Wilson Harris or Édouard Glissant who recuperate figures of colonial resistance in oral traditions and popular memory without "enacting a regressive search for an aboriginal and intact condition/tradition from which a proper sense of historicity is occluded" (173).

14. In Danticat's novel *The Farming of Bones* (1998), however, the Haiti to which the heroine needs to return is configured as a cultural space only.

15. Meso-America defines Québec and Canada as well as the United States. Euro-America includes Québec, Canada, the United States, and a cultural section of Chili and Argentina. Neo-America comprises the Caribbean, including the Brazilian Northeast, the Guianas, Curacao, the southern United States, the Caribbean coast of Venezuela and Columbia, and an important part of Central America and Mexico.

16. See Chris Bongie's *Islands and Exiles* for a discussion of the unexpected similarities between Brathwaite's and Glissant's models of creolization (53–76).

Postscript

1. As critics have amply shown, it is typically the mother who constitutes the symbolic site through which Kincaid works out her relationship to her homeland of Antigua and to Caribbean cultural identity in general. In *In Praise of New Travelers,* for instance, Isabel Hoving demonstrates that it is through the appropriation of the motherly voice that Kincaid engages in colonial mimicry in both

her fiction and nonfiction (*A Small Place*). Similarly, Kristen Mahlis argues that the mother in Kincaid embodies the voice of a colonizing and patriarchal authority against which the daughter rebels. Also see Birbalsingh; Edmondson; and Sugg for an analysis of the trope of homeland as mother/land and the attendant disciplinary role played by the mother in Kincaid's fiction.

Bibliography

Ahmad, Aijaz. *In Theory: Classes, Nations, Literatures.* New York: Verso, 1992.

Alcoff, Linda. "The Problem of Speaking for Others." *Cultural Critique* 20 (winter 1991–92): 5–33.

Alexander, Jacqui, and Chandra Tapalde Mohanty, eds. *Feminist Genealogies, Colonial Legacies, Democratic Futures.* New York: Routledge, 1996.

Allott, Miriam. *Emily Brontë: "Wuthering Heights," A Casebook.* London: Macmillan, 1970.

Alvarez, Julia. *How the Garcia Sisters Lost Their Accents.* New York: Plume, 1992.

———. *Something to Declare.* New York: Plume, 1999.

———. *Yo!* New York: Plume, 1997.

Anderson, Benedict. *Imagined Communities.* New York: Verso, 1991.

Appiah, Kwame Anthony. "Is the 'Post-' in 'Postcolonial' the 'Post-' in 'Postmodern'?" In *Dangerous Liaisons: Gender, Nation, and Postcolonial Perspectives,* edited by Anne McClintock, Aamir Mufti, and Ella Shohat, 420–45. Minneapolis: University of Minnesota Press, 1997.

Armstrong, Nancy. *Desire and Domestic Fiction: A Political History of the Novel.* New York and Oxford: Oxford University Press, 1987.

Arnold, James. "The Gendering of Créolité." In *Penser la Créolité,* edited by Maryse Condé and Madeleine Cottenet-Hage, 21–41. Paris: Karthala, 1995.

Ashcroft, Bill. *Post-colonial Transformation.* New York: Routledge, 2001.

Ashcroft, Bill, Gareth Griffiths, and Helen Tiffin. *The Empire Writes Back.* Routledge: New York, 1989.

Azim, Firdous. *The Colonial Rise of the Novel.* New York: Routledge, 1993.

Balutansky, Kathleen. "Créolité in Question: Caliban in Maryse Condé's *Traversée de la Mangrove.*" In *Penser La Créolité,* edited by Maryse Condé and Madeleine Cottenet-Hage, 101–13. Paris: Karthala, 1995.

Baudrillard, Jean. *Simulacra and Simulation.* Ann Arbor: University of Michigan Press, 1994.

Beckles, Hilary, and Verene Shepherd, eds. *Caribbean Freedom: Economy and Society from Emancipation to the Present.* Princeton, N.J.: Markus Wiener Publishers, 1996.

Behdad, Ali. "Une Pratique Sauvage: Postcolonial Belatedness and Cultural Politics." In *The Pre-Occupation of Postcolonial Studies,* edited by Fawzia Afzal-Khan and Kalpana Seshadri-Crooks, 71–86. Durham: Duke University Press, 2000.

Benítez-Rojo, Antonio. "Three Words toward Creolization." In *Caribbean Creolization: Reflections on the Cultural Dynamics of Language, Literature, and Identity,* edited by Kathleen M. Balutansky and Marie-Agnés Sourieau, 53–62. Gainesville: University Press of Florida, 1998.

Bernabé, Jean, Patrick Chamoiseau, and Raphaël Confiant. *Éloge de la Créolité/ In Praise of Creoleness.* Bilingual edition. Paris: Gallimard, 1993.

Bhabha, Homi. "Of Mimicry and Man: The Ambivalence of Colonial Discourse." In *The Location of Culture,* by Bhabha, 85–93. New York: Routledge, 1994.

———. *Nation and Narration.* New York: Routledge, 1990.

———. "The Other Question: Stereotype, Discrimination, and the Discourse of Colonialism." In *The Location of Culture,* by Bhabha, 66–85. New York: Routledge, 1994.

Biddiss, Michael D., ed. *Images of Race.* New York: Holmes and Meier Publishers, 1979.

Birbalsingh, Frank. "Jamaica Kincaid: From Antigua to America." In *Frontiers of Caribbean Literature in English,* edited by Birbalsingh, 138–51. New York: St. Martin's Press, 1996.

Bloom, Harold, ed. *Heathcliff.* New York: Chelsea House Publishers, 1993.

Boehmer, Elleke. *Colonial and Postcolonial Literature: Migrant Metaphors.* New York: Oxford University Press, 1995.

Bongie, Chris. "Exiles on Main Stream: Valuing the Popularity of Postcolonial Literature." *Postmodern Culture* 14, no. 1 (September 2003). *Project Muse.* 11 January 2004. http://muse.jhu.edu/journals/ pmc/v014/14.1bongie.html.

———. *Islands and Exiles: The Creole Identities of Post/colonial Literature.* Stanford: Stanford University Press, 1998.

Boyce, Carole Davies. *Black Women, Writings, and Identity: Migrations of the Subject.* New York: Routledge, 1994.

Braidotti, Rosi. "Becoming-Woman: Rethinking the Positivity of Difference." In *Feminist Consequences: Theory for the New Century,* edited by Elisabeth Bronfen and Misha Kavka, 381–414. New York: Columbia University of Press, 2001.

———. *Metamorphoses: Towards a Materialist Theory of Becoming.* Malden, Mass.: Blackwell, 2002.

———. *Nomadic Subjects: Embodiment and Sexual Difference in Contemporary Feminist Theory.* New York: Columbia University Press, 1994.

Brathwaite, Edward Kamau. *Contradictory Omens: Cultural Diversity and Integration in the Caribbean.* Kingston, Jamaica: Savacou Publications, 1974.

————. *The Folk Culture of the Slaves in Jamaica.* London: New Beacon Books, 1981.

————. "A Post-Cautionary Tale of the Helen of our Wars." *Wasafiri* 22 (autumn 1995): 69–78.

Brontë, Charlotte. "Editor's Preface to the New Edition of *Wuthering Heights.*" 1850. *Wuthering Heights,* edited by Linda Peterson, 21–24. Boston: Bedford Books of St. Martin's Press, 1992.

————. *Jane Eyre.* 1847. New York: Norton Critical Editions, 1971.

Brontë, Emily. *Wuthering Heights.* 1848. Edited by Linda H. Peterson. Boston: Bedford Books of St. Martin's Press, 1992.

Brown, Wendy. "Feminist Hesitations, Postmodern Exposures." *differences* 3.1 (spring 1991): 63–84.

————. *Politics Out of History.* Princeton: Princeton University Press, 2001.

Bruner, Charlotte, and David Bruner. "Buchi Emecheta and Maryse Condé: Contemporary Writing from Africa and the Caribbean." *World Literature Today* 59, no. 1 (winter 85): 9–14.

Butler, Judith. *Bodies That Matter: On the Discursive Limits of "Sex."* New York: Routledge, 1993.

Caine, Jeffrey. *Heathcliff.* New York: Random House, 1978.

Campbell, Elaine. "Reflections of Obeah in Jean Rhys's Fiction." In *Critical Perspectives on Jean Rhys,* edited by Pierrette M. Frickey, 59–67. Washington: Three Continents Press, 1990.

Casey, Ethan. Review of *Breath, Eyes, Memory,* by Edwidge Danticat. *Callaloo* 18, no. 2 (spring 1995): 524–27.

Cecil, David. "Emily Brontë and *Wuthering Heights.*" 1934. In *Emily Brontë: "Wuthering Heights," A Casebook,* edited by Miriam Allott, 135–43. London: Macmillan, 1970.

Césaire, Aimé. *Notebook of a Return to the Native Land.* In *The Collected Poetry,* translated by Clayton Eshleman and Annette Smith, 32–86. Berkeley and Los Angeles: University of California Press, 1983.

Chamoiseau, Patrick. "Reflections on Maryse Condé's *Traversée de la Mangrove.*" *Callaloo* 14, no. 2 (spring 1991): 389–95.

Chatterjee, Partha. *Nationalist Thought and the Colonial World: A Derivative Discourse?* London: Zed, 1986.

Chow, Rey. *Writing Diaspora: Tactics of Interventions in Contemporary Cultural Studies.* Bloomington: Indiana University Press, 1993.

Cliff, Michelle. "History as Fiction, Fiction as History." *Ploughshares* 20, no. 2 & 3 (fall 1994): 196–203.

Condé, Maryse. *La Belle Créole.* Paris: Gallimard, 2003.

————. *"Cahier d'un Retour au Pays Natal": Analyse Critique.* Paris: Hatier, 1978.

————. *Célanire Cou-Coupé.* Paris: Robert Laffont, 2000.

————. "Chercher Nos Vérités." In *Penser la Créolité,* edited by Maryse Condé and Madeleine Cottenet-Hage, 305–11. Paris: Karthala, 1995.

———. *La Civilisation du Bossale: Réflexions sur la Littérature Orale de la Guadeloupe et de la Martinique.* Paris: Éditions L'Harmattan, 1978.

———. *Les Derniers Rois Mages.* Paris: Mercure de France, 1992.

———. *Heremakhonon.* Washington D.C.: Three Continent Press, 1982.

———. *La Migration des Coeurs.* Paris: Robert Laffont, 1995.

———. "Notes sur un Retour au Pays Natal." *Conjunction: Revue Franco-Haïtienne* 176 (Supplément 1987): 7–23.

———. "Order, Disorder, Freedom, and the West Indian Writer." *Yale French Studies* 97 (fall 2000): 151–65.

———. "The Role of the Writer." *World Literature Today* 67, no. 4 (autumn 1993): 697–99.

———. *Ségou.* Paris: Robert Laffont, 1984.

———. *Traversée de la Mangrove.* Paris: Mercure de France, 1989.

———. *Tree of Life: A Novel of the Caribbean.* Translated by Victoria Reiter. New York: Ballantine Books, 1992.

———. *Windward Heights.* Translated by Richard Philcox. London: Faber and Faber, 1998.

Confiant, Raphaël. *Aimé Césaire: Une Traversée Paradoxale du Siècle.* Paris: Stock, 1993.

Cottenet-Hage, Madeleine. Introduction to *Penser la Créolité,* edited by Maryse Condé and Madeleine Cottenet-Hage, 11–21. Paris: Karthala, 1995.

Dalton, Elizabeth. "Sex and Race in *Wide Sargasso Sea.*" *Partisan Review* 68, no. 3 (summer 2000): 431–63.

Danticat, Edwidge. "AHA!" In *On Becoming American: Personal Essays by First-Generation Immigrant Women,* edited by Meri Nana-Ama Danquah, 39–45. New York: Hyperion, 2001.

———. *Breath, Eyes, Memory.* New York: Vintage Books, 1994.

———. *The Farming of Bones.* New York: Penguin Books, 1998.

———. "A Conversation with Edwidge Danticat." Interview. *Behind the Books.* 10 January 2004. http://www.randomhouse.com/vintage/danticat.html.

Dash, Michael J. *Édouard Glissant.* Cambridge: Cambridge University Press, 1995.

———. "The Madman at the Crossroads: Delirium and Dislocation in Caribbean Literature." *Profession* (2002): 37–44.

———. *The Other America: Caribbean Literature in a New World Context.* Charlottesville: University of Virginia Press, 1998.

David, Deirdre. *Rule Britannia: Women, Empire, and Victorian Writing.* Ithaca: Cornell University Press, 1995.

Davies, Carole Boyce. *Black Women, Writing and Identity: Migrations of the Subject.* New York: Routledge, 1994.

Davies, Carol Boyce, and Elaine Savory Fido. *Out of the Kumbla: Caribbean Women and Literature.* New Jersey: Africa World Press, 1990.

Davis, Wade. *The Serpent and the Rainbow.* New York: Touchstone, 1985.

Drake, Sandra. "All that Foolishness/That All Foolishness: Race and Caribbean Culture as Thematics of Liberation in Jean Rhys's *Wide Sargasso Sea.*" *Critica* 2, no. 2 (fall 1990): 97–112.

Duara, Prasenjit. *Rescuing History from the Nation: Questioning Narratives of Modern China.* Chicago: University of Chicago Press, 1995.

Eagleton, Terry. *Heathcliff and the Great Hunger: Studies in Irish Culture.* New York: Verso, 1995.

———. *Literary Theory: An Introduction.* Oxford: Basil Blackwell, 1983.

———. *Myths of Power: A Marxist Study of the Brontës.* London: Macmillan, 1988.

Eagleton, Terry, Fredric Jameson, and Edward Said. *Nationalism, Colonialism, and Literature.* Minneapolis: University of Minnesota Press, 1990.

Edmondson, Belinda. "Return of the Native: Immigrant Women's Writing and the Narrative of Exile." In *Making Men: Gender, Literary Authority, and Women's Writing in Caribbean Narrative,* 139–69. Durham and London: Duke University Press, 1999.

Eliot, George. "The Natural History of German Life." 1856. In *Essays,* 157–94. New York: Booklover Press, 1883.

Emery, Mary Lou. *Jean Rhys at "World's End": Novels of Colonial and Sexual Exile.* Austin: University of Texas Press, 1990.

Ewbank, Inga-Stina. *Their Proper Sphere: A Study of the Brontë Sisters as Early Victorian Female Novelists.* London: Edward Arnold, 1966.

Fanon, Frantz. *Black Skin, White Masks.* London: Pluto, 1986.

Ferguson, Moira. *Colonialism and Gender Relations: From Mary Wollstonecraft to Jamaica Kincaid.* New York: Columbia University Press, 1993.

Ferly, Odile. "'Giving Birth to the Island': The Construction of the Caribbean in Julia Alvarez's Fiction." *Mots Pluriels: Revue Électronique de Lettres à Caractère International* 17 (April 2001): 1–4.

Foucault, Michel. *The History of Sexuality: An Introduction.* Vol. 1. New York: Random House, 1978.

Frickey, Pierrette M. Introduction to *Critical Perspectives on Jean Rhys,* edited by Pierrette M. Frickey. Washington: Three Continents Press, 1990.

Friedman, Susan Stanford. "'Beyond' Difference: Migratory Feminism in the Borderlands." In *Mappings: Feminism and the Cultural Geographies of Encounter,* 67–105. Princeton, N.J.: Princeton University Press, 1998.

Fuentes, Carlos. "Central and Eccentric Writing." In *Carifesta Forum: An Anthology of Twenty Caribbean Voices,* edited by John Hearne, 209–21. West Indies: Institute of Jamaica, 1976.

Gardiner, Judith Kegan. *Rhys, Stead, Lessing and the Politics of Empathy.* Bloomington: Indiana University Press, 1989.

Gates, Henry Louis, Jr. "Writing 'Race' and the Difference It Makes." Introduction to *Race, Writing, and Difference,* edited by Henry Louis Gates Jr., 1–21. Chicago: University of Chicago Press, 1985.

Gellner, Ernest. *Nations and Nationalism*. Cambridge: Blackwell, 1983.

Genette, Gérard. *Narrative Discourse*. Ithaca, N.Y.: Cornell University Press, 1980.

Gérin, Winifred. *Emily Brontë: A Biography*. New York: Oxford University Press, 1971.

Gikandi, Simon. *Writing in Limbo: Modernism and Caribbean Literature*. Ithaca, N.Y.: Cornell University Press, 1992.

Gilbert, Sandra M., and Susan Gubar. *The Madwoman in the Attic: The Woman Writer and the Nineteenth-Century Literary Imagination*. New Haven: Yale University Press, 1979.

Gilroy, Paul. *Against Race: Imagining Political Culture Beyond the Color Line*. Cambridge: Harvard University Press, 2000.

———. "Route Work: The Black Atlantic and the Politics of Exile." In *The Post-Colonial Question: Common Skies, Divided Horizons*, edited by Iain Chambers and Lidia Curti, 17–30. New York: Routledge, 1996.

Givner, Joan. "Charlotte Brontë, Emily Brontë, and Jean Rhys: What Rhys's Letters Show about That Relationship." In *Faith of a (Woman) Writer*, edited by Alice Kessler-Harris and William McBrien, 105–14. Westport, Conn.: Greenwood, 1988.

Glissant, Édouard. *Le Discours Antillais*. Paris: Gallimard, 1997.

———. *Faulkner, Mississippi*. Paris: Stock, 1996.

———. *Introduction à une Poétique du Divers*. Paris: Éditions Gallimard, 1996.

———. *Poetics of Relation*. Translated by Betsy Wing. Ann Arbor: University of Michigan Press, 1997.

Gregg, Veronica Marie. *Jean Rhys's Historical Imagination: Reading and Writing the Creole*. Chapel Hill: University of North Carolina Press, 1995.

Grossberg, Lawrence. *We Gotta Get Out of This Place: Popular Conservatism and Postmodern Culture*. New York: Routledge, 1992.

Hall, Stuart. "New Ethnicities." In *Black Film, British Cinema*, 27–31. London: ICA Documents 7. ICA, 1988.

———. "Religious Ideologies and Social Movements in Jamaica." In *Religion and Ideology*, edited by R. Bobcock and K. Thompson, 269–96. Manchester: Manchester University Press, 1985.

Haire-Sargeant, Lin. H. *The Story of Heathcliff's Journey Back to Wuthering Heights*. New York: Pocket Books, 1992.

Hamilton, Paul. *Historicism*. New York: Routledge, 1996.

Handley, George. *Postslavery Literatures in the Americas: Family Portraits in Black and White*. Charlottesville: University Press of Virginia, 2000.

Harris, Wilson. "Carnival of Psyche: Jean Rhys's *Wide Sargasso Sea*." In *Explorations: A Selection of Talks and Articles: 1966–1981*, edited by Hena Maes-Jelinek, 125–34. Denmark: Dangaroo Press, 1981.

———. *The Womb of Space: The Cross-cultural Imagination*. Westport, Conn.: Greenwood Press, 1983.

Haubruge, Pascale. "Emily Brontë en Guadeloupe." *Le Soir,* 25 October 1995, 18.

Hearne, John. "*The Wide Sargasso Sea*: A West Indian Reflection." In *Critical Perspectives on Jean Rhys*, edited by Pierrette M. Frickey, 186–94. Washington: Three Continents Press, 1990.

Hoffman, Alice. *Here on Earth*. New York: Berkley Publishing Group, 1998.

Hoving, Isabel. *In Praise of New Travelers: Reading Caribbean Migrant Women's Writing*. Stanford: Stanford University Press, 2001.

Huggan, Graham. *The Postcolonial Exotic: Marketing the Margins*. New York: Routledge, 2001.

Hulme, Peter. "The Locked Heart: The Creole Family Romance of Wide Sargasso Sea." In *Colonial Discourse/Postcolonial Theory*, edited by Francis Barker, Peter Hulme, and Margaret Iversen, 72–89. New York: Manchester University Press, 1994.

Hutcheon, Linda. "Circling the Downspout of Empire." In *The Post-colonial Studies Reader*, edited by Bill Ashcroft, Gareth Griffiths, and Helen Tiffin, 130–36. New York: Routledge, 1995.

Hutchinson, John, and Anthony D. Smith, eds. *Nationalism*. New York: Oxford University Press, 1994.

Jack, Belinda Elizabeth. *Négritude and Literary Criticism: The History and Theory of "Negro-African" Literature in French*. Westport, Conn.: Greenwood, 1996.

James, Louis. *Jean Rhys*. London: Longmans, 1978.

———. "Sun Fire—Painted Fire: Jean Rhys as a Caribbean Novelist." In *Critical Perspectives on Jean Rhys*, edited by Pierrette M. Frickey, 118–29. Washington: Three Continents Press, 1990.

Johnson, Barbara. *The Critical Difference*. Baltimore: John Hopkins University Press, 1980.

Johnson, Dane. "The Rise of Gabriel García Márquez and Toni Morrison." In *Cultural Institutions of the Novel*, edited by Deidre Lynch and William B. Warner, 129–57. Durham: Duke University Press, 1996.

Kaplan, Caren. *Questions of Travel: Postmodern Discourses of Displacement*. Durham: Duke University Press, 1996.

Kaplan, Carla. *The Erotics of Talk*. New York: Oxford University Press, 1996.

Kincaid, Jamaica. *Annie John*. New York: New American Library, 1983.

———. *The Autobiography of My Mother*. New York: Farrar, Straus, and Giroux, 1996.

———. *Lucy*. New York: Penguin, 1991.

———. *Mr. Potter*. New York: Farrar, Straus, and Giroux, 2002.

———. *A Small Place*. New York: Farrar, Straus, and Giroux, 1988.

King, Russell, John Connell, and Paul White, eds. *Writing Across Worlds: Literature and Migration*. New York: Routledge, 1995.

Knoepflmacher, U. C. *Emily Brontë: Wuthering Heights*. New York: Cambridge, 1989.

Knox, Robert. *The Races of Men: A Fragment*. Philadelphia: Lea and Blanchard, 1850.

Kutzinski, Vera. "Borders and Bodies: The United States, America, and the Caribbean." *CR: The New Centennial Review* 1, no. 2 (fall 2001): 55–89.

———. *Sugar's Secrets: Race and the Erotics of Cuban Nationalism.* Charlottesville: University Press of Virginia, 1993.

Lamming, George. *The Pleasures of Exile.* Ann Arbor: University of Michigan Press, 1992.

Lanser, Susan. *Fictions of Authority. Women Writers and Narrative Voice.* Ithaca, N.Y.: Cornell University Press, 1992.

Laurence, Patricia. "Women's Silence as a Ritual of Truth: A Study of Literary Expressions in Austen, Brontë, and Woolf." In *Listening to Silences: New Essays in Feminist Criticism,* edited by Elaine Hedges and Shelley Fisher Fishkin, 156–68. New York: Oxford University Press, 1994.

Leavis, Q.D.L. "A Fresh Approach to Wuthering Heights." In *Lectures in America,* 1:85–152. London: Chatto and Windus, 1969.

Ledent, Bénédicte. "Exile and Caribbeanness in Caryl Phillips's Fiction." PhD diss., University of Liège in Belgium, 1996–97.

L'Estrange, Anna. *Return to Wuthering Heights.* Edinburgh: Pinnacle Books, 1977.

Lewis, Matthew Gregory. *Journal of a West Indian Proprietor Kept during a Residence in the Island of Jamaica.* London: J. Murray, 1834.

Lionnet, Françoise. *Autobiographical Voices: Race, Gender, Self-Portraiture.* Ithaca, N.Y.: Cornell University Press, 1989.

———. "Narrating the Americas: Transcolonial *Métissage* and Maryse Condé's *La Migration des Coeurs.*" In *Mixing Race, Mixing Culture: Inter-American Literary Dialogues,* edited by Monika Kaup and Debra Rosenthal, 65–88. Austin: University of Texas Press, 2002.

Loe, Thomas. "Patterns of the Zombie in Jean Rhys's *Wide Sargasso Sea.*" *World Literature Written in English* 31, no. 1 (1991): 34–42.

Long, Edward. *The History of Jamaica.* 3 vols. London: Lowndes, 1774.

Losing Isaiah. Dir. Stephen Gyllenhaal. Perf. Jessica Lange, Halle Berry, Cuba Gooding Jr., Mark John Jeffries, and Samuel L. Jackson. Paramount Studio, 1995.

Maes-Jelinek, Hena, and Bénédicte Ledent. "The Novel since 1970." In *A History of Literature in the Caribbean,* vol. 2, *English- and Dutch-speaking regions,* edited by James Arnold, 149–99. Philadelphia: John Benjamins Publishing Company, 2001.

Mahlis, Kristen. "Gender and Exile: Jamaica Kincaid's Lucy." *Modern Fiction Studies* 44 (1998): 164–83.

Mardorossian, Carine M. "Double (De)colonization: Feminist and Postcolonial Criticism of Jean Rhys's *Wide Sargasso Sea.*" *College Literature* 26, no. 2 (spring 1999): 79–96.

———. "Opacity as Obeah in Jean Rhys's Work." *Journal of Caribbean Literatures* 3, no. 3 (summer 2003): 133–43.

———. "Rewriting the Postcolonial: Maryse Condé's *Windward Heights.*"

Forthcoming in *Emerging Perspectives on Maryse Condé: A Writer of Her Own*, edited by Sally Barbour and Gerise Herndon. Africa World Press.

———. "Shutting Up the Subaltern: Silences, Stereotypes, and *Double-Entendre* in Jean Rhys's *Wide Sargasso Sea.*" *Callaloo: A Journal of African-American and African Arts and Letters* 22, no. 4 (fall 1999): 1071–90.

———. "Suspect Listener and Unsuspected Storyteller: A Postcolonial Reading of Charlotte Brontë's *Jane Eyre.*" Forthcoming in *ARIEL: A Review of International English Literature.*

———. "Toward a New Feminist Theory of Rape." *Signs: A Journal of Women in Culture and Society* 27, no. 3 (spring 2002): 743–77.

Mayne, Isobel. "Emily Brontë's Mr. Lockwood." *Brontë Society Transactions* 15 (1968): 210–16.

McClintock, Anne. *Imperial Leather: Race, Gender, Sexuality in the Colonial Context.* New York: Routledge, 1995.

McDowell, Deborah. "Transferences: Black Feminist Discourse: The 'Practice' of 'Theory.'" In *Feminism Beside Itself,* edited by Diane Elam and Robyn Wiegman, 93–119. New York: Routledge, 1995.

McLeod, John. *Beginning Postcolonialism.* Manchester: Manchester University Press, 2000.

Melville, Pauline. *The Ventriloquist's Tale.* London: Bloomsbury, 1997.

Meyer, Susan L. *Imperialism at Home: Race and Victorian Women's Fiction.* Ithaca, N.Y.: Cornell University Press, 1996.

Michie, Elsie. *Outside the Pale: Cultural Exclusion, Gender Difference, and the Victorian Woman Writer.* Ithaca, N.Y.: Cornell University Press, 1993.

Mignolo, Walter. "(Post)Occidentalism, (Post)Coloniality, and (Post)Subaltern Rationality." In *The Pre-Occupation of Postcolonial Studies,* edited by Fawzia Afzal-Khan and Kalpana Seshadri-Crooks, 86–118. Durham: Duke University Press, 2000.

Miles, Peter. *"Wuthering Heights": An Introduction to the Variety of Criticism.* London: Macmillan, 1990.

Miller, J. Hillis. "Emily Brontë." In *The Disappearance of God: Five Nineteenth-Century Writers,* 157–211. Cambridge: Harvard University Press, 1963.

Mohanty, Chandra Talpade. "Feminist Encounters: Locating the Politics of Experience." *Copyright* 1 (fall 1987): 30–44.

Moore-Gilbert, Bart. *Postcolonial Theory: Contexts, Practices, Politics.* New York: Verso, 1997.

Mukherjee, Bharati. "Beyond Multiculturalism: Surviving the Nineties." In *Race: An Anthology in the First Person,* edited by Bart Schneider, 129–41. New York: Three Rivers Press, 1997.

Murdoch, Adlai. *Creole Identity in the French Caribbean Novel.* Gainesville: University Press of Florida, 2001.

Naficy, Hamid. *The Making of Exile Cultures: Iranian Television in Los Angeles.* Minneapolis: University of Minnesota Press, 1993.

Nair, Supriya. "Homing Instincts: Immigrant Nostalgia and Gender Politics in *Brown Girl, Brownstones*." In *Caribbean Romances: The Politics of Regional Representation,* edited by Belinda Edmondson, 183–98. Charlottesville: University Press of Virginia, 1999.

Nesbitt, Nick. *Voicing Memory: History and Subjectivity in French Caribbean Literature.* Charlottesville: University of Virginia Press, 2004.

Newson, Adele S., and Linda Strong-Leek. *Winds of Change: The Transforming Voices of Caribbean Women Writers and Scholars.* New York: Peter Lang, 1998.

Ngũgĩ wa Thiong'o. "Borders and Bridges: Seeking Connections between Things." In *The Pre-Occupation of Postcolonial Studies,* edited by Fawzia Afzal-Khan and Kalpana Seshadri-Crooks, 119–26. Durham: Duke University Press, 2000.

Nicholson, Linda. "Interpreting Gender." In *Social Postmodernism: Beyond Identity Politics,* edited by Linda Nicholson and Steven Seidman, 39–68. New York: Cambridge University Press, 1995.

Nyatetu-Waigwa, Wangari wa. "From Liminality to a Home of Her Own? The Quest Motif in Maryse Condé's Fiction." *Callaloo* 18, no. 3 (summer 1995): 551–65.

O'Connor, Theresa F. *Jean Rhys: The West Indian Novels.* New York: New York University Press, 1986.

Olmos, Margarite Fernandez, and Lizbeth Paravisini-Gilbert, eds. *Sacred Possessions: Vodou, Santeria, Obeah, and the Caribbean.* New Brunswick, N.J.: Rutgers University Press, 1997.

Parmar, Pratibha. "Other Kinds of Dreams." *Feminist Review* 31 (spring 1989): 55–66.

Parry, Benita. "Problems in Current Theories of Colonial Discourse." *Oxford Literary Review* 9 (1987): 27–58.

———. "Resistance Theory/Theorizing Resistance, or Two Cheers for Nativism." In *Colonial Discourse/Postcolonial Theory.* edited by Francis Barker, Peter Hulme, and Margaret Iversen, 172–97. Manchester: Manchester University Press, 1994.

Parry, J. H., Philip Sherlock, and Anthony Maingot. *A Short History of the West Indies.* 4th ed. New York: St Martin's Press, 1987.

Pfaff, Francoise. *Entretiens avec Maryse Condé.* Paris: Karthala, 1993.

Philcox, Richard, trans. *Windward Heights,* by Maryse Condé. London: Faber and Faber, 1998.

Phillips, Caryl. *Cambridge.* 1991. New York: Vintage Books, 1993.

———. "Crossing the River: Caryl Phillips Talks to Maya Jaggi." *Wasafiri* 20 (autumn 94): 25–29.

Poovey, Mary. *Uneven Developments: The Ideological Work of Gender in Mid-Victorian England.* Chicago: University of Chicago Press, 1988.

Prakash, Gyan. "Postcolonial Criticism and Indian Historiography." In *Social Postmodernism: Beyond Identity Politics,* edited by Linda Nicholson and Steven Seidman, 87–103. New York: Cambridge University Press, 1995.

Pratt, Mary Louise. *Imperial Eyes: Travel Writing and Transculturation*. New York: Routledge, 1992.

Pykett, Lyn. *Emily Brontë*. Savage, Md.: Barnes and Noble Books, 1989.

Raiskin, Judith L. *Snow on the Canefields: Women's Writing and Creole Subjectivity*. Minneapolis: University of Minnesota Press, 1996.

Ramchand, Kenneth. "Terrified Consciousness." In *The West Indian Novel and Its Background*. 223–37. New York: Barnes and Noble, 1970.

———. *The West Indian Novel and Its Background*. New York: Barnes and Noble, 1970.

Renda, Mary. *Taking Haiti: Military Occupation and the Culture of U.S. Imperialism 1915–1940*. Chapel Hill and London: University of North Carolina Press, 2001.

Retamar, Roberto Fernandez. *Caliban and Other Essays*. Minneapolis: University of Minnesota Press, 1989.

Rhys, Jean. *The Complete Novels*. New York: W. W. Norton, 1985.

———. *Smile Please: An Unfinished Autobiography*. New York: Harper and Row, 1979.

———. *Tigers Are Better-Looking: Stories by Jean Rhys*. New York: André Deutsch Ltd., 1968.

———. *Voyage in the Dark*. New York and London: W. W. Norton, 1982.

———. *Wide Sargasso Sea*. New York and London: W. W. Norton, 1982.

Rich, Adrienne. *Blood, Bread, and Poetry: Selected Prose, 1979–1985*. New York: W. W. Norton, 1986.

Rimmon-Kenan, Shlomith. *Narrative Fiction: Contemporary Poetics*. New York: Methuen, 1983.

Roberts, Diane. *The Myth of Aunt Jemima: Representations of Race and Region*. London: Routledge, 1994.

Rody, Caroline. "Burning Down the House: The Revisionary Paradigm of Jean Rhys's *Wide Sargasso Sea*." In *Famous Last Words: Changes in Gender and Narrative Closure*, edited by Alison Booth, 300–326. Charlottesville and London: University of Virginia Press, 1993.

Rosello, Mireille. *Declining the Stereotype: Ethnicity and Representation in French Cultures*. Hanover, N.H.: University Press of New England, 1998.

———. "'One More Sea to Cross': Exile and Intertextuality in Aimé Césaire's *Cahier d'un Retour au Pays Natal*." *Yale French Studies* 83, no. 2 (1993): 176–96.

Rushdie, Salman. "Imaginary Homelands." In *Imaginary Homelands: Essays and Criticism 1981–1991*, by Rushdie, 9–22. London: Granta Books and Viking, 1991.

———. *The Moor's Last Sigh*. New York: Vintage Books, 1995.

———. *The Satanic Verses*. New York: Picador USA, 1988.

Sagar, Aparajita. "Forays into the Attic: The Postcolonial Fiction Of Jean Rhys And J. M. Coetzee." PhD diss., University of Illinois at Urbana-Champaign, 1991.

Sagar, Keith. "The Originality of *Wuthering Heights*." In *The Art of Emily Brontë*, edited by Anne Smith, 121–60. New York: Barnes and Noble Books, 1976.

Said, Edward. *Orientalism*. New York: Random House, 1979.

Sarup, Madan. *Identity, Culture, and the Postmodern World*. Athens: University of Georgia Press, 1996.

Savory, Elayne. *Jean Rhys*. Cambridge: Cambridge University Press, 1998.

Sedgwick, Eve Kosofsky. *Tendencies*. Durham, N.C.: Duke University Press, 1993.

Sharpe, Jenny. *Allegories of Empire: The Figure of Woman in the Colonial Text*. Minneapolis: University of Minnesota Press, 1993.

Sinclair, May. *The Three Brontës*. London: Hutchinson, 1912.

Spear, Thomas. "Jouissances Carnavalesques: Représentations de la Sexualité." In *Penser la Créolité*, edited by Maryse Condé and Madeleine Cottenet-Hage, 135–53. Paris: Karthala, 1995.

Spivak, Gayatri Chakravorty. "Can the Subaltern Speak? Speculations on Widow Sacrifice." In *Marxism and the Interpretation of Culture*, edited by Cary Nelson and Lawrence Grossberg, 217–313. London: Macmillan, 1988.

———, trans. "Draupadi," by Mahasweta Devi. In *In Other Worlds: Essays in Cultural Politics,* by Spivak, 179–97. New York: Routledge, 1988.

———. "A Literary Representation of the Subaltern: A Woman's Text from the Third World." In *In Other Worlds: Essays in Cultural Politics,* by Spivak, 241–69. New York: Routledge, 1988.

———. *The Postcolonial Critic: Interviews, Strategies, Dialogues*. Edited by Sarah Harasym. New York: Routledge, 1990.

———. "The Rani of Sirmur." In *Europe and Its Others. Proceedings of the Essex Sociology of Literature Conference,* 1:125–51. Colchester, Eng.: University of Essex, 1984.

———. "Three Women's Texts and a Critique of Imperialism." *Race, Writing, and Difference*. Edited by Henry Louis Gates Jr., 262–81. Chicago: University of Chicago Press, 1985.

Stewart, Maaja A. *Domestic Realities and Imperial Fictions*. Athens: University of Georgia Press, 1993.

Stone, Donald S. *The Romantic Impulse in Victorian Fiction*. Cambridge: Harvard University Press, 1980.

Stoneman, Patsy. *Brontë Transformation: The Cultural Dissemination of Jane Eyre and Wuthering Heights*. New York: Prentice Hall/Harvester Wheatsheaf, 1996.

Strachan, Ian Gregory. *Paradise and Plantation: Tourism and Culture in the Anglophone Caribbean*. Charlottesville: University of Virginia Press, 2002.

Sugg, Katherine. "I Would Rather Be Dead": Nostalgia and Narrative in Jamaica Kincaid's *Lucy*." *Narrative* 10, no. 2 (May 2002): 156–74.

Suk, Jeannie. *Postcolonial Paradoxes in French Caribbean Writing: Césaire, Glissant, Condé*. New York: Oxford University Press, 2001.

Sutherland, John. *Is Heathcliff a Murderer? Puzzles in Nineteenth-Century Fiction*. New York: Oxford University Press, 1996.

Taylor, Patrick. "The Quest for Identity: Négritude." In *The Narrative of Liberation: Perspectives on Afro-Caribbean Literature, Popular Culture, and Politics,* 151–83. Ithaca, N.Y.: Cornell University Press, 1989.

Thackeray, William Makepeace. *Vanity Fair: A Novel without a Hero.* New York: Signet Classic, 1981.

Thiébaut, Claude. *Guadeloupe 1899: Année de Tous les Dangers.* Paris: L'Harmattan, 1989.

Thieme, John. *Postcolonial Con-Texts: Writing Back to the Canon.* London: Continuum, 2002.

Thomas, Sue. *The Worlding of Jean Rhys.* Westport, Conn.: Greenwood Press, 1999.

Tiffin, Helen. "Mirror and Mask: Colonial Motif in the Novels of Jean Rhys." *World Literature Written in English* 17 (1978): 328–41.

———. "Post-colonialism, Post-modernism, and the Rehabilitation of Post-Colonial History." *Journal of Commonwealth Literature* 23, no. 1 (1988): 169–81.

Urquhart, Jane. *Away: A Novel.* New York: Penguin, 1995.

Van Ghent, Dorothy. "Dark 'Otherness' in *Wuthering Heights.*" In *Emily Brontë: "Wuthering Heights," A Casebook,* edited by Miriam Allott, 177–83. London: Macmillan, 1970.

von Sneidern, Maja-Lisa. "*Wuthering Heights* and the Liverpool Slave Trade." *ELH* 62, no. 1 (spring 1995): 171–97.

Ward, Humphry. "Introduction to *Wuthering Heights.*" 1900. In *Heathcliff,* edited by Harold Bloom, 9–10. New York: Chelsea House Publishers, 1993.

Ward, Maryanne. "Romancing the Ending: Adaptations in Nineteenth-Century Closure." *Journal of the Midwest Modern Language Association* 29, no. 1 (spring 1996): 15–32.

Weissman, Judith. *Half Savage and Hardy and Free: Women and Rural Radicalism in the Nineteenth-Century Novel.* Middletown, Conn.: Wesleyan University Press, 1987.

Weathcroft, John. *Catherine, Her Book.* London: Cornwall Books, 1983.

Whipple, Edwin. "Novels of the Season." *North American Review* 141 (October 1848): 358–59. Reprinted in *Heathcliff,* edited by Harold Bloom, 5–6. New York: Chelsea House, 1993.

Wiegman, Robyn. *American Anatomies: Theorizing Race and Gender.* Durham: Duke University Press, 1995.

Wilson, Lucy. "Women Must Have Spunks": Jean Rhys's West Indian Outcasts." In *Critical Perspectives on Jean Rhys,* edited by Pierrette M. Frickey, 67–75. Washington: Three Continents Press, 1990.

Winnifrith, Tom. *The Brontës.* New York: Macmillan, 1977.

Winterhalter, Teresa. "Narrative Technique and the Rage for Order in *Wide Sargasso Sea.*" *Narrative: The Journal for the Study of Narrative Literature* 2, no. 3 (October 1994): 214–30.

Woolf, Virginia. *The Waves.* London: Grafton Books, 1977.

Wyndham, Francis. "An Inconvenient Novelist." *Tribune,* 15 December 1950, 16–18.

Wyndham, Francis, and Diana Melly, eds. *Jean Rhys Letters, 1931–1966.* London: André Deutsch, 1984.

Yelin, Louise. "In Another Place." In *Reading Sites: Social Difference and Reader Response,* edited by Patrocinio P. Schweickart and Elizabeth A. Flynn. New York: MLA, 2004.

Young, Robert. *Colonial Desire: Hybridity in Theory, Culture, and Race.* New York: Routledge, 1995.

———. *Postcolonialism: An Historical Introduction.* Cambridge: Blackwell, 2001.

Index

New World Studies

Vera M. Kutzinski
Sugar's Secrets: Race and the Erotics of Cuban Nationalism

Richard D. E. Burton and Fred Reno, editors
French and West Indian: Martinique, Guadeloupe, and French Guiana Today

A. James Arnold, editor
Monsters, Tricksters, and Sacred Cows: Animal Tales and American Identities

J. Michael Dash
The Other America: Caribbean Literature in a New World Context

Isabel Alvarez Borland
Cuban-American Literature of Exile: From Person to Persona

Belinda J. Edmondson, editor
Caribbean Romances: The Politics of Regional Representation

Steven V. Hunsaker
Autobiography and National Identity in the Americas

Celia M. Britton
Edouard Glissant and Postcolonial Theory: Strategies of Language and Resistance

Mary Peabody Mann
Juanita: A Romance of Real Life in Cuba Fifty Years Ago
Edited and with an introduction by Patricia M. Ard

George B. Handley
Postslavery Literatures in the Americas: Family Portraits in Black and White

Faith Smith
Creole Recitations: John Jacob Thomas and Colonial Formation in the Late Nineteenth-Century Caribbean

Ian Gregory Strachan
Paradise and Plantation: Tourism and Culture in the Anglophone Caribbean

Nick Nesbitt
Voicing Memory: History and Subjectivity in French Caribbean Literature

Charles W. Pollard
New World Modernisms: T. S. Eliot, Derek Walcott, and Kamau Brathwaite

Carine M. Mardorossian
Reclaiming Difference: Caribbean Women Rewrite Postcolonialism